WOMEN
&
FRIENDSHIP

WOMEN & FRIENDSHIP

JOEL D. BLOCK, Ph.D.
AND
DIANE GREENBERG

Franklin Watts New York Toronto 1985

Library of Congress Cataloging in Publication Data

Block, Joel D.
Women & friendship.

Bibliography: p.
Includes index.
1. Women—Psychology. 2. Friendship. 3. Interpersonal
relations. I. Greenberg, Diane. II. Title. III. Title:
Women and friendship.
HQ1206.B46 1985 155.6'33 85-13800
ISBN 0-531-09707-2

*We are indebted to the many women and men who gave
generously of their time and permitted us to briefly
enter their personal lives. Their wisdom, candor,
and rich experiences made this volume possible.
Ellen Joseph, our editor, took a personal interest
in the book; her talents enhanced the work,
and for this we are grateful.
The librarians at the Half Hollow Hills and
Shoreham–Wading River public libraries aided in the
gathering of research materials; their initiative
and resourcefulness are greatly appreciated.
Once again, Alice Castellucci has painstakingly and
with great personal care typed the manuscript and
offered helpful suggestions as the book evolved.
Our thanks for her concern and extraordinary competence.
The cooperation and loving support of our families,
Gail, Abbey, and Fred Block and
Bill and Alicia Greenberg, provided encouragement;
they created the environment needed to
give this work our best effort.*

DI

OTHER BOOKS BY
JOEL D. BLOCK, Ph.D.

Lasting Love:
How to Give it, How to Get it,
How to Keep it

Friendship:
How to Give it, How to Get it

To Marry Again

The Other Man, the Other Woman:
Understanding and Coping
with Extramarital Affairs

CONTENTS

WOMEN
&
FRIENDSHIP

For the world's most inspiring people—
our families and friends.

INTRODUCTION

Female friendship has been one of the best-kept secrets of our society. There appears to be much more to say about women's relationships with men and children than about their relationships with other women. In Western cultural tradition, being a wife and mother forms the basis of a woman's identity. By comparison, friendship and female solidarity have largely been ignored. There has been a plethora of books on man-woman relationships and the mother-daughter bond. It is rare, though, to read of the electricity that suffuses female friendship, of the feelings women develop for one another that intensify their existence. Friendship remains a vast, fertile area of women's lives that is unexplored.

Not that the void in academic research and popular literature reflects reality. To the contrary, women have a rich heritage of friendship that is older than the civilizations of Greece and Rome; it is from the literature and philosophy of these cultures—where women were not allowed to be citizens—that we get many of our ideas about the nature of their bond. Women have been told throughout history that their lives are empty without men. Yet, for many women, friendship provides the essential psychological nutrients on which their life feeds.

The popular media, unlike academia, have recently caught on to the importance of women's friendships. In the last few years there has been a spate of movies, plays, and television shows depicting women as friends. Two of the hottest television series this past season involved women friends. "Cagney and Lacey" portrays two policewomen who are caring friends as well as loyal partners. The comedy "Kate and Allie" involves two divorced women who share an apartment and each other's lives. Instead of the unreal relationship of Lucy and Ethel, we have Alice and Vera, and Laverne and Shirley, not just using each other as comedy foils but exhibiting clear love of each other. On the stage recently we saw Nell Dunn's *Steaming*, about a group of women from upper class to blue collar who frequent a steambath and become friends by recognizing their ties in a society that indoctrinates them all into living for men, and Wendy Wasserstein's *Isn't It Romantic?*, in which a young woman searching for independence gives up the nice Jewish doctor in her life but continues to rely on and appreciate her girlfriend.

The flow of women's friendship in films is almost a tidal wave. After years of MASH buddies and Sundance Kids, of Diners and Midnight Cowboys, the women are getting their day on the screen; from *Julia, The Turning Point,* and *The Goodbye Girl* to *Entre-Nous, Nine to Five,* and *Swing Shift,* a central theme is friendship between women. A decade ago, who would have thought that the big embrace at the end of a movie would be, as it is in *Swing Shift,* between two women reunited in friendship?

Yet women's friendships are sometimes less than loving; they are a complex arrangement that often involves disappointment, jealousy, anger, competitiveness, and betrayal. Indeed, for women close friendship has been cited as a nearly impossible achievement. According to popular culture, women don't trust each other, women don't work well for other women, and women are inherently in competition for the available men; it is men to whom they turn for love, support, and validation. And there is some truth here: What woman doesn't remember being stood up by a female friend who received a last-minute invitation from a man? What woman hasn't heard another spread spiteful gossip?

This negative view of women's friendship, whether held by men or by women, is not too surprising given the press this relationship has received over the years. History rarely celebrates female friendship as it does male camaraderie. Rather, it is filled with endless portrayals of women as each other's best enemies. Competing for men, from whom they have historically derived their identity, they are depicted as fierce rivals. Even the synonyms for *friend* and *friendship* are mainly rooted in male experiences: *fellow* and *fellowship, brotherhood* and *buddy, billy.* The thesaurus offers thirteen famous friends starting with Achilles and Patroclus, Castor and Pollux, and Pylades and Orestes and ending with Soldiers Three and the Three Musketeers. Where are the women?

But this negative characterization of women has historically been distorted and overblown. In fact, we have found that friendships between women are deeper, more enduring, and more plentiful than those between men. Women's education for their sex role prepares them for relating to others intimately, whereas male sex-role conditioning prepares men to act invulnerable and competitive.

Because women are so often uninhibited about sharing their genuine feelings and concerns with each other, they are often able to move beyond competitive barriers. Women offer support for each other during their worst times as well as their best; they will admit weaknesses and faults to each other and will share defeats as well as victories. In short, women dare to be vulnerable with each other. And this vulnerability brings with it the joy and pain of intimacy. Like mother-daughter relationships, female friendships are seldom bland. They are intensely loving, sustaining, and supportive; when they have gone amiss, they are envious, deceitful, and treacherous. Intimacy, it appears, breeds intensity of feelings.

When a man uses the word *friend* he is likely to be talking about someone he does things with—a teammate, a fellow hobbyist, or a drinking buddy. These activities constitute the fabric of the friendship; it is a "doing" relationship in which similarity of interests is the key bond. Women opt for a warm, emotional exchange in which communication flows freely; activity is mere background.

Because of the contrasts evoked by their conditioning and diverse expectations, women and men react to the friendship experience differently. If an atmosphere of discovery and delight pervades many female friendships, an atmosphere of guardedness characterizes many male relationships. One woman who cherishes the emotional sharing and support she receives from her female friends put it this way: "Men fix things, but women fix each other."

Women's friendships are especially sustaining in these times of social upheaval when the very concept of womanhood is being redefined, when mores and expectations are thrown into the air like a crazy deck of cards and the queens come tumbling back to earth in totally new patterns. The ties that bind women in friendships are crucial. Every day the changes accelerate: More and more women enter the work force; 11.8 million women live alone; according to 1983 U.S. Census statistics, widows outnumber widowers by five to one, and almost one in two marriages ends in divorce. Women have realized that in our impersonal, disconnected society, friendships may be more a necessity than a luxury. To put the matter more bluntly, in the modern world, friendships are not optional. For women, this may be especially true.

As marriages or other housekeeping arrangements dissolve, women friends most often substitute for ex-husbands or ex-lovers in many aspects of day-to-day life. As families are separated by geography or the "generation gap," friends substitute for the family circle. As women consciously reject the idea of relying totally on husbands for financial and emotional support, they turn to the job market for their paychecks and to their women friends for emotional sustenance. With increasing numbers of women working outside the home, friendships are blossoming between union buddies, lunch-hour squash pals, and business colleagues.

In many ways, friendship is even more critical to women than to men. Women, as do any "minority," need like people for support. Surely, while their needs, ideas, hopes, and fears are in flux, women will turn to other women.

The abundance of women's groups bears this out. These groups range widely in scope from consciousness-raising groups to La Leche League meetings, from divorcées' and widows' programs to breast-surgery rap groups, from Christian womanhood groups to feminist collectives. What they have in common is women united with women. As one woman, a forty-four-year-old librarian and mother of three, stated:

> Two years ago I joined a women's consciousness-raising group. This proved to be an enormous step toward getting to know myself and other women from a totally different perspective. The women in the group are stimulating, alive. They are a challenge to my antiwoman bias. Ironically, these women aren't extraordinary. They may well be the same women I rejected as friends all these years. I look at my own womanhood differently now; I am more sympathetic to my own struggle in a man's world. Consequently, I relate to other women's lives more sympathetically.
>
> When I look more closely at those neighborhood parties I so dreaded, for example, I have a different view of things. The women clustered in the "recipe-swapping" corner frequently were squeezed out of the men's conversations and looked to each other for support. Those conversations among women, as meager as they may have seemed to me, were often their only acknowledgment as human beings of worth—they shared a common struggle. Other women, those I characterized as rivals, simply wanted a different way to say, "I want recognition also." I can understand that; it no longer seems con-

temptuous. Actually, it's quite human. These days I work on my relationships with other women. I invest in them. And you know what? They ripen. I have a few good, close friends. I am quite pleased with that.

And in less formal ways, women are meeting and bonding around their changing needs and are cultivating lasting friendships that transcend any one issue. One woman who recently returned to the work force after five years as a homemaker explained:

My old friendships have been dissolved through either relocation or divorce and the changes that brings. Some have just fizzled out, and we have gone our separate ways. Living in a neighborhood where people pretty much keep to themselves, I felt quite isolated and unhappy. The thought of moving even occurred to me—maybe to a co-op or to a friendlier community or something—but my husband wouldn't hear of it. I held out as mother and homemaker for a while, but when being alone all day started to feel like jail, when I would practically taste my longing for close friendship with another woman, I made up my mind to find a babysitter and return to nursing. What I was looking for was friendship; developing a close relationship was my main objective. As a matter of fact, I quit my first job even though it had obvious benefits—good salary, convenience, pleasant conditions—and took a lower-paying position with a longer commute in a bustling, active teaching hospital. I did it simply for the increased opportunity to meet a wide range of other women.

A forty-year-old woman, a college instructor who had gone through a bitter divorce, confided:

If I had made an effort to make friends with women when I was married, I would have had someone to confide in, and maybe, just maybe, it would have taken the pres-

sure off my spouse to be always available to me. Maybe
I would have hung on to my marriage, then, or at least
I would have been better able to cope when we did break
up. Since I've been separated, I've developed lots of
friendships with women, and I am very close with one
of them. The two of us check in with each other everyday as if we were members of AA. In the future, if I
ever marry again, I would never depend solely on my
husband for friendship. I need women friends to keep
me whole.

And a thirty-eight-year-old woman, a housewife and mother of
two young children, revealed that she was comforted by a woman
friend after terminating a devastating extramarital affair that almost cost her her marriage:

I felt I had no right to be comforted. I didn't even want
to admit what I had done, but my friend Tess, after putting together the clues concerning my depression, said
"You know, if you had an affair, I don't think it's the
most awful thing in the world. You're still the same
sensitive person that I always knew. Nothing could
change that." And then, my hurt and anger came tumbling out spontaneously, and Tess listened and gave me
tissues and tea. We spent the entire afternoon together
talking, and we created a bond that day that I feel is un-
breakable. It's five years now since I confided my secret
to her, and to no one else. The affair, I realize now,
was almost meaningless compared to my friendship with
Tess.

Lest it appear that friendship in the female world is only or even
primarily a kind of crisis relationship, the following experience
is offered.

My friend Barbara was a painter, writer, and rebel. We
met through a mutual acquaintance who felt we would

be drawn to each other. I, too, was involved in the arts and was inclined toward feeling a kinship with another artist. My first meeting with Barbara confirmed what I had been told about her. She was a marvel, a woman with an inner glow and eyes that danced with playfulness—a quick-witted woman with enormous charm. Her temperament was by turns tough and tender. She had this sense of inner strength mixed with a transparent vulnerability. Her face could express "Elaine, I'm disappointed" one moment, and in the next she would be filled with compassion. What life! She seemed bold, not ashamed of anything about herself; she was open about her "blemishes," contradictions, and self-doubts.

Over the course of this friendship, Barbara and Elaine formed an intense mutual admiration society. Just as Elaine prized and respected Barbara, Barbara was taken with Elaine's strong character and integrity—her ability to stick to her principles regardless of the cost. Elaine was married to an alcoholic who at times was abusive, not only to her but to her two children. Barbara was bitter about this. She felt the hurt Elaine tried to keep hidden. This was the only source of conflict in their friendship; Elaine wouldn't discuss Barbara's negative feelings about Elaine's husband. While Elaine did not tolerate any abuse to her children, she seemed undeterred by her husband's drinking.

Eight years after they met, almost to the day, Barbara was diagnosed as having liver cancer. She died within three months. Nearly six years later, Elaine can't get past the anniversary of Barbara's death without crying or becoming morose. Barbara's death made Elaine keenly aware of how much her friend meant to her. With Barbara, she had felt completely relaxed, without a need to censor her thoughts and feelings. She felt free to ask favors and do favors. They traveled together, played together, and enriched each other. They trusted each other. As Elaine said to Barbara shortly before her untimely death, "We have incorporated ourselves, you and I, into each other's psyches."

Women and Friendship celebrates women's unique bonding as friends. It explores the patterns of friendships among women, examines the roots of the myths about women and friendship, and attempts to discover how friendships are formed. The book probes whether friendships can exist between the sexes, how marriage and divorce affect friendship, how friendships affect marriage and divorce, how mentors and protégées become friends, how friendship changes during the different stages of life, and how the women's movement and other societal changes are affecting women and their friendships.

The book is based on several hundred interviews and the available social science literature, of which there is an astonishing paucity. Data are given where numbers are particularly surprising or enlightening, but in the main the significant findings of our research are presented through and supported by the words of women themselves. Their voices are certainly more colorful and persuasive than any statistics.

For the most part, everyone has to puzzle out her own friendship needs, but this book will be helpful. We did discover connections; certain patterns in friendships began to emerge. Myths were shattered. Current doctrines were challenged. These new discoveries are valuable guideposts and are gladly shared.

CHAPTER

1

KINDRED
SPIRITS IN
AN UNKIND
WORLD

Terri Carr was leading what she considered a very fortunate life, including a loving husband, three kids who never gave her much aggravation, plenty of neighborhood friends, and a large family living nearby. When her fiftieth birthday rolled around, Terri studied the options for a celebration: a large family party, an extravagant vacation with her husband of almost thirty years, or maybe an expensive dinner and a hit show. Instead, Terri chose to mark her birthday by celebrating her friendship with women, in particular her friendship of more than forty years with five friends she had stayed close to since childhood.

They rented two rooms in the newest hotel in her city, ordered a chocolate cake to be served at poolside, and later had an adult pajama party in their rooms. All weekend, they basked in their joy of each other.

It seemed especially appropriate to Terri to choose to be with close friends for the landmark occasion. These were the women who had shared all the landmarks of her life; they were her past. They had shared report-card day in grade school and the first fumblings of dating in high school. They had started a sorority together in college and still laughed about the afternoon teas they held for mothers, who all came wearing hats. After they married and were one another's bridesmaids, they were young mothers themselves, sharing brand-new experiences, and although sometimes none of them knew the correct answers, they advised one another on domestic matters.

Though they all were married and had families, their friendship added another layer to the fabric of their lives; it had enriched each one's experiences because there were five others to share them with. Without this circle of close friends, "life would have been like going to see a good movie alone," Terri explained. When they or their families achieved success, when Phyllis won a scholarship and Elaine got a job, the achievements were validated by friends who cared. When tragedy struck, when Roberta became widowed and when Claire went into the hospital for a major operation, these friends shouldered some of the burden.

They especially needed each other as they negotiated the unique circumstances faced by women: the isolation of the job of housewife, a job that comes with no training manual. When women started to become "liberated," these friends, who could discuss their most intimate fears and dreams with each other, helped one another adjust to the new world. They were the cheerleaders when Sonny went back to school; they advised one another on returning to the job market middle-aged and female.

All through the birthday weekend, Terri kept noticing the response of strangers they met. The management considered the event important enough to send the birthday cake free. The local newspaper thought the event unique enough to send a reporter. The reservations clerk, a woman, was especially solicitous. In the hotel restaurant they were congratulated by the women at neighboring tables as if they had just won a lottery.

To Terri, it was not such a big deal. At first she failed to understand why the celebration would have meaning to anyone but her friends. Her friendships were so interwoven with her lifestyle she had lost sight for a moment of their uniqueness. But the response is not surprising. To women who had enjoyed close friendships as Terri had, the reaction validated their own close feelings toward their friends. For the males who encountered the friends that weekend, the sight of six caring women was an awakening, for they had believed the conventional wisdom that women can't be loyal to one another.

Terri's bonds with her friends were deep and enduring. Our research has shown that, like Terri, many women are able to sustain lifelong, close friendships with each other. The psychological literature indicates that women are at least as capable as men of deep friendships, and maybe even more capable.

In writing the book *Friendship: How to Give It, How to Get It,* psychologist Joel Block found that many more women are on intimate terms than is commonly supposed. Out of nearly 1,100 women questioned, the majority had a close friend, and most who did not yearned for such a relationship. It was a rare woman who was so totally obsessed with the role of homemaker and mother or so enmeshed in her career that she completely ignored the need for friendship. Such relationships were not nearly so bountiful for the thousand or so male participants in the study. The majority did not have a close buddy with whom they could talk intimately. Trust, a basic ingredient of friendship, appeared to be a rare commodity among men.[1]

Other researchers agree. Alan Booth of the University of Nebraska studied the friendship patterns of eight hundred adults in two major cities and found that both working-class and middle-class women had more solid and emotionally satisfying friendships than did working-class and middle-class men.[2] In another investigation, Mirra Komarovsky scrutinized a number of blue-collar marriages and found that six out of every ten wives she interviewed had good friends, but only two out of ten husbands enjoyed close nonfamilial relationships.[3]

Differences in the number of women and men who have friendships or in the number of friends they have may be notable, but even more important is the contrast in the quality of these relationships. Here the two sexes clearly travel different friendship paths. Women more often than not share intimate styles of interaction. Girls are traditionally raised to openly express their emotions, to be less concerned about exposing their vulnerabilities than boys, and to be nurturing. Thus, women's sex-role socialization prepares them for relating on an emotional level. Men, because they have been exposed to sex roles that are constraining ("It's every man for himself") are less prepared for friendships. Closeness with others—particularly with other men, who are regarded as adversaries to be conquered or avoided—is an unaffordable luxury for many men.

In an investigation bearing on the issue of friendship quality, Paul Wright, after more than a decade of researching same-sex friendship, reports in the journal *Sex Roles* that there is no sound basis for the contention that women's friendships are inferior to those of men. Wright notes that for men, friendship tends to be a side-by-side relationship, with the partners mutually oriented to some external task or activity; for women, friendship tends to be face-to-face, with the partners oriented to a personal knowledge of and concern for one another. Women, Wright concludes, tend to be more sensitive than men to the overall quality of their friendships.[4]

Women also share a bond unique to them. Unlike men, they are steeped in the physicality of menstruation, fertility, and birth. Men do not swallow birth control pills or use contraceptive devices. Men do not become pregnant, have abortions, or give birth. Women share an awareness of their bodies that is uniquely female and, as such, is a link to one another. Indeed, Johanna Dobkin Gladieux found in her research reported in *The First Child and Family Formation* that for many women, satisfaction with pregnancy has a stronger association to friendship factors than to marital relationship factors. Apparently, the empathy between women, sharing a common biology, is stronger than the support offered by a man, whose understanding of the pregnancy experience is limited.[5]

Even more startling is another finding by sociologist Robert Bell. When American women were asked to specify the three persons they would most like to be with, the husband was mentioned by 64 percent, the mother or daughter by 67 percent, other kin by 38 percent, *and a woman friend by 98 percent.*[6]

Perhaps it is women's ability to quickly understand and empathize with each other that makes them sought after as friends, as the story of Beth, age twenty-eight, indicates. Having recently arrived in New York, Beth was invited to a small gathering by her new neighbors. At one point in the evening, she found herself alone with an older woman. The older woman spoke of her work and of her fear of losing her position to a younger, more energetic woman. Beth, who felt restless in her job, empathized and admitted her own plight. Although these two women could easily have become adversaries, they did not. Rather, by the time they were joined by other guests, they had plunged into deep conversation. It is difficult to imagine two men becoming as quickly intimate about so sensitive a subject.

SISTERHOOD DENIED, BROTHERHOOD AFFIRMED

If literature is the cosmic mirror that reflects the ways of the world, it is understandable that myths about women's friendships should take hold. From the beginning men have been portrayed as loyal, caring friends. Mythology, often used as the imagery to reflect contemporary issues, is bereft of tales of women as friends. To match the story of Damon and Pythias, whose friendship was so strong that one was willing to die for the other, there is the myth of Demeter and Persephone, but they were mother and daughter, and Demeter's crusade to retrieve her daughter from Hades was acceptable to society in terms of mother love rather than friendship. Unlike Damon and Pythias, the goddesses and demigoddesses of classical mythology are forever embroiled in disputes over a man. They are duplicitous, jealous, conniving wretches. In the body of Greek literature that has set the standard for the Western world, women finally form an alliance in *Lysistrata,* but not for their love of each other. Their alliance was a political one to bring their men home from a war.

And what weapon did these women use? Why, sex, of course. They agreed to withhold their charms. (Unfortunately, it didn't work.)

In the Bible, once again, there are no hymns to females as friends, only as wives, mothers, and devotees of the Lord. The friendship between David and Jonathan is lionized in the Scriptures. The closest women friends come to such recognition is in the story of Ruth and Naomi. While Ruth vowed, "Whither thou goest I will go," the basis of this loyalty is again family rather than friendship since they were mother-in-law and daughter-in-law. Women fare no better in biblically based literature such as the miracle plays. In these plays, which had formed the standard fare of theatergoers in the fifteenth century, mankind had a second shot at writing women friends into biblical history. Mrs. Noah in one of the miracle plays is typical of the result.[7] Mrs. Noah, who was not in the Bible, appears in the miracle play as a gossip who has to be dragged kicking and screaming aboard the ark because she doesn't want to leave her friends behind. Who were her friends? Gossips like her. Such were social expectations that the bond between women had to be a union based on chatter.

Modern Western literature, until very recently, has been no less of a disappointment on the subject of women's friendships. In *A Room of One's Own,* Virginia Woolf wrote: "I tried to remember any case in the course of my reading where two women are presented as friends. . . . They are confidantes, of course, in Racine and the Greek tragedies. They are now and then mothers and daughters. But almost without exception they are shown in their relation to men. It was strange to think that all the great women of fiction were, until Jane Austen's day, not only seen by the other sex, but seen only in relation to the other sex."[8]

Woolf had read of Hamlet and Horatio, Romeo and Mercutio, Hal and Falstaff, and Antonio and Bassanio. She had been raised on *The Three Musketeers* and Kipling's *Odes to Male Camaraderie,* on Mulvaney, Ortheris, and Learoyd in *Soldiers Three.* Even the Little Women had a best friend who was a boy. One can't help wondering if Emma Bovary had some secret woman friend in whom she confided. Knowing what we know about women and friendships, she must have, but the concept either never occurred to Flaubert or was considered and dismissed.

Although women writers portrayed women's friendships, these alliances were tortured or doomed, destructive or manipulative, motivated by lesbianism or threatening to heterosexual lovers. Janet Todd's book *Women's Friendship in Literature* discusses eighteenth-century writing from England and France. Although she was able to find several friendships in literature, they are uniformly distressing relationships. In Samuel Richardson's *Clarissa,* the protagonist literally dies because of her attachment to Anna Howe, which she can fully accept only on her deathbed.[9] In Jane Austen's *Mansfield Park,* the heroine does her utmost to avoid friendship.[10]

Modern literature is hardly more tolerant of women's friendship until the late 1970s and the 1980s. We can hardly conjure up one play involving women as friends. Sociologist Sally Ridgeway did a study of women's roles in the most popular Broadway comedies over the past five decades and found that only two, *The Voice of the Turtle* and *The Women,* portrayed women friends. Many were competitors in the race to catch a man but not friends.[11] What is more, the two plays Ridgeway cites involving friendship between women are hardly flattering.

In *The Voice of the Turtle* by John Van Druten we meet two women, Sally and Olive, who are actresses and friends, friends who see the world together, joke together, and tell each other their secrets. Then Bill comes along. He had gone out with Olive, the older and wiser of the pair. He is now in town on leave. A few minutes after Olive makes a date with Bill, another of her loves calls. She makes excuses to Bill and leaves him with Sally, warning her not to steal him away. The two, of course, fall in love. After they express their devotion in the third act, Bill says to Sally, concerning Olive: "I'm afraid that's the end of a beautiful friendship." Sally answers: "I'm afraid . . . for *me,* too." And Bill answers: "Well, it can't be helped."[12] Sally and Olive's long relationship is buried in three lines.

Clare Boothe Luce's *The Women* is far more damaging to

the claim that women can be friends. The play revolves around a group of Park Avenue matrons and one unmarried intellectual who lie and connive, breaking up each other's marriages and discussing their friends with the tongues of snakes. The crucial act in the play involves Sylvia, the most vicious of the group, and Mary, the sweet mother-wife, who, Sylvia has discovered, is having an affair. Sylvia learned of this from her chatty manicurist. Sylvia has enticed Mary into going to her manicurist, knowing full well Mary will divulge the confidence to her. And she does. In one scene, set in Reno where Mary has gone to get a divorce, she advises one of the other divorcées, Peggy: "When you get back, don't see too much of your girlfriends for a while." And Peggy answers: "Oh, I won't, Mary. It's all their fault we're here." [13] In another scene Sylvia tells the women that her analyst has told her "women are natural enemies." To which Mary answers: "As if any woman needed to go to a psychoanalyst to find out she can't trust women." [14]

Lillian Hellman at least acknowledged female friendship in *The Children's Hour*. The two protagonists, who together run a girls' boarding school, are friends in the deepest sense of the word. But given the society in which they live, their friendship is ultimately destroyed by charges from a disgruntled student that they are lesbians.

Yet from diaries and letters written by women over the centuries we know that female friendships did exist. Why, then, have their meaningful friendships been ignored or distorted through the ages?

THE POWER OF PATRIARCHY:
KEEPING
SISTERHOOD IN ITS PLACE

Most classical literature was written by men. Most of these male writers could not begin to fathom the relationship between two women. It was not so much that male writers ignored female friendships as that they didn't understand them. Most men, in fact, are aliens in the world of female friendship.

Then, of course, there is the denigration of women by many men and some women that characteristically leads to an unfavorable view of friendship. On the psychological front, Freud believed that in essential ways females were inferior to males and therefore wished that they were male. Freud was a product of a society that valued males more than females, so his bias toward women does not come as a surprise. But are contemporary American attitudes so different? Cultural ambivalence about women's equality in American society is alive and well. Notably, this is reflected in the discrepancy between the incomes of females and males for the same work, a reminder that women aren't worth as much as men.

Despite lip service paid to female equality, only a small minority of women have risen to the top ranks of business. And, although more than half of all women work outside the home, the large majority of women continue to be primarily responsible for homemaking and child care. Even our language reflects the lower status of women in our society. One researcher, Muriel Schulz, found that American slang has as many as one thousand phrases and terms that denigrate women, including obscene terms, while there are few words with negative connotations to describe men.[15]

The psychological literature also reflects women's second-class role. Until very recently, few psychologists studied women's relationships with other women. Most often it is the lives and work of men that are highlighted. Psychological theories have been more concerned about men than women. Men in war under the stress of combat and men as aggressors or competitors are subjects that have fascinated scholars. Male-female relations, particularly sexuality and most recently sexual differences, is another focus. But interest in female-female relationships has been scant.

Perhaps the most crucial driving force behind the bad press and negative stereotype of female friendship is an old issue: power. More often than not, men have it and women don't. Naturally, those who have power want to keep it. An alliance of women could be conceived as quite a threat to the patriarchy.

If a woman could depend on other women, she would have less reason to depend on her man. If a woman loved another woman, she might love her spouse less. If a woman could join with other women, who knows what power they might wield?

The recognition of women together seriously threatens the preservation of the status quo. In *Between Women: Lowering the Barriers,* psychologist Paula Caplan discusses a particularly dramatic example reported in the international news. The story concerns the arrest of the Yorkshire Ripper. As reported, the police sent a guard to the house of the suspect's wife because they feared an angry mob of women might try to harm her. Yet absent from the story was any mention or even hint that an angry word had been uttered about the accused man's wife. It would seem plausible, Caplan notes, that many women might shudder in horror and sympathy for the wife; either she stayed with a man she knew was disturbed, or she unknowingly lived with a man filled with hatred and violence. The media, however, chose to report the conventional notion that angry women would turn against another woman.[16]

The assumption in this example is that women's behavior can easily be characterized by one mind and one set of predispositions, which is, of course, unrealistic. All too often one group, in an effort to quiet the fears of another group, attaches simplistic labels to complex behavior and assigns the out-group individual to a very limited, and limiting, category.

On a cultural level, Americans are "materialistic," Germans are "orderly," the English are "distant," the French "passionate," the Italians "emotional," and so on. Rather than capturing the complexity of a culture, this sort of labeling simplistically jams everybody into some pigeonhole. And, of course, the sexes are labeled. Women are "passive," "catty," and "domestic"; men are "aggressive," "fiercely independent," and "strong." Characteristically, the in-group descriptors are more favorable than the adjectives for the out-group. For example, the success of an in-group member (male) is attributed to competence, while a successful out-group member (female) is considered a hard worker. Predictably, since most accomplishments and characterizations of women are devalued, their friendships are similarly demeaned.

HISTORY:
HER STORY, HIS STORY

Friendships among women do exist in fact if not in fiction, despite the soft underside many of these relationships have from being kicked in the belly by society. We are familiar with our mothers' friendships, which flourished despite Clare Boothe Luce's contention that women are natural enemies. We know of friendships in earlier centuries not from what novelists wrote but from what the women wrote themselves in letters and diaries that were fortunately saved. We know that at least since medieval times, when ties expanded past closed fiefdoms and family circles, women have befriended women and gathered together in groups.

So strong was the need for comradeship that women turned many of their household chores into social occasions. With all other social outlets barred, women compensated by washing together at streams, organizing sewing circles, and communally putting up food for the winter. The social communication of the sewing bee should be viewed as hardly less valid than male gatherings at pubs and clubs.

On the American frontier there was an intense need for comradeship among women. Here couples lived away from the institutions of civilization and often away from the extended family. Without relatives, women had to turn to women from other families for advice and support. And that is friendship. Without a family to educate them on childbearing and child rearing, young women sought whoever was around for advice, solace, and aid.

In preindustrial America, women fulfilled a number of roles for one another that have since been relinquished to men. Gynecological and obstetrical services, for example, were often provided by women on the American frontier. Women also attended to other physical and psychological problems that were later attended to by mostly male physicians and psychotherapists. Marriage, childbirth and child rearing, care of the sick, and care of widows were once women's domain.

Indeed, for those women who could not seek solace and support from each other because of the lack of transportation in a sparsely populated land, the price was great. Accompanying the loss of female friendship came psychic casualties: Fear, depression, mental breakdown, insomnia, and suicide haunted that first generation of prairie women. The erosion of their very spirit dramatically documented the cost of their deprivation.

Evidences of friendship in the Victorian era are documented in Carroll Smith-Rosenberg's remarkable essay "The Female World of Love and Ritual." The essay includes letters written by women to their closest friends from 1760 to the 1800s.

Smith-Rosenberg writes of Sarah Butler Wister and Jeannie Field Musgrove, who met in the summer of 1849, when Jeannie was sixteen and Sarah two years younger. Sarah kept a bouquet of flowers before Jeannie's portrait. "If the day should come when you failed me either through your fault or my own, I would forswear all human friendship thenceforth," Sarah wrote Jeannie.[17] After Sarah married, she wrote: "I shall be entirely alone [this coming week]. I can give you no idea how desperately I shall want you."[18] Jeannie began her letters with the salutation "Dear darling Sarah!"[19]

Molly and Helena met at school, the Cooper Institute School for Design for Women in New York City, and became close with each other and each other's families. One letter Smith-Rosenberg quotes reconstructs something of their relationship. "I have not said to you in so many or so few words that I was happy with you during those few so incredibly short weeks but surely you do not need words to tell you what you must know. . . . We know we can amuse each other for many idle hours together and now we know that we can also work together. And that means much, don't you think so?"[20] Molly wrote.

It is hard for contemporary women to read these words without surmising a sexual entanglement in these friendships, but Smith-Rosenberg discounts this idea. This was just the way Victorians wrote: openly, emotionally, and unashamed of their friendships. She writes of how rural women of that period would pay each other extended visits "even dislodging husbands from their beds and bedrooms so that dear friends might spend every hour of every day together." [21]

Smith-Rosenberg says that "women who had little status and power in the world of male concerns possessed status and power in the lives and worlds of other women." [22] She concludes: "The regularity of their correspondence underlines the sincerity of their words. Women named their daughters after one another and sought to integrate dear friends into their lives after marriage. As one young bride wrote to an old friend shortly after her marriage: 'I want to see you and talk with you and feel that we are united by the same bonds of sympathy and congeniality as ever.' " [23]

The female friendship of the nineteenth century, the intimate, loving friendship between two women, is an excellent example of the type of historical phenomenon that most historians are familiar with, that few have thought much about, and that virtually no one has written about. It is one aspect of the female experience that, consciously or unconsciously, they have chosen to ignore.

In this century, women met and became friends through various clubs that were organized for women only in the face of their almost total disbarment from the business and social institutions of male society. Around the turn of the century the educated woman enjoyed social commerce at university alumnae clubs and the PTA (which was formed not to buy playground equipment or bake cookies but out of concern with child labor and child abuse by parents; the organization became linked to schools because they were the logical base from which to lobby and organize).

During this period, organizations like the National Council

of Women, the YWCA, and the League of Women Voters were organized. None of these organizations was founded for its social potential, but, in fact, sociability was the inevitable by-product and perhaps the key to the first "old girls' network" in America. It was also during this period that women began organizing to fight for the right to vote. But by and large, as was usual among women, the foundations of these organizations were in social service, whether it took the form of registering voters, raising scholarship money, or supporting neighborhood settlement houses, where, not incidentally, immigrants and poor women gathered to learn homemaking skills and to become literate. Yet these clubs indeed served the women themselves in that these social groupings offered a way for women to socialize—to meet people outside their family circles and to make friends.

One can only speculate on why men's clubs were held in esteem while women's clubs became the butt of jokes. The term *clubwoman* itself is loaded with negative baggage, the image of the overweight, overage housewife diddling around with good works as reflected in Helen Hokinson's famous cartoons.

FROM VICTIMS
TO VICTIMIZERS

Possibly many of the current misconceptions about women and friendship are rooted in the post–World War II period, when women were swept from their defense jobs to make way for the returning veterans. *McCall's* magazine then touted marital "togetherness" as the goal of a woman's life.

Some scholars believe female friendships did go through some rocky times during the 1950s. The immersion in home and family, they contend, separated women from the outside world and from one another. Among middle-class families, a woman's best friend was supposed to be her husband. Previously it had been thought acceptable for two or more generations to live together in the same household, but now more affluent families, the daughters and sons of immigrants, started their migration from city tenements to single-family homes in the suburbs. The homemaker's energy turned away from the extended family and from the female friends she had made at work during the war to her husband and children again. Since women had less contact with one another, housework and child care became the individual responsibility of each woman to be borne alone; grandmothers, or aunts, or women friends were no longer readily available to many women. And as women produced less tangible products at home, their work became devalued, and along with it, they became devalued by society and, inevitably, in their own eyes.

Certainly, women still had friends during this period, but considering the derision of women in general, their relationships with each other would also be trivialized. We all succumb easily to society's image of ourselves, and millions of women regarded themselves as "only a housewife," or "only a woman." The highest compliment given a woman in this decade was that she thought "like a man."

This negative self-image certainly would be an impediment to friendships with other members of the same class. Like Groucho Marx saying, "I wouldn't join any club that would have me as a member," women would reject one another's friendship. A negative self-image can lead to self-hate. To make matters worse, a woman may not only hate herself and others of her sex, but she may be distressed by these feelings. She is badly torn. Her conflict makes for uneasiness with herself and a lasting sense of insecurity.

Studies of intragroup prejudice have bearing on this issue of women's self-hate. Some Jews, for instance, refer to other Jews as "kikes," blaming them exclusively for the anti-Semitism from which all Jews suffer. Class distinctions within other groups— "lace-curtain Irish" looking down on "shanty Irish," well-educated blacks snubbing their noses at poorly educated blacks— serve the same purpose.

In a dramatic demonstration of rejection of one's own, the late psychologist Gordon Allport in his classic text *The Nature of Prejudice* cited studies of Nazi concentration camp victims.

At first prisoners tried to keep their self-respect intact, but after two or three years of unusual suffering and after other ego defenses had failed, they identified with their oppressors as a form of adjustment. They imitated the guards, wore bits of their clothing for symbolic power, and turned against their fellow prisoners and became anti-Semites.[24]

While antifeminism is not nearly as extreme as conditions in a Nazi concentration camp, the process of viewing women as a wholly different and inferior species to men has one similar outcome: Some of the victims become victimizers.

Clearly, the struggle for women to accept each other as friends has not been easy, nor is it over. Many women are seeking serious relationships with one another based on mutual respect, a healthy exchange of ideas, and the simple enjoyment of each other's company. Others still form relationships for reasons that are less than noble: so they can have a sympathetic shoulder to lean on when a man is unavailable or a willing listener to brag to when romance and career are going well, or simply to fill empty time on those occasions when there is nothing better to do.

And there is betrayal. "Oh, betrayal, you mean like the cheating between a man and a woman," several women responded, as if sexual infidelity is the only source of deceit. But betrayal comes in many forms: the betrayal of confidences, exploiting a friend, "innocent" deceptions, breaking commitments. Women can be competitive and unfaithful as friends; to portray them as always loving would be simplistic. For instance, here is an instance of betrayal revealed to Joel Block in his research for *Friendship: How to Give It, How to Get It*.

One evening at a party, Caroline went into one of the bedrooms to lie down for a few minutes. She swung open the door and found Patricia, a friend for many years, and Walt, another friend's husband, talking. Their manner gave them away; standing so close and talking so seriously, they were clearly involved in a romantic intimacy. Patricia knew the instant she saw Caroline that her adventure had been discovered. Patricia couldn't be sure of Caroline's loyalty; the possibility existed that she might try to hurt her. She was frightened; if the affair were made public all hell would break loose. Some form of action had to be taken. Caroline related:

At first Patricia stopped by to see me less frequently; then she didn't come by at all. Then, suddenly, she was too busy to spend time with me when I dropped by her place. At first I really didn't notice the change. It may seem odd, but I didn't connect what was happening to the party incident. To me, there was no point going into details of that with Patricia. But when her avoidance of me finally registered, I challenged her. I asked if she felt awkward with me. She denied any uneasiness. Nothing was wrong, she said, "I've just been busy." In the coming months, a relationship I had thought of as supportive just stopped. Patricia never offered an explanation, and I didn't push any further. Patricia just wasn't the type to be probed; she would only solidify her position, and we would end up further apart.

By the time summer rolled around, Patricia had cut me off completely. No phone calls, nothing. Then something else started to happen. I began to have a vague feeling of being an outsider among my own friends—mutual friends of Patricia's and mine. Then it hit me. The thought came like a jolt, while I was out for a walk by myself: Walt's wife was very suspicious; Patricia was terrified. An ingenious solution would be to find a target to deflect the suspicion. That was me! Since Walt's wife was already wary and not about to be soothed, at least Walt and Patricia could protect their relationship by offering me as a sacrifice. And if I went public with what I know, who would believe me now? Patricia had spent months spreading rumors, laying the groundwork. I felt absolutely victimized. I was humiliated. How could I ever trust another woman again?

Suddenly, little things that occurred over that year

started to make sense. Comments that friends made—
"Haven't seen you around your old haunts; keeping pretty
busy?"—fell into place. I wondered why Uta, Walt's
wife, snubbed me; I walked right by her, looked straight
at her, and said hello, and she just stared through me.
Intimacies with other friends had turned into polite social conversation. Now it all came together. I was a de-
coy in a vicious plan. It was a nightmare. I was terribly
hurt. After some months, with my feelings at least par-
tially repaired, I moved out in search of new friends. I
missed the daily intimacy and companionship of my old
friends and was unsure that I would find it again, but I
refused to have anything to do with them. As far as I
was concerned, I had no friends left. Patricia saw to that;
she made a clean sweep.[25]

Mary Wollstonecraft, who showed us in her novels how difficult
the road was for women friends, defined the problem of wom-
en's friendship and its relation to the status of women in *A Vindication of the Rights of Woman:* "I know that a little sensibil-
ity, and great weakness, will produce a strong sexual attachment,
and that reason must cement friendship; consequently, I allow
that more friendship is to be found in the male than the female
world, and that men have a higher sense of justice. . . ,"[26] These
don't seem like the words of the feminist she was, until her
thought is completed: "How can woman [sic] be just or generous, when they are the slaves of injustice?"[27]

It is no accident that Betty Friedan's experiences during the
post–World War II period gave rise to her first stirring that there
was rampant among women a profound dissatisfaction with their
lot. Her analysis of the problem took the shape of the seminal
work of the new feminist movement, *The Feminine Mystique.*

In the 1960s the feminist movement opened a floodgate of
understanding, and finally the secret was out of the bag: Women
have value, to themselves, to each other, and to society. And as
women began to value themselves they began to value their work,

whether outside or inside the home. They began to value their aspirations, even if they entailed nonfamilial roles, and they began to value their friends.

Lynne, who graduated from a large northeastern university in 1958, when the purpose of a college education for women was only half-jokingly defined as winning a "Mrs." degree, said:

> I was surely a product of my time. I studied to be a buyer, a career appropriate for women. I planned to work but, of course, only until I had a child. I never even entertained the question of whether I should work once I had kids. It wasn't even a thought. All through college I had friends, mostly in my sorority. Girlfriends were basically to pass the time until I had a real relationship, I thought.
>
> It's only now I realize how happy just being with friends made me and how much support they gave me through awful times, like trying to diet off twenty pounds, when they cheered each ounce I lost, or the time two of them stayed up all night with me, helping to type a paper. But there wasn't a time I wouldn't break a date with a friend if I got a chance to go out with a guy. And only recently did I realize how important one special friend was in my life. Her name was Marlene and we roomed together my junior year. It was my happiest year of college, but I never credited Marlene for being the reason. She moved out of the sorority house in our senior year to live in a special dorm for students in a program that combines the last year of college with the first year of law school. I was very lonely that year. I remember feeling unattached to the sorority. I felt vague, as though I was floating through the year. There simply was no model for me to weigh the loss of a best friend against. At least not as a grown-up. I knew little girls had best friends, but I thought they weren't important to adults. I think it was no accident that my other close friend was

a male, a guy who was my best friend's friend. To be accepted by him was very satisfying to me. Actually, I still see him often, and I'm glad he's my friend, but I'm a bit embarrassed now about how little I realized Marlene's friendship meant to me.

When I graduated, I saw a lot of my college friends. Then I met Robbie, and in less than a year's time we were married. I stopped calling my own friends and socialized only with his friends and their wives. I became quite close to several of them, but it wasn't ever like Marlene. Now she lived in Florida and I lived in Manhattan, so our contacts were rare. It was easier to integrate her into my life because our meetings were infrequent. I saw her when we vacationed in Florida. The rest of my college friends, who lived nearby, I just erased.

After I was divorced I renewed my friendship with Jenny, another old college friend. One day I just looked her up in the book and called. What a happy reunion! To this day, we remain friends. Even though I'm married again, I consciously kept her as part of my life, not letting the rest of my friends go this time. I'm not embarrassed to let my husband know they are important to me. No, women friends count. I thank the women's movement for teaching me that.

Indeed, women's friendships are ready to come out of the closet. Today many women will dare to choose a woman friend's company over a spouse's company or a lover's or male friend's company. More and more, women are realizing that their friendships are necessary for their survival, just as women are necessary for the emotional survival of their spouses, lovers, and male friends.

CHAPTER

2

WHAT
DO WOMEN
WANT?

Women's wants have baffled men from the beginning of time, but surprisingly, the answer to Freud's famous question has evaded women themselves until recently. The beginnings of an answer emerged when pioneer feminist Betty Friedan described "the problem that has no name" in *The Feminine Mystique*. Homemakers who had willingly hidden behind a barricade of suburban chain-link fences in split-level homes, women who were split in spirit between their families and obvious discontent, along with masses of single women who worked in low-paying, dead-end jobs while waiting for men to rescue them, broke free.

Women finally realized what they lacked as they tried to fill their lives caring for their husbands, bosses, children, and homes. They lacked identity: the unique part of themselves that would allow them to be wholly accountable for themselves and to feel fully alive.

Women, at last, knew what they wanted: the freedom to choose their own identity.

To gain that identity has been a long and arduous process in a world where men are accustomed to viewing women as help-mates, nurturers, and caretakers. It is a process of discovery that women are still struggling with, but they are no longer alone in their discontent. For with their emerging identity, women have united in their commonality—their similar frustrations and desires. And they have discovered their needs are as important and powerful as men's needs. Women are now less reluctant to acknowledge that after the children have been tended to, after the husband is fed and the house has been cleaned, the nurturers need nurturing, and the caretakers need caring for, too. Depleted emotional energy, they have found, can best be replenished by frequent supportive contact with other women. Often their friendships are celebrated as cherished alliances that provide a unique understanding of each other and an irreplaceable emotional connection. Women acknowledge that they share experiences that are uncommon to men, experiences that create a feeling of belonging beyond the love of men.

As well as a defense against sexism, women's friendship serves as an escape from it. In a society where women are routinely restricted in so many ways, friendship among women is one of the few "equal opportunities." It is a relationship women choose, with people they choose, and within the boundaries they choose. In friendships, women face none of the gender-based legal and social barriers confronting them in almost all other relationships.

Edith, a fifty-four-year-old teacher, said she understood, when she was a young mother in the late 1950s and early 1960s, that without women friends her life would be boring and empty. She explained:

> I lived on a park bench on West End Avenue in Manhattan when my children were small. I was there more than in my apartment. My husband owned a pharmacy in Harlem, and he worked late every night. I'd sit on the park bench, watching my children play and talking to my women friends, the other women on the block, endlessly. Those were the happiest times in my life.
>
> My women friends are very important to me; they

are actually more important than my family. My husband is loyal, but I could never talk to him the way I talk to my women friends. There is a mutual experience and reaction that only women can share together. And women have experience at listening and talking that men don't. If I didn't have to take sexual needs into account, and if I had a choice of spending the rest of my life on a desert island with my male friends or with my female friends, I'd definitely take the women. By the way, when I moved to suburbia with my husband, my city friends bought me a park bench. I was lonely for a while when we moved, but since friends are a priority, I joined groups, I became active in the community, and I had parties until I could find women whom I could talk to, really talk to.

For the vast majority of women we spoke with, women friends were more responsible to their emotional needs than men friends. A thirty-nine-year-old journalist said she had both male and female friends but felt far more comfortable about revealing intimate concerns with her women friends. "It's just not the same, somehow, talking to men. And I am infuriated by women who think men are better friends than women. They think they become more important by associating with important men, as though power rubs off. It doesn't. Women together are powerful. For me, the 1960s and the emergence of the women's movement was a changing point; I finally realized intellectually and emotionally that women were important, that I wasn't simply marking time with my women friends, waiting for a man to come along."

WOMEN FRIENDS:
THE NURTURERS' NURTURERS

Women have always depended on each other as friends; their socialization leaves them ideally suited to fulfill this role for each other. Mothers, after all, have traditionally raised daughters to be nurturers; sons, however, are taught that independence and competitiveness are ideal male characteristics.

The role of nurturer is so well instilled in girls from infancy that preschoolers who are not interested in cuddling dolls are cause for concern. Young girls, who need nurturing themselves, are encouraged to care for others, including younger siblings and their parents. A preadolescent girl, for instance, will proudly serve her father dinner or take pleasure in helping her mother fix her hair. Today, when both parents work in more than 50 percent of households with children under eighteen, young girls, more than boys, are required to care for younger children every day after school. Girls are expected to be more mature and less of a nuisance than boys. And sometimes girls are deprived of the nurturing they are expected to give.

Later in life, the demand to nurture continues for women. It is women who are expected to care for elderly parents. Women are expected to be caretakers of their own families as well, and if a woman and her husband should part, she is expected to care for the children on her own. When she does not, she is often viewed as selfish or strange, and she is sometimes scorned by other women.

Women who have not received as much emotional sustenance as they required in childhood will crave nurturing as adults. They usually do not receive this nurturance from their spouse or minor children, so they will turn to other women to fill this need. Thus, women friends are especially important to each other.

Not only do women seek each other out, they tend to be drawn to relating in general. Evidence suggestive of this tendency appears in a study by Michael Argyle and Adrian Furnham reported in the *Journal of Marriage and the Family*. Women, more than men, Argyle and Furnham found, derived satisfaction in relationships in which they were able to give and get emotional support, discuss personal problems, and simply be with another person. Women also derived more satisfaction from being with friends of either sex, siblings, neighbors, and adolescent children, while men got more satisfaction from being with spouses and work superiors.[1] Perhaps it is because women are reared to value their nurturing role and to be in touch with their emotional selves that they find pleasure in emotional intimacy. Men rely primarily on their spouses for such intimacy.

Aside from an emotional sensitivity that is fostered in women from early childhood, often making intimacy easier for them than for men, women are drawn to other women as friends because of common biological circumstances.

Katherine, a thirty-seven-year-old homemaker, often depended on women friends for emotional sustenance and support. But after she had a hysterectomy at thirty-two, she found new meaning in female friendships: "I felt devastated, as though my worth as a woman was no longer there. Even though I didn't want any more children, just knowing I was still fertile gave me a sense of worth. I felt mutilated and somehow ashamed. Neither my male doctor nor my husband could understand my feelings. They told me to be thankful for the family I had. But they didn't understand my mourning. Only women understood that, and only women would listen to me and cry with me. And it was only with the help of my women friends that I began to come out of my postoperative depression."

While the circumstance precipitating Katherine's depression—psychologically provocative surgery—is one activator of depression, other less dramatically activated depressive episodes are an all-too-familiar experience for women. In fact, study after study has shown that women are at least twice as likely to suffer from depression as men. Most assuredly, woman's role in American society and the way she is socialized to think about herself contribute to the negative feelings she is likely to have about her life. Women are often taught to be responsible for others' needs; when a woman cannot fulfill the needs of all those close to her, which is an impossibility, she suffers from guilt, self-blame, and a feeling of helplessness.

Since the beliefs underlying these disruptive feelings—that women must be self-sacrificing, all-nurturing caretakers without complaint or regret—are often reinforced by society, they remain unchallenged. To confront these unrealistic notions, still operative even in our enlightened age, is to break with tradition, which is no small task. Yet the uncritical acceptance of impossible standards is conducive to depression; a woman's energies, in effect, are directed to "doing good and feeling bad."

Another case in point, Sara's story of a depression she was not even aware of, exemplifies the plight of many women. Caretaker to two demanding children, in charge of the menial, monotonous household chores with little or no praise for her hard work and certainly no hope of pay or promotion, it is not surprising that she felt helpless.

An attractive thirty-two-year-old homemaker, Sara felt as though she was in a stupor most of the time. Even before she arose in the morning, she felt listless, apathetic, and unable to plan her day. Her two preschool children nevertheless required her to be awake and alert despite her longing to retreat from life.

Ever since she had quit her job as a teacher to rear her children, Sara had no time or energy to make friends; the friends she had were her husband's. In the evening, when her husband came home and she was finally able to put the children to bed after dinner, she would try to carry on a conversation with him. But most evenings, she was too tired to talk, or Ted was too tired to listen. Sara would then collapse in front of the TV, where she usually fell asleep. She had no energy or enthusiasm for sex. With the waning of sexual pleasure, the emotional connection to her husband died, too. Ted could not understand her malaise. After all, she had everything, didn't she? A nice home, good kids, a husband who loved her and supported her.

It was at a boring dinner party that Ted's colleague secretly slipped his business card into Sara's pocket. Later that evening, in the privacy of her bedroom, she looked at it. Don had written "Meet me for lunch?" on the back of the card. Sara did not sleep well thinking about the implications of Don's invitation, but she was surprised to find that she was not listless the next morning. She greeted all her boring tasks with a new nervous energy, and while her children took their brief afternoon naps, she decided to call Don.

Sara's subsequent two-year affair with Don, which resulted in a separation from her husband and six months of psychotherapy for both her and Ted before they were able to begin to live together in harmony again, might have been averted if she had recognized her symptoms of depression. What Sara sought from her affair with Don was a friend more than a sex partner. She needed relief from her boredom and loneliness. If Sara had sought some relief from her routine or some definition of her own identity through social contacts, her depression might have eased and her marriage might not have fallen apart.

One of the best remedies for depression is a support system of friends. If women justifiably feel depressed because of their second-class status in a man's world, they cannot turn to men to rescue them. Nor can they escape from their depression through the excitement of an affair; for a time, an affair may make a woman feel exuberant and sexually attractive again, but soon the fantasy fades, and severe depression is likely to set in. In contrast, women are quite capable of providing the emotional refreshment and mental stimulation needed to sustain each other through monotonous days. It is other women who can safely provide the emotional connection that is lacking in a marriage until a woman is on solid ground again in her relationship with her husband. If change is what a woman requires, it is other women with similar needs—whether it is the need for a job, an education, a night out, or a divorce—who can provide her with the strength to satisfy her ambition.

Women may be vulnerable to depression, but unlike men, they have a resource to overcome the blues: each other. The same quality that enriches their friendships—a willingness to acknowledge and disclose personal feelings—can act as a powerful antidepressant. Many men also suffer from depression. Frequently, though, their symptoms are camouflaged by alcoholism, overwork, a tendency to brood (which is accepted in men but not in women), or some other form of denial. Ironically, this pattern of coping with depression, more characteristic of men than of women, also typifies men's friendships. That is, friendships distract men from everyday problems, but they lack substance.

Highlighting the therapeutic potential of women's friendships is a study conducted by Ladd Wheeler, professor of psychology at the University of Rochester. Wheeler found that women and men are both less lonely when they spend time with women. The data revealed that whenever a female was involved in interaction, both individuals disclosed more about themselves, and the interaction became distinctly more intimate.[2]

Perhaps it is women's overlapping histories that bring them together, nurturing each other. Women share similar experiences: managing a household, common problems with men and children, and the growing struggle to combine family and career. But it is not merely a shared experience that enriches women's friendships; the years of suffering from prejudice, the years of repudiation by their own sex, and the alienation from each other have resulted in a bond strengthened through adversity. Indeed, women's friendships have been forged in fire and are emerging with an enviable luster.

DIFFERING FRIENDSHIPS:
VARYING COMMITMENTS

Each friendship is unique; each reaches its own level of intimacy, depending on the needs of the two friends and the indefinable chemistry between them. Most of the women we interviewed had few intimate friends—friends with whom they shared their innermost thoughts and feelings—but they also enjoyed a wider circle of casual friends who were able to fulfill different needs.

Joanne, a forty-two-year-old high school teacher, described her two closest friends, whom she depended on for daily emotional and intellectual stimulation, as her "inner circle" of friends. Another circle of friends was comprised of women to whom she felt a lesser degree of closeness—coworkers and neighbors she had known a long time, women she enjoyed socially but with whom she did not share secrets. Several more concentric circles of friends were comprised of women she was decreasingly less intimate with, until the final circle contained only nodding acquaintances.

Like most women, Joanne could fairly easily leave friends in the outer circles, but if she had to move away from her two closest friends, she would mourn in the same way as if she had lost a loved member of her family. Several women interviewed said they felt a sense of security and well-being was derived from their closest friends. "As long as my friends are part of my life, even if I don't get the chance to see them very often, I feel secure," said a forty-year-old journalist.

Robert R. Bell, in his study *Worlds of Friendship*, found that men interact with others more often in terms of roles than women do; women are likely to view another as a whole person whereas a man may view another man as a business associate, a running partner, or a drinking pal. A woman is likely to let each category overlap.[3] For example, a woman's coworker may also be the woman with whom she goes to exercise class, as well as a friend with whom she often socializes. Women may also have more difficulty than men separating sexual intimacy from emotional intimacy because of their propensity to see others in global terms rather than categorically; for women it is easier to focus on the whole person in a friendship—not just one facet of the individual.

Nevertheless, women, as well as men, do seek different friends to serve different purposes. The following is an analysis of different forms of friendships women experience, although some friendships may overlap with others:

Special-Interest Friends
Some friends have a particular interest in common and get together mainly to share this interest. This group includes tennis partners, friends who belong to political groups, and those who

share hobbies like playing bridge, collecting Chinese porcelain, or skydiving. Some special-interest friends may attend French cooking classes together or go to Broadway plays, but they usually do not see each other in any other context. They are not intimate friends; their talk is mainly about the interest they have in common.

A twenty-five-year-old dental assistant commented: "There is a woman I met at aerobics class that I've become friendly with, and now we always go to class together. We socialize later in the locker room, and sometimes we'll go out for coffee together, but our friendship is limited. I guess we don't have the chemistry it takes to be closer."

Convenience Friends

Other friends are friends of proximity; they live next door, or they work with us, or they share the same car pool, but we are not emotionally close to them. A woman will gladly lend her convenience friend a hand; she may drive her to the supermarket when her car is in the repair shop because she knows her friend would do the same for her. But we often do not have the desire to be close with convenience friends.

One woman told us she became friendly with whoever was placed next to her desk in her office. She commented: "I don't know if it's just accidental that all the women they rotated in next to me were especially likable or I considered them likable just because they were next to me. What I mean is, would I have chosen any of them as friends if, say, they worked in another department and I met them casually in the cafeteria? I wonder sometimes if it's not the luck of the draw that breeds the friendship."

Convenience friends become friends because, like Mount Everest, they are there. For example, Fran, a forty-eight-year-old homemaker who relocated to another state when her husband's business moved, despaired over the loss of her close friends. At her new home, she immediately became friendly with Jean, a neighbor; the two women often shared their morning

coffee together and socialized as a foursome with their husbands, and they occasionally helped each other when favors were
asked. But even though Fran and Jean saw each other often, the
relationship was never as close as with her old friends. Her new
neighbor was a convenience friend who, as Fran realized years
later after she moved again, was "my friend only because of my
loneliness and our physical proximity."

Business Friends

Increasingly, women are making friends at work. Two social
workers who met when the elder one, Bernice, hired Liz as her
junior associate began their relationship on a casual basis.

"I didn't expect friendship to develop," Bernice stated. "We
were in such a small office together that I figured we would have
to get along, but the closeness we shared was a surprise to me.
There wasn't any effort in it—or so it seemed. It was like falling off a log."

Liz commented: "Soon after Bernice hired me, I went through
a painful divorce. I couldn't wait, during this period, to go to
work each day and talk with Bernice. In fact, my ex-husband
wanted me to work with him and give ourselves a new start; I
gave it brief consideration but decided not to leave my job or
my friends, especially Bernice. She sustained me."

Life at the office, however, is not all cooperation and en-
dearment. For today's woman, a career might be born of necessity and a strong desire to succeed. Competition in the marketplace and the fight for the top rung on the corporate ladder are
no longer an exclusively male domain. Sometimes, for women
as well as men, the workplace can be characterized more as a
war zone than as a fertile ground for friendship. One woman in
a highly competitive sales position, for instance, acknowledged
that she sometimes becomes friendly with coworkers simply "to
pick their brains, find out their angles, probe for a new sales
idea."

Thrown into an arena governed by men, will women fall prey
to the same pressures and become alienated from each other?

Like most men, women are finding their self-worth is becoming tied to their income and career success. These women have set themselves the most ambitious goal of all: combining friendship and professional success.

Crisis Friends

Sometimes friendships develop among women who find themselves at a major crossroads in life at the same time. The mortar of their friendship may be childbirth, illness, career, divorce, or widowhood. Through a shared crisis two women are bound in an intense and intimate bond. The immediate emotional release involved in these relationships, however, often fails to evolve into a full, enduring friendship.

One woman remembered a friend she had met at college several years ago; Ellen, like her friend, Lydia, had recently gone through a divorce and decided to return to school before reentering the job market. Each woman desperately needed someone to listen in a caring, nonjudgmental manner. They spoke of their bitterness, their mixed feelings of sadness, apprehension, and relief. Each, for the first time, shared the stories of her failed marriage. But when summer vacation arrived, although they agreed to keep in touch, neither pursued the relationship.

"We were like strangers in the night," Lydia said. "Maybe we're too embarrassed now about all the intimate revelations to be friends; perhaps it was too much too soon—a case of emotional overload. Or maybe we just want to forget that part of our lives. I, for one, want to move on. I've met a new man; I have a new life. I don't want to look back."

Some women, like Lydia, give up a crisis friend with the crisis and eventually move beyond both. Others tire of the daily emotional strain. One woman, for example, pulled away from a crisis friend when her frequent calls became too much to bear, running the gamut from alimony problems to a squabble with the next-door neighbor. She became a "foul weather" friend, seldom inquiring as to her friend's welfare.

Occasionally, two women joined by crisis will begin a

friendship journey that goes beyond the original source of their coupling. Their friendship broadens and flourishes because they appreciate each other as more than fellow survivors. In this instance, the crisis has merely acted as a catalyst. The basic ingredient for intimacy—that indefinable chemistry—was in place, waiting to be discovered.

Intimate Friends

Whether joined through crisis or random meeting, it is with intimate friends that women are apt to share much of their private lives, to celebrate their joys, and to commiserate over sorrows. A young woman, interviewed several years ago by psychologist Joel Block for *Friendship: How to Give It, How to Get It* expressed the meaning of this kind of relationship:

> There are friends I have grown up with and with whom I have shared important parts of my life—my memories, our hometown, our youth. And then there are friends I met later in life with whom I share more than a common history; with these friends, there is a real exchange of thoughts and feelings. These are the people who enhance my ecstasies, who will fly with me. With these friends, I am able to break down barriers, to go beyond common experience.
>
> When I am with such an exceptional companion, times stands still. It is for these people I reserve the glowing hours that are too good not to share. I don't need cigarettes, food, or liquor; I get caught up in the experience. We seem to be parts of the same mind. The next day and for several days I feel more energetic, very optimistic. The effort of sharing, at getting involved, leaves me with an increase in power.[4]

Many kinds of friendships have a place in women's lives. But the experience of close friendship is the rarest of all; all others, valuable as they may be, pale by comparison. Close friendships allow women to be more open and spontaneous, more insightful, less bound by conformity, and less hidden behind the masks of their existence.

WOMEN'S FRIENDSHIPS
AND THE LIFE CYCLE

Any woman who has ever been a friend, wanted a friend, or lost or loved a friend recognizes the friendship experience as a recurring and significant theme in her life. As one forty-two-year-old woman put it, "My longing for friendship was the same at age five as it was at age thirty-five—what changed over the years was the intensity of my desire and what I want from friends."

In a study bearing on the desired ingredients of women's friendships, psychologist Sandra Gibbs-Candy and her colleagues found three factors to be important throughout the span of fourteen to eighty: intimacy, defined as the sharing of secrets and disclosure of personal feelings; status, which was described as feeling important when being with a friend; and power, defined as having influence with a friend. Of these factors, intimacy was regarded as most important.[5]

Many researchers suggest that the ability to be intimate is crucial in childhood as well as in adulthood and is necessary for normal psychological development. While women typically find this intimacy through their female friends, men most often seek it with their wives, if at all. Perhaps a man's sole reliance on his wife for some semblance of intimacy accounts for his prolonged suffering in the event of her death. Widowers appear to have more difficulty adjusting to single life than widows; more widowers than widows remarry after a spouse's death, and more widowers than widows commit suicide.

According to Gibbs-Candy's study, status in a friendship is most important for adolescent girls, for women in their late forties, and for retired women. A weakened self-image may be a factor in influencing the need for status in a friendship. Adolescence is a time when a girl's developing identity and sexuality are untried and on shaky ground; she often seeks friends to shore up her self-confidence in these areas. A middle-aged woman who has performed the traditional wife-mother role may sometimes suffer from an identity crisis similar to a teenager's; her career of bearing children is over, and she must find a new identity. Similarly, changes in a middle-aged woman's sexuality, the cessation of menstruation, and other physical changes related to the aging process may temporarily diminish her self-image. Friends may be sought at this difficult juncture for a lift in status and strengthened identity. Retired women as well may search for identity and validation through friends.

While power is also a factor throughout women's friendship cycles, Gibbs-Candy reports a progressive decrease in its importance with age. With growing maturity, it appears, women develop more respect for individuality and consequently become more accepting of differences. At its best, this entails appreciating a friend's unique identity rather than becoming locked in a power struggle for change. Older women in general will be more tolerant of their friends' differences. They accept friends for who they are rather than trying to change them.

Other researchers have found various factors —altruism, communion, and emotional expression, for example—to be important ingredients in women's friendships, varying in significance at different life stages. Clearly, what women search for in their friendships varies as their lives evolve. As each life stage is approached, friendship is interwoven into the new challenge, changing and ripening in the process. However, although each life stage—childhood, adolescence, adulthood, or old age—holds mystery and uniqueness, common elements also emerge.

Childhood

Friendship in childhood is not a mere luxury; for optimal functioning it is an imperative. These early friendships, as psychologist Harry F. Harlow demonstrated in a famous study, are vital for a child's social development. Professor Harlow raised a group of baby monkeys, the primates closest to humans, with cloth surrogate mothers, another group with unaffectionate mothers, and a third group with no mothers at all. Those monkeys from each of the three groups allowed to form affectionate relationships with peers initially showed some maladjustment but eventually improved. Baby monkeys deprived of adequate mothering and of contact with peers for about six months became social isolates with enduring socialization problems.[6]

There is no question among authorities on child development that friendless children are more susceptible to emotional disturbances. Childhood friends are our first link with the world outside our family. They help us begin the process of separation from our parents; they teach us by their reactions acceptable social behavior; we learn in friendship to look with the eyes of another person, to listen with another's ears, and to feel with another's heart. If a child grows up without comrades, she is not likely to develop the ability to identify with other people. Such a child will have difficulty considering the needs of others as an adult. Friendship is training for living in a social world.

Especially for girls, friendships serve as an important step in separating from the mother. Although the separation process is difficult for both sexes, it is particularly tough for females. Their main caretaker is of the same sex, a situation that leads to fusion more than to individual functioning. While boys are encouraged by our society to be independent, girls are expected to be dependent and to fulfill others' needs. Finding the answer to "What do I want?" is not as easy for girls, conditioned to ask the more nurturing question "What do others want from me?" Hence, friends help a girl better understand her own needs and wants by exposing her to differing values and beliefs and by helping her separate from her mother. By acting as a sounding board for ideas that may not be acceptable to a girl's parents, friends enable a girl to expand her range of thinking and behavior.

In addition to the rich opportunities for self-exploration and personality expansion that can be part of the early friendship experience is the delightful support girls can provide for each other.

While watching her eight-year-old grandchild play with her friends, an energetic sixty-three-year-old grandmother began to think about her own childhood friendships: "When I was about eight, my granddaughter's age, I had lots of girlfriends. I lived in an apartment house loaded with other kids. As soon as I came home from school, I ran to my group of friends; we were inseparable. We adored each other and provided support for one another. When someone had a falling out with her parents, we always took her side; we echoed each other's opinions about particular teachers; we helped each other with homework and made sure no one was left out of activities. We were really quite sensitive and concerned with each other."

As preadolescence approaches, emotional sharing with friends becomes more important than enjoying cooperative activities together. But even in younger girls' play groups, researchers have consistently found that girls more often interact as pairs, while boys characteristically interact in larger groups. Apparently, socialization strongly affects the male-female patterns of friendship in our culture. We have traditionally regarded intimacy among boys as undesirable but encouraged it in girls.

Preference for friends of the same sex among boys and girls begins as early as two or three years old and continues through adolescence. Women spoke of their "first friend" in especially tender terms: "We loved each other"; "We couldn't imagine anything or anyone coming between us"; "We were always together and thinking of each other"; "Janice and I were like sisters." The events and contexts of childhood—embracing each other with tenderness, walking arm in arm, whispering confidences to one another, sleeping at each other's houses—are cherished memories to many women.

Adolescence

Adolescent friends depend on each other for emotional support and security the way younger children need their families to survive. Rita, a middle-aged secretary, recalled that her friends were her "security blanket" in her teen years. A homemaker in her thirties remembered that her friends in adolescence provided her with "a kind of consolation" during the confusing years of puberty. Friends, she said, were "like family," yet they allowed her a wide range of expression—an important step toward independence and identity formation.

Adolescents of both sexes work through their concerns about sexuality and independence by discussing them with same-sex friends. Girls, in particular, seek intimacy through friendships with each other to replace the loss of intimacy with their family as they struggle to reformulate these ties, eventually break away, and negotiate the world on their own. Adolescents feel more comfortable confiding in each other than confiding in adults. During this stormy period, girls tend to seek one-to-one relationships in their quest for emotional support; boys, in contrast, are more likely to opt for larger groups.

E. Douvan and I. Adelson, in a study based on two large national surveys of adolescent girls (ages eleven to eighteen) and boys (ages fourteen to sixteen), found girls fourteen to sixteen wanted their friends to be loyal, trustworthy, and a source of emotional support. In contrast to younger girls, teens fourteen and over selected friends on the basis of personality and responses, rather than on external qualities such as where they lived or what activities they could share.[7] Intimacy becomes intense during these mid-teenage years as girls endeavor to cope with their strong self-doubts, their sexuality, and their place in the world. Because of the intensity of these relationships, jealousy and hurt feelings run rampant, littering the landscape with discarded friends.

As adolescent girls mature, they become more sure of their identity and more focused on pursuing romantic relationships with boys. Their same-sex friendships decrease in intensity. Competition for male attention is evident at this age, and to maintain a solid friendship, girls abide by an unwritten code: "Do not become interested in the boy I am dating."

For less secure young women, competitiveness for male attention causes deviousness among female friends. Eileen, a public relations director in her late twenties, recalled the pain of loneliness in her teenage years in an interview with Dr. Joel Block for *Friendship: How to Give It, How to Get It*:

> From junior high school through high school, my close friends were mainly girls. I had a special friend whom I walked arm in arm with; we confided in each other and faithfully held each other's secrets in confidence. Life at the time seemed full of secrets; the secret of pubic hair, of wanting to defy our mothers, and, of course, the big secret of sexual relations. But after junior high school, I stopped having one special girlfriend in whom I confided. In fact, by the time I was fifteen, I didn't discuss my personal feelings with anyone. I no longer had close friends. I remember, in spite of all my girlfriends, feeling lonely, as if the surrounding world were hostile and impersonal.
>
> When I was about seventeen, I started to date. This is when friendship was replaced by the dream of Prince Charming. Occasionally I even dared talk about my Prince Charming fantasies with other girls, but our conversations were guarded; there was an underlying rivalry between us. We became more and more private. This saddened me because I had begun to miss the closeness of friends. I was really mystified by the whole dating process and wanted very much to talk to someone about my feelings. It was very frustrating because other girls seemed very unwilling. It was always a case of "Sure, I'd love to, if there isn't anything better to do." This meant, "as long as a boy doesn't call."[8]

It was not until Eileen was in her mid-twenties that she again felt a closeness with women. By that time she and most of her friends were married. Competition for men was no longer an issue dividing them. However, adulthood, marriage, and careers posed new dilemmas, different challenges to friendship.

Adulthood

Mental health professionals have repeatedly found that women who suffer from a wide range of dangerous symptoms, ranging from low self-esteem and a sense of "missing something" in their lives to clinical depression and suicidal tendencies, hardly ever regard their lack of a support system to be at the core of their problems. Yet when these women eventually understand the barriers they have set against friendship and the possibility of its importance in their lives, they are often able to be helped. Once they make the giant leap of self-discovery by starting to make friends, they feel more self-satisfied and happier.

A case in point is Alexandra, a thirty-five-year-old financial analyst who had no female friends because she was brought up to believe that women were her competitors for men and scarce career positions. To protect her interests, she attempted to become "very much like the traditional male." She contained her feelings, threw herself into her work, and attempted to hold her own in talking about sports and business. Despite male acceptance, Alexandra felt a sense of emptiness:

> I guess I believed all the stereotypes about women; bitchiness, weak, empty-headed, the whole thing. It wasn't until I had a minor breakdown—if a breakdown could be considered minor—that I started to come to my senses. What I mean is I didn't go into a hospital, but I felt I was close. I went into therapy with a woman, I'm not sure why. Considering how I felt, you'd think I'd choose a man, but I felt sure I wanted to see a woman. That was a new beginning. I worked out my adolescent anger with women, went through the traditional anguish about my parents, and most important of all, came to respect and probably love the therapist, a very wise, compassionate, and tough lady. She helped me unite with other women. I came away from therapy with a stronger sense of myself, more clearly defined, increased respect for myself as well as a deeper appreciation of what it is to be a woman. Now, in my thirties, I'm drawn to women.

> I'm not ashamed to celebrate my friendship with other women. They add a richness to my life I've never experienced in the male world.

One would think Alexandra would have shed her underlying dislike, rivalry with, and envy of other women like an old skin as she left adolescence and entered adulthood. Yet for her and many other women, there is an undertone of competition and comparison, even between the best of friends. Husband, children, and career take center stage in this adult drama. In the movie *The Turning Point,* two former friends—one a dancer, the other a homemaker—have made opposite choices in the classic family-versus-career dilemma. They finally confront their envy of each other in a violent brawl.

Perhaps the source of these adult rivalries is the fact, so common in the lives of women, of being propelled into the role of nurturer before they themselves have received adequate nurturing. We see the effect of early deprivation, the feeling that one will never get what one wants and needs, in the way some women attempt to hold each other down. They often have difficulty accepting their female friends' successes.

Intensifying the tangle of emotion facing the adult woman are the events of marriage and career. The American dream of husband and family is sought by most women. Shouldering the combined weight of family and career allows precious little time for the pursuit of friendship. For those married women who don't make time for friendships, contact with old friends drops off and new, less intense friendships form with neighbors or wives of their husbands' business associates. One thirty-one-year-old copy editor who juggles a career with the needs of her husband and children, expressed these sentiments: "In college I was very social and made some very solid friendships. I've kept a few of them, but from a distance. I don't have the time nor a strong inclination at this point in my life to pursue these old friendships—or new ones for that matter. I'm not interested in superficial relationships, and I am just too busy with the daily grind to be involved in lives outside of my family. The weekdays fly by in a blur; the weekends are spent preparing for the week! No, my energy for friendship is not there now; at this point in my life I have other priorities.''

A married woman who values friendship and maintains old ties or forms new ones of substance rather than convenience or diversion often is faced with a husband who is unsympathetic to their friendship needs. More to the point, he is likely to resent the time taken away from him when his wife chooses the company of her female friends. Indeed, when we asked one forty-six-year-old woman if she ever felt guilty about leaving her husband or children to go out with a friend, she replied: ''I always feel guilty, but I spend the time with my friend anyway. If I didn't I'd resent my family. I really need my friends to keep my sense of self.''

In light of these not uncommon sentiments, when a woman turns to a woman friend for help or understanding, that friend had better be available. If the price of friendship is so high that she must suffer criticism from her husband to keep it, the reward must be worth the effort.

Many women become submerged in raising a family or building a career, or both, in their twenties and thirties. As they enter their mid- to late thirties and their careers become more established and the children are becoming more independent, the longing for friendship rises to the surface. In the middle years, the forties and fifties, women often have more time to pursue friendships and more inclination to do so. Friendships at this stage of life are especially crucial for women. When children leave home, when signs of aging are difficult to ignore, when health problems become familiar concerns, the support and sharing provided by female friends who are going through the same season in their life can alleviate stress and reinforce fading self-esteem.

Women providing support for each other can go a long way toward repairing the emotional deprivation experienced in their lives. Increasingly, women are viewing themselves as individuals, not as half a couple. Indeed, for women to feel proud of a friend because she is making great strides in her career or because she is fulfilled is no minor achievement. As one woman, typifying these sentiments, said: "My friends are more of what I want to be. One is smarter than I, another is better looking, and still another is more artistically inclined. I'm not jealous of them in any way; I love them too much, and I know they appreciate my qualities, too. I feel good about myself, but I believe there is room for growth; when I try to become just a little more like my friends, I believe they are helping me to stretch myself. Because of them, I am more."

Old Age

One out of three American women over sixty-five lives alone, compared to one out of seven men. Since the life expectancy of American women, on the average, is about eight years longer than men's, elderly women have come to depend on each other for the emotional strength needed to weather the vagaries of old age. At this stage of life, illness, bereavement, feelings of uselessness or helplessness, and loss of self-esteem can easily lead to despair if experienced in isolation. At this point, the time that can be the loneliest, friends can make the difference between depression and a cheerful acceptance of life.

A study by Marjorie Fiske Lowenthal and Clayton Haven published in the *American Sociological Review* revealed that 72 percent of women age sixty to sixty-four had confidants, compared to 50 percent of men in that age group.[9] Consistently, studies have shown that more elderly women than men of the same age have intimate friends or confidants. As women age, they turn to each other for emotional support, just as they did in earlier years.

The ability to make and keep intimate friends is a skill that should be cherished by older people, because friends appear to be more important than family for the aged in helping to maintain morale. A study by Greg Arlings reported in the *Journal of Marriage and the Family* indicated that in old age, life satisfaction is linked more to contact with friends than with kin.[10]

When an elderly woman lives with her adult child, it is most often out of necessity rather than choice. Interaction between elderly women and their children often is viewed as an obligation rather than as a pleasurable exchange. The dependency of an aging parent may prove burdensome for both mother and child. Most of us, women and men, are uncomfortable with the aged; they present us with a portrait of what we fear we will become. Further, the addition of an elderly parent into a household often becomes a source of marital conflict. Sensing this, the older woman is more likely to turn to an equal, a female friend, to confide in and to socialize with than to kin.

Friends made at earlier stages of life act as social insurance for old age, when friends are harder to meet. Illness, lack of mobility, retirement, and widowhood result in fewer opportunities for meeting friends. For the older woman who has built a traditional life around caring for her husband and children, the death of her spouse can be potentially devastating. Yet here, too, friends can ease the grief.

A forty-year-old photographer explained that both her father and her father-in-law died within a year's time. Her mother, she said, always had many women friends whom she would confide in, but her mother-in-law depended on her husband for friendship. She commented: "The difference between the two, in the way they handled mourning, was striking. My mother got through it relatively easily by speaking to her friends whenever she felt down, by reminiscing with them, by not being afraid to cry in front of them. But my mother-in-law had a hard time because she always stayed pretty much to herself. Her center of life was her husband, and she had no other friends. I don't think she knew how to make friends, and she did not maintain her old ones after she married. It has been more than two years now since my father-in-law died, and she still is in a depressed state."

A woman's retirement may narrow her field of friendship, but even a woman who has never worked outside the home may feel the strain on her friendships when her husband retires. She may have depended on the wives of his work friends for a social life, and as these friendships dissolve, she may be left with fewer social contacts. In addition, a retired man who has developed few interests to fill his increased leisure time after retirement may depend on his wife for amusement and emotional sustenance; his dependence may leave her less free time to spend with her women friends. This dilemma can be a source of marital conflict as one sixty-five-year-old woman reported:

> When my husband first retired, three years ago, he constantly wanted me available to him to talk, have lunch, take walks, and so on. He left me practically no free time. I had to give up my bridge club, and I saw my friends less and less. Then I realized that I was becoming quite irritable. I told my husband he would have to find his own friends, because I had my own life and my own friends, and I liked it that way. My attitude forced him to change. He eventually became interested in photography and gardening, and he took some courses in which he eventually made his own friends.

Both women and men tend to make fewer new friends as they age; however women, more than men, appear to retain friends they formed in earlier stages of life. A seventy-two-year-old widow spoke of her varied friendships throughout her life:

> I've gone through many different plateaus in my life, and I've met many different friends. I met friends at school, and I met friends when I first married and had children. These friends have gone their own way through the years; I have not kept in touch with them. But in middle age, when my husband died, I met some friends who helped me through that trying time; they understood what I was going through more than my doctor, who gave me tranquilizers for my grief. My friends were better for me than any tranquilizer. In late middle age, I went back to work, after I had stayed home with the children for more than twenty years, and I met women friends at work who helped me to adjust. Now that I'm retired, I haven't met

any new friends, but I still see the friends I made in mid-life, and I still see my friends from work. They have stuck with me through my ups and downs.

Although age variation in friends is common in early to middle adulthood, in old age, as in adolescence, friends are more often of similar age. This is especially true of retired people. When an elderly woman lives in a young neighborhood, she usually has fewer friends than a woman of the same age who lives in a retirement community.

James E. Montgomery, in a 1972 study of housing patterns of older families, found that interaction among and morale of the elderly were significantly higher among those who lived in age-homogeneous communities than among those who lived in communities with neighbors of varying ages.[11] While some younger people may criticize age-segregated housing as a way of isolating the aged, in fact, this kind of housing appears to reduce their isolation.

Just as some young single women may share housing to cut costs and maintenance and to provide company for each other, older women may benefit by such living arrangements. Although society condones this kind of arrangement for single career women—as long as it is for an interim period, while they are establishing a career or looking for a husband—it is considered strange for two or more older women to pool their resources and share living facilities. The aged are expected to maintain their independence at almost any cost or to turn to kin for help, it seems. Yet it is the mutual dependence of friendship that blunts the edge of loneliness for elderly women.

EVOLUTION OF FRIENDSHIP: ONE WOMAN'S STORY

There are many ways to discover the nature of a person. Psychologists have their ink blots, uncovering weaknesses more than strength, and physicians have X-rays, revealing form but not substance. So how do we know a person? For women, friendship may be the answer. In fact, the old adage "You can judge a man by the company he keeps" is more apropos of women. While friendship is a mere shadow in the lives of men, it is center stage for women. Woven into the fabric of every woman's life is the thread of friendship.

Melanie, a forty-four-year-old interior designer, spoke of her friendships throughout her life. Her story is unique, yet it contains many of the problems and struggles all women experience, along with the joy and power of the bond of sisterhood. Melanie's story, in many ways, is every woman's story:

> When I was a child, I felt the more friends I had, the more secure I would be. I sought the acceptance of friends as a barrier against the problems of the world. Not that my childhood friendships bring fond memories to mind. Most vividly, I recall lots of testing, never really trusting the loyalty of my friends: I felt unsure of their feelings for me and I held back in relation to them. I liked girls better than boys as friends, and from fourth grade through high school, I remember being a member of a lot of different groups. It's strange, but I never really had a very intense relationship with a girl the way most teenagers did. The intensity was just not there. I remember feeling a competitiveness, vying for boys' attention. Maybe that got in the way of being close.

Melanie's mother strongly influenced her daughter's attitude toward friendships in her early years. A strong, competitive career woman who had separated from her husband when her daughter was six years old, she had no intimate female friends. She considered independence a more admirable goal than friendship. By her attitude she taught Melanie that too much closeness was often too painful to bear, that close relationships were demanding and often led to disappointments. And true to her principles, her relationship with her daughter was a seesaw of balanced distance;

if Melanie tried to move closer to her mother, she would find her mother backing away, yet if Melanie withdrew completely, her mother would draw her closer, in an effort to remain in control. As a result, Melanie's early friendships lacked stability and intimacy.

I got married shortly after I finished high school to a guy I thought I loved, the high school athletic star. We moved into a little apartment in New York City, downtown. I felt very isolated for a while, even with my husband home in the evenings. I had two babies within three years, and I was absorbed in raising my family. When the children got older, I met a few women through the children's nursery school group. They were bright, interesting women, very cosmopolitan. I liked them a lot, and I felt better about myself among them, almost as though I were somebody else—more than a housewife and mother. I got pretty close to a divorced woman, Connie, a bookkeeper, and we started to go to an encounter group together one night a week.

After five years of marriage, I knew I had made a mistake, and I initiated a separation; my women friends helped me get through that difficult time. I actually thought I was through with life, that no one would want me anymore, that I was all washed up, even though I was only twenty-eight years old. My friends helped me to gain a different perspective; they helped me to understand my strengths.

I'd spend a lot of time with Connie, who was a smart woman with a sense of humor. I'd tell her about my dates, and she'd offer her advice when I asked for it, but she never talked about any of her dates—if she had any. Soon I realized that she began to resent talking about my romances. I sensed that she was exploring the idea of lesbianism, after she dropped a few hints about women enjoying each other's sexuality. I loved Connie as a friend, but I knew I could never have a sexual relationship with another woman. I told her so, and that ended our friendship. I didn't want it to end, but she took my refusal of a sexual relationship as a personal rejection.

Saddened and shaken by her failed relationship with Connie, Melanie felt she needed to discover who she was before she risked any further hurt in future relationships. She withdrew into raising her children for a while, then joined a consciousness-raising group where, after several months, she felt the emotional safety and acceptance she needed to explore in depth some of the crippling beliefs she had learned about women and their relationships. She came to understand that closeness to other women was not necessarily dangerous, that if she lit the flame of friendship with care and cautious trust and let it ignite slowly, her chances of being burned were minimal. She also came to learn, through a new friendship, that she could not interfere with the autonomy of her friends, nor could she demand their exclusive attention.

At my consciousness-raising group, I met Sonya, a beautiful accomplished woman—a dancer who had recently been divorced. At the time, we were both struggling single parents. Sonya and I almost immediately became friends. There was a strong attraction between us, and I felt I wanted her all to myself. I was jealous of her friendships with other women. Sonya and I have so much in common. If I buy a new pair of shoes, Sonya is likely to buy the same shoes, without knowing I bought them. Frequently, we find ourselves thinking about the same things. Sonya eventually introduced me to a male friend of hers, Walt. He is the man I am living with. Now that Sonya has married again, and I am settled, a lot of our competitiveness is gone. I find I can now share Sonya with her other friends, and I have other friends, too. I realized, after Sonya got angry with me because of my possessiveness, that I couldn't own her. It's unhealthy to depend on one person for everything.

A new phase of life started for Melanie when she moved to the suburbs with Walt. She missed her women friends in the city, especially Sonya, with whom she talked on the telephone two or three times a week. Every two or three weeks, the two women would get together for lunch, even though they now lived fifty miles apart. Melanie still needed close contact with Sonya because she was unable, at first, to form any deep attachment to anyone in the suburbs.

> My new neighbors were not what I expected. In my encounter group and in consciousness raising, I had learned to express myself. I was used to intimacy, used to feeling sharp. But I had to learn to pull back. The women I met in the suburbs had obviously not heard of consciousness raising, or if they had, they wanted nothing to do with it. I resented not being able to be myself with them. It's hard to keep your mind sharp if you don't express your thoughts. I had communicated differently with my friends in the city. We had always said exactly what we felt. With my new neighbors, I was totally out of touch with my feelings. They were speaking another language, and I think I was threatening their status quo. Then I joined an amateur theater group, and I met women there who were more outgoing, easier to talk to, not so uptight.

Because of the influence of her friends at the theater, Melanie started her career in interior design. Several women noticed how expertly Melanie designed stage sets, and a few of them asked her for advice in decorating their own homes. Melanie, ready for new challenge and a sense of autonomy in her life since her children were reaching the age of independence, enrolled in courses in architectural and interior design.

When I was ready for work, my theater friends came through with valuable contacts, and I was able to get enough work to establish a lucrative part-time business. Walt was happy for me, and supportive, but I don't think I would have had enough confidence in myself to establish a business of my own if it weren't for the encouragement of my friends. I'm so glad I've been able to get beyond my mother's difficulties with friendship. I've gained so much in the process. I used to think women were not very important in my life, but now I can't imagine my life without them.

Over four decades Melanie was able to overcome her earlier prejudices about women as friends. She was able to trust women, to become close to them without becoming possessive or overbearing, and to find pleasure in their company. In the process, Melanie's vision of herself became more positive.

Friendship is interwoven into the pattern of each woman's life. Whether it is woven loosely or with tighter bonds, with rough, tangled thread or with threads smoother than satin, it most surely influences a woman's perceptions and feelings about herself and the world. Friendship for women is indeed a powerful tool that, if used well, can mend grief and strengthen self-esteem, as well as enhance the enjoyment of life.

CHAPTER

3

FROM GREETING TO INTIMATE MEETING: THE SIX STAGES OF FRIENDSHIP

Most women who have intimate friends claim that their friendships "just happened" spontaneously and naturally. In reality, friendship is not a matter of pure chance; friends either consciously or unconsciously choose each other. Neither does friendship occur at first meeting. Our study shows that women's friendships pass through very distinct phases not unlike the steps one goes through after the death of a loved one, as described by Elisabeth Kübler-Ross, or the stages in the development of a healthy personality, noted by psychologist Abraham Maslow. In the six stages of friendship, each woman in the relationship must be willing to proceed to the next step or the friendship will atrophy, dissolve, or, at best, remain a bland acquaintanceship.

Although close examination of the stages of friendship may be disenchanting to some, because they fear the dissection removes the "mystery of love," the opposite is probably true. By exploring the steps in the growth of a friendship, we can more fully understand how we make friends and why we find certain acquaintances more attractive than others, and we can more readily overcome the difficulties we may have in making or keeping friends. When the ingredients of a friendship are understood, the relationship is heightened, not diminished.

THE SIX STAGES
OF FRIENDSHIP

Come-ons versus Put-offs

When two women first become acquainted, they will most often be civil and polite to each other; eye contact and some conversation, usually impersonal, will be made. Perhaps the women will shake hands, a custom inherited from men. But if the women's personalities "click," as Terry, a thirty-five-year-old scientist, put it, or if, as Marianne, a forty-four-year-old artist said, "her feelings match yours," or if for one of countless reasons the women feel attracted to each other, one of them, either the more assertive one or the one more desirous of friendship, will make an overture concerning a future meeting. Usually these overtures are vague, to minimize the risk of rejection.

"Perhaps we can get together for coffee sometime?" and "I'd like to know more about your job, when we both have more time" are indefinite overtures that leave room for "maybe" responses. "I'd like to have you as my friend" is a direct approach that may be too risky for most to handle gracefully. At this stage of the relationship, not enough is known about each other to determine whether two women will be friends. Only the possibility exists.

Even at this initial stage of friendship, a woman must have a sense of self-esteem that is strong enough to withstand the risk of possible rejection. She must be willing to reveal something personal, enough of herself to create an interest.

Such overt and initial disclosures will be made, however, only if a mutual interest is evident. When body language and indifference reveal boredom, no further effort at friendship is likely to be made. Indeed, to protect herself against rejection or ridicule, the one who is shunned may avoid future meetings with the decidedly unfriendly acquaintance.

Maureen, a twenty-one-year-old college student, had such an experience: "At the beginning of the term, I met a woman who I thought I would be interested in knowing better. She was a graduate student, and I thought I could be helpful to her since she was taking an undergraduate course which she had missed and I had completed. In turn, maybe she could help me with some of my other courses. But when we were introduced, she made it clear she did not want any help. She didn't even look at me, and she directed her conversation totally toward a mutual friend; it was clear she felt superior to me or, at best, was not interested in pursuing a relationship."

It is usually more productive for a woman to make overtures of friendship to someone she considers her equal. This decreases the possibility of exploitation. For instance, the woman who has more to offer in the way of money, status, talent, and so on may use the abilities of the less powerful woman in some way without adequate compensation, or the woman with less to offer may try to use the friendship for her own advancement. While some of these unbalanced couplings do evolve into friendships, many preclude closeness. They are often characterized by the need to feel superior or an attempt to achieve self-esteem by association.

Another element that may destine friendship to an emotional roller coaster is the psychoanalytic concept of transference—the tendency to bring feelings and conflicts from a past relationship (usually with a parental figure) to bear on a current relationship. In women's relations with each other the most prominent earlier bond, that of mother and daughter, may come into play. An initial attraction may include, for instance, an unconscious identification with one's mother; consequently, to some extent, a woman may transfer to her friend the still unresolved needs, conflicts, and expectations between her and her mother.

One such tumultuous relationship existed between twenty-five-year-old Diana and twenty-seven-year-old Syrelle, inseparable friends. They worked together in the research department of a cosmetics firm, usually took their vacations together, and often double-dated. Syrelle was content with her life, but Diana was growing and wanted more for herself than her present job provided. She considered going back to school for an advanced degree in chemistry. Syrelle, threatened by Diana's ambitions and the possible loss of the friendship, tried to discourage her: "How could you work all day and study at night? Why bother? Chemists don't get paid well enough to warrant all this effort." After a while, Diana began to feel "sucked dry" and "emptied" by Syrelle's complaints and her neediness. Moreover, she strongly resented Syrelle's attempts to undermine her confidence.

Syrelle's tactics were pushing Diana away. When she was with Syrelle she felt constricted, oppressed. She didn't want to be burdened by Syrelle's need for her or have to deal with her dependency. This was particularly painful because it reminded Diana of her mother's dependency. Diana's mother was a housewife whose life revolved around her family. She had never adjusted to Diana's leaving home or to her husband's death several years before. She now lived through Diana, desperately needing her to fill the void in her life, unconsciously discouraging Diana's independence and autonomy.

Syrelle's insecurity and her feelings of abandonment, envy, and attachment played right into Diana's vulnerability. In her anxiety, Diana felt she could maintain her selfhood only by fighting off these two women who desperately needed her.

Common Ground:
Uncommon Chemistry versus
Superficial Sociability

Like men, women select friends from a very large pool of acquaintanceships. In a study conducted by Michael Gurevitch at the Massachusetts Institute of Technology, researchers asked a varied group of individuals to keep track of all the different people with whom they come in contact in a 100-day period. On average, each person listed about 500 names. Social psychologist Stanley Milgram, who cites the Gurevitch study in a *Psychology Today* article and who has conducted a number of experiments dealing with communication through acquaintanceship networks, has found similarly that the average American has anywhere from 500 to 2,500 acquaintances and associations. From these hundreds of people, however, few real friends are chosen.[1]

On what basis is the friendship choice made? How do women select friends from a large pool of acquaintances? It is easy enough to say that friendships are likely to be built around common interests and values. But that isn't sufficient to fully explain close relationships. Many of a woman's acquaintances have similar interests and values compatible with her own, yet she forms strong ties with only a few of them.

In fact, personality characteristics need not be alike; some dissimilar personalities seem to complement each other in friendship. Said Jenny, a thirty-two-year-old physics teacher: "As a graduate student, I used to be very friendly with two other women. Actually, the three of us were almost inseparable, yet we were all very different. I was studious, practical, and outdoorsy, Miranda was a dreamer and very correct and feminine, and Beth was a chain smoker and known as a tough-skinned, aggressive go-getter, but we all got along. I think each gave the others a different point of view, or some of what was lacking in the others. Perhaps if we had lived with each other, friction would have developed, but our friendship gave us enough distance to appreciate our individuality."

We know that at this point, the honeymoon phase of friendship, risks and rewards are relatively unknown, which adds an excitement to the relationship. Women will try to size each other up concerning their intimacy potential; they will try to determine the emotional accessibility of the potential friend. It is also evident that in the formative phase of friendship there is a tendency to see only the other's virtues. At some later point, perhaps when inflated expectations have left open wounds, there is a tendency to find only faults. If a relationship survives this critical moment there is the possibility of becoming true friends.

But there seems to be no satisfactory answer to the question, On what basis does a woman choose a friend? Like religion, friendship demands an initial leap of faith or daring that may be developed or eventually disavowed. Beyond social class and age factors, which virtually every study affirms to be important, the reasons why two women join in friendship cannot be fully accounted for. The basis for friendship choices remains a mystery.

Mutual Respect versus Disparaging Comparisons

Many of us are unaware of the tremendous pressure we put on mates, children, and friends to duplicate our feelings. It is often as if we decide, "If you want me to like you, then you must feel as I do. If I feel your behavior is bad, you must feel so, too. If I feel a certain goal is desirable, you must feel so, too." A budding friendship precludes the demand "You must think, feel and act like me." Rather, it is characterized by respect and acceptance of a friend as a separate, unique person without demanding that she be otherwise. To respect and value another's individuality includes accepting not only those characteristics that are considered socially desirable but also traits that might be called faults.

For women in particular, identity struggles and fragile feelings of self-worth are especially troublesome. Being able to express the various facets of her personality without the fear of harsh judgment is crucial to a woman's growth. A sound friendship permits the expression of anger, childishness, and silliness as well as affection. If there is no danger that we will be condemned if we drop our mask of maturity, we can be as we really are, weak when we feel weak, scared when we feel confused, childish when the responsibilities of adulthood seem too heavy.

What does the experience of acceptance feel like? Sheila, a forty-eight-year-old high school English teacher, had been separated three months when she met Helen, a woman with whom she developed a stormy but beneficial friendship:

When I met Helen one of my strongest and most persistent feelings was pain, not just emotional pain but actual physical pain—nausea, headaches, and the like. I remember saying once that when my husband left me for another woman and I became a statistic, one of the "displaced homemakers," it was as if a knife was put into me and was being turned around each day to cut up my insides. My first reaction to Helen was one of surprise at her sensitivity and awareness of what and how I was feeling, even when I expressed it inarticulately or hardly at all. Then I began to get the feeling that not only was she sensitive but she also cared about me. It seems crazy but I fought desperately against this feeling. I was firmly convinced that to give in to her respect for me meant to sell my soul; there was a high price for allowing another person into my life. Indeed, I was still reeling from the last time I had yielded.

I tried demonstrating to her how unworthy I was— how selfish, inadequate, and nasty. I tried hating and attacking her. I told her that she couldn't possibly think well of me, that I was defective. I suspected that she was being deceitful and cruel in pretending that she liked me. But she was always there, treating me with respect; she was a firm, strong pillar which I beat on to no avail and which merely said, "You are a worthwhile human being." She saw past my bullshit yet she didn't condemn me for it. Not that she was a saint; she expressed anger, outrage, and frustration. She engaged me and fought ferociously, but she always did so in a way that didn't belittle me. Her words were strong yet soft; somehow the sharp edges were removed. She conveyed that I was a person acting in an obnoxious manner, not an obnoxious person. In other words, I was not disqualified or considered garbage because of my foibles.

As I look at it now, I was putting all my faults and felt inadequacies on the line so that I could be done with the process of rejection. And Helen calmly (and sometimes not so calmly), by her respect for me as a person, peeled off layer after layer of my armor. Slowly, it became clear that it was safe; I realized that I am the one who makes the ultimate judgment of my worth. That sounds like a simple, common-sense statement. Yet my appreciation of that dictum has given me such a sense of peace that it is awesome. I feel elevated, freer, not only more respectful of my self but also of women. In my relationships with other people, I try to see them as individuals struggling with the same things as I do. They do not have to fit my image; each of us has a right to struggle in our own unique manner. Keeping this in mind, my tolerance for individuality has been expanded and my friendships, as a result, are much richer.

It should not be construed from the foregoing that acceptance of another woman's individuality is the same thing as liking. Obviously, we may not like all facets of another person, but by acceptance we acknowledge and respect the fact that she is still worthwhile. It is the attitude that expresses: "I may not like these qualities in you, but that doesn't make you less of a person." Women with this characteristic tend to be flexible and adaptable to change and to accept other women even when they disagree with them. At this stage, a new respect and admiration develops for each other. Friends need not be role models, nor need they be extraordinary in their accomplishments; we admire them simply for their ability to care for us, to be our friend.

The feeling of being respected can be obtained only in human relationships. It is found in varying degrees among mature lovers, wise parents, and their children as well as some educators and their students. However, because of their shared life experience, women are in the best position to offer this rich nutrient. And it is precisely this feeling of being valued that promotes full relationships with other women.

Trust versus Mistrust

Trust is a very sensitive issue for women. The tradition of jealousy, of fighting over men—whether or not this depiction is a true representation—has not left women untouched. Combine this with the discrimination women experience professionally and the exploitation many women currently face at home, and nothing is more unsettling for a woman than not knowing where she stands with those closest to her. Having a trusted ally, a confidant, a person who will comfort and console, becomes all the more important when you are not society's favored child.

Trust in another requires consistent and dependable behavior, the absence of deceit, and the confidence that the other individual will act decently and with good intentions. Trust doesn't reside *within* a person (as a trait does); it is developed *between* people as a result of their experiences together. If Anne's behavior is consistent, unambiguous, and honest, Betty will feel trust because she can depend on this behavior.

All deceptive maneuvers sabotage the building of trust between friends and prevent them from knowing each other more intimately. The common practice of telling "little white lies" in order to protect a friend's ego more often than not limits intimacy. Beyond the benevolent explanation of the deception ("for my friend's sake") is the deceiver's attempt to protect herself; by being deceptive, she avoids confrontations. If she is discovered, however, sustaining an open, trusting relationship becomes more difficult. It is also probable, in some instances when the deception has not been discovered, that the deceived friend intuitively suspects that the truth is not being told and consequently becomes suspicious of her friend's motives.

Trust also involves loyalty. For example, when a writer tells a fellow writer and friend about an idea for a book, she expects her friend not to use the idea to get an assignment of her own. Trust in a friendship means that the friends are more important to each other than any other benefit, professional, social, financial, or otherwise, that could be a consequence of the friendship.

Often, trustworthiness, loyalty, and the ability to genuinely care for another's welfare are tested in a crisis. When a career woman is in danger of losing her position, or when she is suddenly on financially shaky ground because of illness, divorce, or other misfortune, the friends she can depend upon and trust will be supportive. Others will drift away.

While it is apparent that trust will be drained by deception and disloyalty, the effect of inconsistency on trust is less obvious. For example, if a woman tells her friend that she is very important in her life yet by her daily behavior communicates only selfishness, lack of consideration, and irritability, how can the friend trust her? She may want to believe that she is cared for, and her friend's words may be very flattering, but her friend's behavior speaks forcefully and belies her words. If a woman tells her friend that she trusts her implicitly to watch her children yet innumerable times when the children are in the friend's care voices her concern about their welfare, will the friend feel trusted?

Building toward greater honesty and thus toward increased trust therefore involves not simply saying what one believes but also acting on those beliefs. To be counted on, one must demonstrate consistency of behavior. Being predictable and consistent do not, however, preclude change. Indeed, a person who remains the same throughout a long-term friendship would be hard to take even for the most tolerant among us; the boredom would be overwhelming. If trust is to be maintained, it must be based on both friends' willingness to be open, so that each knows where she stands with the other and can depend on what the other says, *even in changing circumstances.* One may not necessarily like what one's friend says or does, and there may be distress surrounding certain changes that are occurring; but if there is no deception, no betrayal of trust, change can be understood, accommodated, or modified. Only then can change occur with the fear of the unknown minimized.

Self-disclosure versus
Self-enclosure

The capacity and willingness to open oneself to another—to expose vulnerabilities, weaknesses, and, more positively, hopes and dreams—is a powerful bonding force between two women. When a friendship reaches this stage, it is considered close and loving; the sharing of one's innermost feelings is an act of both courage and love.

Mutual disclosure cannot be forced, however, nor can it come too early in a relationship. If disclosures are made too soon, a potential friendship may end before it has had a chance to flourish. The woman who reveals her problems or sensitivities early in a relationship may be under considerable stress; she may actively be seeking someone who will act as her psychotherapist. The acquaintance on whom she has chosen to do this emotional unloading usually does not become a friend, because emotional dumping before caring or trust is established is a way of using another, a way of taking advantage of an empathetic person. It is not a shortcut to friendship.

The woman who will bare herself emotionally at first meeting is not highly regarded. Her self-disclosure may be judged an act of desperation rather than one of courage or love. Such compulsive self-revelation is meaningless in relation to friendship because it is devoid of feeling for the would-be friend. Without caring and trust developed carefully over time, self-revelation is considered a violation, a personal intrusion.

In contrast, never knowing what a companion thinks, feels, and wants can be quite distressing and unpleasant. This is not to say that the sheer amount of openness or self-disclosure in a friendship is an index of its intimacy. Such factors as timing, interest of the other person, appropriateness, and the effects of the disclosures on either party must also be considered.

It is also evident that while most women desire a close friendship, they also fear that in the process of meeting someone and becoming intimate, they may be found undesirable. For some women, this fear of rejection results in the formation of a false front, a mask to avoid being known. Hidden behind this mask is usually the conscious or unconscious belief that to be one's real self is dangerous, that exposure of real feeling will lead to being unwanted: "If people found out what I was really like, they wouldn't want any part of me." One woman who felt this way described her dilemma, how confused and empty she had become regarding her own convictions:

> During grade school, I had fantasies of being accepted by girls I admired, but I never approached them. I selected my friends from those who approached me. In high school I was considered shy; I was aware of people I really wanted to know, yet I would form friendships with people who were not my first choice. Now I am more selective, but I still play it safe and cautious. I still experience a tension when I'm with other people. I'm more relaxed by myself. I realized recently that when I'm alone I don't have to perform; this accounts for the reduction in tension. Over the years I have developed a knack for determining what kind of individual the other person likes and then pretending to be that individual. Even if this puts my companions at ease it creates a tension within me; since they have an inaccurate concept of me, I am left with the burden of maintaining the phoniness.
>
> When I'm in a social situation, a party for instance, I can be lively and appear to be having a good time, but all the while I'm putting on a little drama, creating the illusion that I'm bright and interesting so that other people will see me as attractive. I am always aware of being judged; it is very important for me to gain the approval of someone I admire. Sometimes I even surprise myself

by taking positions that I don't really feel if I think that would please somebody I want to impress. It's been so long since I stood up for my convictions that I don't know what I feel or what my convictions really are. I haven't been honestly myself. I don't know what my real self is; I've lost touch with my inner experience.

One of the few times that I allowed myself to be off guard, I couldn't handle it. I was involved in a group discussion and my face was flushed, my tone communicated anger, I was shaking my finger at this other woman. Yet when one of the other people said, "Well, let's not get angry about this," I replied with sincerity and surprise, "I'm not angry! I don't have any feeling about this at all! I was just pointing out the logical facts." The other people in the group, seeing my obvious anger, broke out in laughter at my statement and I was utterly embarrassed. My defensiveness, my unwillingness to be myself, kept me from acknowledging my anger at that other woman.

This woman is beginning to discover that her behavior and even her feelings do not flow naturally but are a facade behind which she has been hiding. She is discovering how much of her life is guided by who she thinks she should be rather than by who she is. Still more disturbing, she recognizes that she exists in response to the demands of others, that she seems to have no direction of her own.

Frequently, when women relate in an inauthentic, contrived manner there are signals to this effect. An atmosphere of strain, artificiality, anxiety, and tension prevails. In the company of such women we often sense that what is being said is almost certainly a front, a cover-up for the fear that they are unworthy. We wonder what she really feels or thinks. We wonder if she knows what she feels. We tend to be wary and cautious with such an individual. The contact leaves us feeling empty.

It is only natural to want to be liked and appreciated, but being unnatural in order to accomplish this ultimately inhibits closeness and results in self-alienation. Those women who are stuck in this behavior, not occasionally but as a continuing, repetitive pattern, may meet many people and boast of a wide circle of friends, but essentially they remain unrevealed and hence unconnected. Self-enclosure and lasting friendships do not mix.

In contrast to guarded behavior, open, interpersonal behavior is not burdensome, planned, or deliberately assumed. Rather, it is spontaneous. Such behavior, in the long run, turns out to be flexible and versatile; the contact feels good and is fulfilling. To pick an easily recognized example, consider the infant. If an infant expresses affection, anger, contentment, or fear there is no doubt in our minds of the specific experience. The infant is transparently fearful or loving or angry. There is no deception. Perhaps that genuineness is why so many people respond warmly to infants. We feel we know exactly where we stand with them.

Intimacy versus Alienation

The final stage of friendship, sometimes called love, is characterized by the presence of mutual interest, common ground, mutual respect, trust, and self-disclosure. The term *intimacy* suggests closeness but also refers to a friendship that tolerates periods of distance and conflict as well as warmth and closeness.

The German philosopher Schopenhauer told a story of two porcupines huddled together on a cold winter's night. As the temperature dropped, the animals moved closer together. But then there was a problem; each kept getting "stuck" by the other's quills. Finally, with much shifting and shuffling in changing positions, they managed to work out an equilibrium whereby each received maximum warmth with a minimum of painful pricking from the other.

Intimate friends have something in common with the huddling porcupines. They want to achieve and maintain a kind of equilibrium: warmth and intimacy but without the continuous "pricking" that can become agonizing in a close relationship. The attainment of this proper distance is what creates the keen enjoyment of an intimate friendship.

For a woman to share intimacy with another woman, she must first have a strong sense of self. She must have successfully gone through the process of separation from her mother in childhood and adolescence. If separation did not occur, a woman may fear becoming too emotionally close to another because she unconsciously believes she will be subsumed by the other, thereby losing what little identity she has. In an overly dependent intimate relationship between two women, either one or both women may be substituting the friendship for the mother they never had or a mother to whom they never felt sufficiently close to fulfill their dependency needs.

This final stage of friendship provides the most rewards but also requires the most commitment and obligation. Friends who have reached this stage are beyond the honeymoon of friendship. They experience feelings of joy and heightened self-esteem when they see each other, but there is no intense need to see each other often. Perhaps because much of the risk is gone in the relationship—each knows for certain that she is accepted by the other—there is less need for continual contact and repeated reassurances of friendship. Sometimes friends who have reached this stage of intimacy do not see each other for months or even years because they have moved away. When they meet again, the friendship is automatically renewed as if no time had passed.

Friendship, at this stage, has usually surmounted physical as well as emotional boundaries. Touching—hugs, kisses, affectionate hand-holding, or back patting—are welcome gestures at this stage, while they may have been threatening earlier in the relationship.

Intimacy also requires the giving of affection through words and actions. It means being able to say to a friend: "I think you are wonderful, and I am so glad I know you." It means being able to praise, to be nonjudgmental but honest. It means accepting each other totally without trying to change each other. It means being able to tolerate anger and each other's differences.

The intimacy of women's friendships is like a dance. If one partner becomes indifferent to the music or totally dependent on the other to lead the way for a substantial period, the equilibrium is damaged. Each dancer must be responsible for herself while interacting with the other. Sustained periods of heavy dependence and fierce independence threaten the partnership. Interdependence, on the other hand, fosters grace and balance.

CHAPTER

4

FINDING FRIENDSHIP: FROM BACKYARD TO BOARDROOM

In the impersonal, bureaucratic world of work or in the every-family-for-itself suburbs, women turn to each other for support and intimacy. No longer do women gain emotional sustenance from the extended family, as they did at the turn of the century. The ethnic enclaves of immigrant neighborhoods were breeding grounds for poverty and conflict but also for helpful, loving family relationships. At that time, three generations living together in cramped quarters often provided a family with all the closeness and intimacy they required. But today the ideal of the independent nuclear family breeds loneliness and alienation and the consequent greater need for friends.

As more women delay marriage to pursue their careers, and with more single women living alone, the need for friends to replace family is compelling. One thirty-five-year-old single woman, a lawyer, said: "My family is far away, my lovers come and go, but my friends seem to remain forever. I depend on my friends to help me in times of crisis today the way I depended on my family when I was growing up. I could not survive without them, nor would I ever try to. If I married or moved I'd always be friends with the few women who have sustained me through my adult years.''

Fortunately, women do have more opportunity than ever before to meet a variety of new friends. Because women's spheres are less restricted than in preliberation times, they are free to meet friends today not only through their husbands or families but on their own. Besides neighborhood friends and family friends, women may choose friends at work, at special-interest or professional groups, through networking, through travel, through planned social occasions such as cocktail and dinner parties, which are now more often integrated with single women as well as couples, or by "chance" acquaintance. The probability of a random meeting's sparking a friendship is greater, because it has become more acceptable for women to travel alone, dine alone in restaurants, or be seen in a number of public places unescorted. It is also acceptable now, certainly among young, liberated women, to introduce themselves to a stranger, male or female, if they choose to be sociable.

A thirty-three-year-old business consultant said she met one of her best friends on a flight from New York to California: "Nora sat next to me by chance and we started to talk about a book she was reading. She was going to the Olympic Games, as I was. It was something I did whenever major track events or the games were in the U.S. My husband was too busy with his law practice to attend with me, so I told him I'd go alone. I'm so glad I did, because I met Nora. We still see each other regularly in New York.''

MAKING FRIENDS ANYWHERE: CITY, SUBURBS, COUNTRY

Convention has it that a large metropolis is the most difficult place to initiate a friendship. The population is so large that any resident is anonymously lost.

The reality is that a metropolis is one of the best places to meet friends, more advantageous for many women than the suburbs or rural areas. Sociologist Claude S. Fischer, an expert on personal networks in cities, determined that the large population in cities is conducive to friendship.[1] Since urbanites have a much larger number of people to choose from, they are more likely to meet one with whom they click. In addition, there is a multitude of specialized subcultures in cities, including social, recreational, and professional groups that are generally not part of the suburban or rural culture. For example, in a large metropolis, by seeking out the right resources, you might find a group of women interested in eighteenth-century American antiques or a club devoted to French wine tasting, because in a large pool of, say, five million people, even if just one-tenth of one percent were interested in these subjects, there would be more than enough of them to form a group. But in a small village of five thousand, chances are you would be the only individual interested in a New England double gateleg table or in paying the price to taste a 1961 Bordeaux.

Besides the laws of probability being on your side when trying to meet friends in the city, another factor comes into play: economics. Research has shown that people of high socioeconomic status are more likely to have friends than those lower on the scale. Apparently, money and leisure facilitate friendships. In the city, the population generally has a greater range of income than in small towns.

Naturally, there are exceptions. Some bedroom suburbs of cities are bastions of affluent life, replete with women's luncheons, cocktail and dinner parties, and dining out in groups. If women carefully choose a suburban area where their neighbors have similar values and share similar family incomes, they can make friends as quickly as women in the city.

Jacqueline, a thirty-seven-year-old homemaker, recounted her friendship experiences in the city, suburbs, and country: "As a young family, we always had lots of friends in the city. We lived in an apartment house there, and many of our neighbors were friends. When my husband and our two young children and I moved to an affluent suburb, we also had no difficulty making friends. Most of the families in the neighborhood were our age, and they had children the same age as ours. The women were active in the PTA, the garden club, and the country club. It was no problem to make friends if you joined that social circuit. I had lunch with my women friends several times a week, and we frequently went shopping together.''

When Jacqueline's husband was transferred to a new office in a rural area, the family was eager to meet new friends in the small village they now called home, but they were disappointed. ''In the suburbs, we lived in a development where families grew together,'' Jacqueline said. ''My neighbors there had the same concerns as I did, since their children went through the same stages together. We were all very sociable and child-centered. Now we live in a very diverse neighborhood. Across the street, we have two gay men as neighbors, around the corner is a divorced woman with her children, and next door to us is an elderly couple. We don't have enough in common with the neighbors to be friends with them. And the few women I do meet through my children don't seem to be too sociable. Maybe they moved to the country because they are solitary people.''

If friendship is a priority for a woman who has to relocate, it is as imperative for her to investigate the neighbors she will have as it is to check out property values and shopping areas in her neighborhood. Friendships in small suburban or rural towns with a diverse population are less likely to occur than in large cities or in small neighborhoods with a homogeneous population.

You can make the first effort to get to know your neighbors by inviting them over for drinks or dinner, or if you prefer a more casual approach, you can ask them some ice-breaking questions about the neighborhood. Where is the nearest beauty salon? What cleaners do they use? Are there any outstanding restaurants in town?

One study done in London's Hyde Park found that people

who walked their dogs talked to more people for a longer time than people who walked through the cosmopolitan park alone.[2] If, like most people, you have difficulty starting conversations with strangers you would like to get to know, owning a pet might be a social lifeline for you.

Psychologist Karen Franck compared the length of time it took people who moved to New York City and newcomers to a small upstate town to make friends and found that those in New York City took longer to form their friendships, although both groups of newcomers eventually made the same number of friends. In large cities, more of an effort is required to form relationships, since strangers are less likely to befriend you.[3]

In any event, if you want to make new friends, you will find them anywhere. A thirty-eight-year-old scientist who is also a world traveler said she was able to make friends with women whenever she went from New York to California, from Sweden to Spain, or from rural areas to metropolitan areas. Her secret? She explained:

When I was a teenager, I was very shy. I was afraid that I just couldn't fit in, that I was somehow inadequate to make friends. Maybe it had to do with being an only child, and an overprotected one at that. Consequently, I never tried to make friends. I looked down when I walked through the streets or in the halls in school. I never dared to start a conversation with a stranger. Finally, when I was feeling particularly sorry for myself one day because no one invited me to the high school prom, my mother had a talk with me. "You're able to make friends," she said. "You're intelligent and good-looking and come from a good family. I dare you." I was pretty competitive with my mother—she was a highly educated and attractive woman—so I took her dare. I smiled when I walked into a room filled with people, and I tried to make eye contact with at least one person in a room. When someone looked friendly, I initiated a conversation. If I experienced rejection, I didn't take it personally. I just thought maybe the person had had a bad day or wasn't ready for new friends. Now I realize that your own attitude is what is most important in making friends—your own openness—not your location or what the other people are like.

CAN WORK AND FRIENDSHIP
MIX FOR WOMEN?

Throughout American history, women have worked just as rigorously and steadfastly as men, and whether they have worked on farms, in the home, at factories or in offices, they have made friends at their jobs. Today, when more than 50 percent of women over age sixteen work in the United States, when more than 20 percent have been able to propel themselves into managerial and professional positions, women encounter new, unanticipated difficulties in maintaining their friendships at work.

Just when they need each other most to fight the feminist battles of the workplace, when they need to band together to demand equality with men in terms of pay, when they need to demand the same status and the same promotions as men, when their work warrants it, when they need support from each other, and relief from loneliness in the male-dominated business world, in many instances they have let each other down. Why?

The answer is multifaceted, but it does contain two basic elements: first, the hunger for power, and second, the ambivalence many women have concerning power and success in the marketplace. While women have always worked, before the 1960s few ever considered competing with each other, just as competing with men was totally foreign. Women spent their work lives in traditionally female, noncompetitive jobs. They were teachers, nurses, secretaries, waitresses, and sales clerks—certainly not presidents, vice presidents, or board members, not the power brokers of industry.

Even during World War II, as men enlisted and women took over their jobs, they regarded their new position in the labor force as temporary. The 1950s brought the return of "family stability.'' The housewives moved back to their homes, while men assumed their former roles as breadwinners. Women who were not content to remain at home were considered odd or maladjusted.

As recently as the 1960s women have come to realize that ambition, the drive for power and recognition, is not a sex-linked trait. Women can be just as determined as men in their pursuit of success at work, but because of their traditional upbringing, which has allowed success only in certain feminine domains— at home and in traditionally female jobs—many are still ambivalent about achieving success. Those who are independent enough and determined enough to go after the brass ring, to strive for the power that had previously been a prize hoarded by men, are also most likely to understand that the rules of work and the rules of friendship are often in conflict. Those women who are ambivalent about career success are likely to be confused about their friendship aspirations at work.

Because they have been socialized to be caring, loyal, and trusting helpers rather than single-minded and independent go-getters, today's working women do not usually know how to blend friendship and competition, nor are they sure that the two are compatible. As a result, they may avoid friendships in competitive work situations or react in a shocked or hurt manner when a female coworker does not live up to traditionally feminine behavior expectations in a work setting.

When we asked women: ''Can coworkers be friends?'' the majority answered affirmatively. But when we asked if they could maintain a friendship in a competitive work situation, many were in a quandary. Some had not considered the question before, because, by their choice of friends, they were able to avoid sticky competitive complications. Anita, a forty-two-year-old artist, said: ''I've always had friends in the art world, but I actually never considered my friends as competitors. Come to think of it, I guess I have the edge over all of them in my career. I never realized that before.''

Madeline, a thirty-six-year-old teacher, said, ''I always had other women teachers who were my friends. We were not in competitive situations. But I do remember one friend—when she was offered a summer position, and I wasn't, even though we had both applied at the same time, I was a little envious of her. After she started working that summer, and I stayed home, I didn't see too much of her.''

"Friends at work? Sure, I have them," a twenty-eight-year-old scientist responded. "I just make sure I don't get too close to them, and that work isn't the only thing we have in common."

Women who have been reared to be cooperative, friendly, and careful not to hurt feelings become anxious when faced with conflict and competitiveness—inescapable realities of the business world. Not knowing what to do, they either try to avoid conflict, become passive or immobile when faced with it, or charge ahead full force into the competition, heedless of compromises, politics, and friendships. They are not experienced with the nebulous middle ground of men's business dealings.

Women have not realized, as have men who have been socialized to deal with competition, that conflicts can be resolved, that coworkers can confront each other or take opposing sides on an issue, fight it out, and still remain friends. Arguments and anger have always been considered unfeminine, and for women friends to be comfortable confronting each other, as the rules of success in the marketplace demand, is no easy task.

For example, Iris and Cheryl, two ambitious women who worked side by side in the marketing and sales department of a large conglomerate, might not have wrecked their friendship over a disagreement at work if they had had the career experience of men. Iris had started work as a saleswoman for the company about a year before Cheryl; Iris had always been a hard worker, well-liked by both her coworkers and her superiors. When Cheryl was hired, Iris was expected to train her. She did more than that; Iris helped her to land some excellent accounts, traded office gossip with her, and frequently was her lunch companion.

After they had become good friends, the two women were

surprised to hear that the firm's executives were considering a reorganization of the sales department. First, however, they wanted several key employees' opinions regarding how to divide the work load and how to best attract new accounts. Both Iris and Cheryl were asked if they would like to be on the employees' advisory board that would meet for several sessions with the firm's top executives. Both women were thrilled to have the opportunity.

The company's chiefs wished to know from the employees whether they would prefer a higher base pay with a lower commission percentage than they currently received, a lower salary with a higher commission, or the same base pay and commission as before. Cheryl opted for a higher base pay, because she never did as well as Iris in getting new accounts, and she preferred the security of a more substantial salary. Iris preferred the status quo. After much discussion, the women opposed each other in a final referendum. The majority voted with Cheryl. Iris, instead of understanding that there are winners and losers in every decision of the business world and that she could not react to business decisions as personal affronts if she wished to keep co-workers as friends, was furious with Cheryl.

"If she were a true friend, she would have been appreciative of everything I did for her," Iris remarked. "I showed her the ropes. If I hadn't shown her how to get an account and how to please the bosses, she'd be nowhere."

But Cheryl vehemently disagreed. "I don't owe Iris anything. She trained me, sure, but that was part of her job, and I took it from there. If I was successful, it was my own doing. I work hard. I have to look out for myself when my livelihood is concerned."

Iris did not understand the rules of the business world. She could not separate work conflicts from friendship. Like many successful men, she could have controlled her anger and learned to take business decisions less personally. She would then feel less alone, less embittered at work, and increase her chances for success at work and at friendship.

Perhaps this basically male idea of friendship appears two-faced to some women. It may not be the ideal of feminine friendship, but if friendship and ambitious career goals are to coexist, compromises and the ability to handle win-lose situations with grace and dignity will have to become part of women's social skills.

Betty Lehan Harragan, in her book *Games Mother Never Taught You: Corporate Gamesmanship for Women*, asserts that the structure of the business world is derived from the military, while its everyday functioning is governed by the rules of team sports.[4] Since women are relative strangers to both fields, they will be at a disadvantage in business until they learn to play by men's rules. In the military, the hierarchy is supreme: Officers are saluted, enlisted men do the dirty work, and complete obedience to a superior is mandatory. In sports, even young boys are taught to play to win; it is unheard of—both unmanly and un-American—to slack off in your efforts to win. Yet boys on competing teams resume their friendships after the game is over.

At the other extreme, to be utterly ruthless, autocratic, and opportunistic at the expense of others won't get women very far in business or friendship. That's not playing fair. If women do decide to play the game of business the way men do, they will abide by the rules, and they won't play dirty. Work and friendship will coexist, but the rules of one will not interfere with the rules of the other. Women will not seek love and acceptance through work, nor will they expect friends to abide by their business decisions.

A middle-aged, highly competitive male advertising executive offered his opinion on friendship and work: "Your goal at work is to make money, to get ahead of the other guy, not to be the most popular guy in the office. Women have to learn that they can't let friendship interfere with work."

Women have traditionally defined themselves through their relationships with their husbands, their children, their parents, and their friends so that their self-esteem, to a large extent, depends on the approval of others. Approval is sought at almost any price. To keep a valued friend's approval, a woman may sometimes put her own career in jeopardy. Myra, for example, could have saved herself problems with her supervisor if she had realized that putting her friend's needs at work above her own was unprofessional.

Myra and Roz both worked in the large public relations department of a utility company, but their friendship preceded their working together. They were college chums, and Roz had joined the firm first. After an unsuccessful attempt at full-time free-lance writing, Myra, with an excellent academic record and a good word from Roz, was also hired by the same firm as public relations representative. The women's friendship blossomed; they joked together, commiserated over their work load, and basically enjoyed each other's company.

But when Roz's marriage started to fall apart, the personal stress she was undergoing showed in her efforts at work. She had difficulty concentrating, and she was forgetful; she misplaced several important reports and forgot several appointments.

Myra genuinely cared for Roz; they had been confidants for many years, and the bond they shared as friends could not easily be broken. Roz asked Myra to "cover" for her temporarily, just until she could "get her head straight." Myra started doing much of Roz's work as well as her own, which she actually didn't mind for a few weeks. But soon her own work began to suffer, and when her supervisor reprimanded her for not finishing some assignments on time, Myra told Roz that she could not be responsible for her any longer. Although Myra thought the friendship might suffer for a time, she was surprised to find that Roz accepted her decision with equanimity. She showed some annoyance at first, but she soon started to produce her usual quality of work. The friendship resumed on a firm footing.

Myra, if she had been more attuned to successful work habits, would have realized immediately that shouldering someone else's responsibilities while allowing her own work to suffer was career suicide. It is also disabling for a friendship; when one woman feels she is being taken advantage of by another and says nothing, resentment and hostility are bound to develop. It is better to risk a lack of acceptance for a time than to take the uncomplaining, good-girl course as Myra did.

To avoid conflicts, some women may choose to be loners at work and find their friends elsewhere. But this social isolation on the job is not beneficial personally or professionally. Management generally recognizes the value of employees who get along easily with coworkers; in most instances, the ability to work cooperatively with others is praised and rewarded in the business world.

Besides, women who are friendly with each other at work can compare notes. They ask each other questions that cannot be asked of strangers. "Am I giving Mr. Smith the wrong impression, or does he call you 'sweetie,' too?" "Am I just slow, or do you feel so bogged down that you feel like giving up, too?" Or, "Hey, I just got a 7 percent raise this year. What about you?"

In addition, jobs are usually accomplished more efficiently if coworkers perform them in a friendly, cooperative spirit. Aside from benefiting the employer, which generally benefits workers indirectly, coworkers have found that cooperation pays off in more direct ways. From the time labor unions began, workers have understood that if they stick together, they can better protect their rights. From another viewpoint, it's more pleasant to be friends than enemies at the office. It's healthy to commiserate, to laugh together, and to encourage each other. Friendly relations on the job offer a healthy release from the pressures of the workplace.

Apparently, many women have already discovered the advantages of friendship at work. Janet Lee Barkas explored the friendship patterns of a sample of unmarried women aged twenty-three to forty on an Upper East Side block. The group averaged one best friend, four close friends, and nine casual friends. When the women's best friends were not of long standing such as those they'd met at school, they were most likely to be work friends.[5] For coworkers who recognize the different roles of workers and friends and do not confuse the two, friendship is indeed possible. But will employees and their bosses ever be friends?

Although it is easiest to be friends with a coworker who holds about the same job status, many women said it is entirely possible to be friends with the boss, but only if you keep your priorities straight. The boss must be treated with due respect on the job; she must be given her authority. In social situations, the boss is no longer in power, so she may be treated as a friend, if she has shown that she wishes the relationship with her employee to progress in that direction. However, keeping social expectations and work expectations separate and not letting difficulties from one sphere of the relationship affect the other is, admittedly, difficult.

Some women thought it was easier to befriend a male superior. Perhaps these women are not accustomed to someone of their own sex assuming a position of authority, and consequently, it is hard for them to take a female boss seriously. For instance, when thirty-eight-year-old Yvette finally landed a management position in a firm where she had worked for twelve years, some of her women coworkers, who were also her friends, gave her a party. She was delighted to share the pleasure of her success with them, but when she started her new position as their supervisor, she noticed that the women joked that Yvette "would understand" if work was late, because she had been late a few times herself when she worked alongside them. They said, "Yvette, I know you're not really going to make me do that," when they were handed assignments they did not like.

Yvette took her position seriously, and she expected her friends to do the same. Those who treated her like a boss on the job remained her friends. Those who tried to take advantage of their relationship with her by shirking their work responsibilities were written off her list of intimates, nor were they included in the list of those who received raises or promotions.

If a woman is fortunate enough to be friends with the boss, it is poor practice to use the friendship as an excuse for not doing her best work if she wishes to keep her friendship and her job.

Also, it is wise to be discreet. Bragging to coworkers about friendly relations with the boss often creates envy, not respect. On the job, envy can be turned into vicious office gossip, isolation, and a deliberate lack of cooperation from coworkers— not the kind of interoffice relations needed to get ahead.

Women need not mold themselves into men's doubles if they are to succeed at work while maintaining friendships in the marketplace. Nevertheless, as long as men hold the power, they are calling the shots; their rules, basically, have to be followed. But as women gain more power at work, they can use their own sensitivities to combat the rigidity of elitism and the insult of sexism, to give breaks to other women who through steadfast efforts and shining talent show they deserve them, and to be more tolerant of confused or anxious women who are attempting to find the difficult balance between work and friendship.

NETWORKING
AND FRIENDSHIP

While consciousness raising helped to save women from emotional isolation in the 1960s, in the less radical 1970s networking rescued the ever-increasing multitudes of working women from professional isolation. Clearly, women needed to rescue each other in a marketplace where the annual average earnings of full-time female workers were only 56 percent of men's average earnings in 1977. Five years later, the median full-time female worker earned 62 cents for every dollar a comparable male earned. Certainly, women continue to need each other to help offset the effects of isolation and discrimination in the workplace.

Discrimination against women still prevails on the job, although not as blatantly as in former years when women poured the coffee and took notes at board meetings, and certainly never tried to interfere with men's power and privileges. Today, while a few women are making high-powered decisions in boardrooms rather than deciding who takes cream in his coffee, many men still exclude women coworkers from their informal but highly influential lunches, conferences around the water cooler, and golf games. Erma, a thirty-five-year-old stockbroker complained: "I'm never invited. I've dropped a few hints, but it's as though I'm not even there."

To offset women's loneliness and lack of information in the workplace and to establish valuable contacts, networking has more formally kept women on top of the career heap in the same way as men's less formal alliances. A sampling of some network groups reveals their diversity: Career Advancement Network, Columbus, Ohio; Forum for Executive Women, Philadelphia, Pennsylvania; the New York Association of Women Business Owners, New York, New York; Architectural Secretaries Association, Richardson, Texas; and the Women's Equality Action League, Washington, D.C. Literally hundreds of local, national, and international networks are available in almost any field.

Networking is essential for any woman intent on getting ahead in the business world, since so much of success depends on who can help you rather than what you can do. According to the U.S. Bureau of Labor Statistics, almost half of all jobs are secured through personal contacts.

What about friendships? Surely, intimate friendships may result unexpectedly from joining women's networks. But remember, the goal of networking is not friendship; it is business advancement.

Although Mary Scott Welch, in her book *Networking: The Great New Way for Women to Get Ahead,* praises networking for its professional usefulness to women, she admits that the main purpose of networking goes against the feminine consciousness: Networks are set up so that women can use each other.[6] Using a person for your own goals is the very antithesis of women's friendships, even if it is mutual. Friendship, as most women perceive it, is a relationship established for the pure joy of knowing another person, enjoying time together, and sharing intimacies with her, regardless of what she can do for you in any practical sense. Meeting friends at networks, then, may be dif-

ficult at best and impossible at worst, if this definition of friendship applies.

Women must understand that the rules of business, rather
than the principles of friendship, apply to networking. It would
be just as inappropriate, for instance, for a woman who has just
met a new contact at a network meeting to discuss intimacies of
her personal life as it would be for a successful businessman at
a golf game to discuss his impending divorce. Rules are rules in
old boys' clubs and in new girls' networks. It is best not to mix
business with pleasure and not to mix networking with friendship.

Nevertheless, occasionally when women trade mutual favors or offer each other advice concerning their business decisions, they may grow to like and respect each other beyond their
roles as colleagues. With time and more privacy than a networking atmosphere offers, two women who started as network
contacts may eventually become friends.

It is important for those women who decide to join a network to advance their career and to meet contacts who might
possibly turn into friends to make sure they join an appropriate
group. So-called vertical networks welcome any woman who is
interested in greater job success, while horizontal networks in-
vite women who may work in different fields but hold the same
job title or status. Within these categories, some networks are
further specialized by occupation.

Horizontal occupational networks may be elitist, but even in
vertical networks, some old-time members may resent newcomers. A twenty-six-year-old free-lance journalist remarked: ''I
thought the women's network I joined would help me in my career, but it backfired. I tried to get to know some respected jour-
nalists in the club, but they wanted nothing to do with me. I
guess they figured I'd have nothing to contribute to them, so why
should they help me?''

Professional jealousy and elitist attitudes stem from insecurity in a competitive job market, and unfortunately, women are

just as prone to these frailties as men. But women must remember that the more they are willing to help each other, the more women will be successful, and the greater their collective power will be. Women must be willing to come to each other's aid if they are to be a viable force in the marketplace.

CAN HOUSEWIVES AND CAREER WOMEN BE FRIENDS?

"If you enjoy what you're doing with your life, then it will be easier for you to make friends," said a forty-five-year-old biologist and former housewife. The statement applies to both career women and housewives. If a housewife is content in her role as nurturer of her husband and children and caretaker of the home, and if a career woman is truly excited by her work, there is no reason why the two, if there is some chemistry between them, can't become friends. But if one is subconsciously or consciously discontented and envies the other, friendship between the two would be hard to fathom.

Joyce, a thirty-four-year-old former teacher who had opted to quit her job when she became a mother for the first time, did not have difficulty keeping or making friends with career women afterward because she had a variety of interests. "If I were only interested in the baby's colic, and keeping the kitchen floor clean, I'm sure I'd have difficulty making friends with working women. But I've kept up my interest in so many things—art, politics, tennis, books. I have no trouble holding a conversation with anyone."

Because she has not defined herself totally by her roles of wife and mother, Joyce has a plethora of friends, including housewives and career women. But she is unusual. More often, housewives complain of loneliness and a lack of contact with career women. The solitary nature of a housewife's work explains part of her difficulty in making friends, but often the difficulty is more deep-seated. It is insecurity—a lack of confidence and self-esteem that society fosters by viewing the housewife's role as menial and inconsequential, a job requiring no special skills (in reality, it requires numerous skills) and therefore not worthy of financial remuneration. While professional recognition and monetary rewards, as well as prestigious prizes and appreciative bonuses, are provided for worthy workers in all other fields, no prize or reward is given to the housewife for keeping the cleanest home, cooking the best meals, or raising the most stable, healthy, productive children. The rewards of a housewife are supposed to be inherent in her doing, in her giving.

Ask any man what he would say to an employer who suggested he work a minimum of twelve hours a day, not for pay but for the sheer joy of giving, and you can guess with certainty that his answer would be full of negative superlatives or positively obscene expletives.

Particularly distressing to housewives is the all-too-often-asked question "What do you do?" This strikes an especially sensitive chord when asked by career women who have children and are therefore housewives, too. It is natural to feel inadequate when faced with someone who holds the same kind of job but holds another one as well and seems to be succeeding at both.

Fortunately, since the feminist movement has helped to free women from devaluing themselves, most homemakers today would recoil from the answer "I'm just a housewife." A few respond tongue-in-cheek, when asked what they do. "About what?" they'll reply, or "I do the best I can." More serious-minded women might answer, "I'm proud to say that I'm a housewife."

The prevailing attitude that paid work is challenging and housework is boring is changing as more women go to work for a living. Few women's jobs are exciting, challenging, or well paid. One woman who had been a housewife while her children were preschoolers and returned to work as a nurse out of financial necessity commented: "Work is not glamorous. When you have to work full-time, there is little time left for other interests or for friends. I wish I could still be a full-time housewife."

While time for socializing is difficult to come by for working women with families, some full-time housewives have a different problem that hampers friendships: lack of money. Geraldine, a teacher who opted to stay home to rear her children while her friends went back to work after they had their babies, found that she could no longer afford to go to luncheons or to the theater with her women friends, as she often had when she worked. After she quit work, she and her husband often stayed home and watched TV on Saturday night rather than joining friends for a meal out and a movie. They also refused invitations to some dinner parties, because, she said, "We just didn't have the funds to reciprocate."

To be friends, housewives and career women will have to recognize and be tolerant of each other's difficulties concerning friendship. When Harriet, a housewife, calls Zoe to arrange a dinner date, if Zoe has to work late, Harriet will have to understand the priorities of business. Conversely, if Zoe calls Harriet because she would like to spend an evening together, and Harriet says, "Not tonight, my husband's coming home late and I just can't afford another sitter this week," her friend will have to recognize that family and finances often present problems when a housewife wishes to continue a friendship with a career woman. But if the friendship is strong, and if each of the women has a strong sense of herself and of her value to others, neither career demands, family demands, money, or time limitations will destroy it.

CHAPTER

5

CAN WOMEN
AND MEN
BE FRIENDS?

One hundred fifty years ago, when American women and men were building civilization out of wilderness on the western frontier, the dichotomy between the sexes was strongly defined. As recently as thirty years ago, vestiges of the sexism of pioneer days still pervaded opposite-sex relationships. In the 1950s, a woman who befriended a man was regarded by some of her peers with suspicion. To open oneself emotionally to a member of the opposite sex was viewed as a prelude to a sexual involvement. If emotional intimacies could be shared, it was assumed that physical intimacy was also enjoyed—or soon would be.

Today new frontiers in opposite sex relationships are starting to be explored. Friendships between women and men are more frequent, and they are on the threshold of social acceptance. The onset of women's liberation marked hostility and alienation between the sexes, but we are now starting to reap the harvest of years of turmoil. Both women and men are beginning to view each other more as people than as sex objects. As men come to regard women as their equals in work settings, they are becoming more accepted as social equals. With the sexes having more contact with each other on the job and in coed dormitories and other living arrangements, they have opportunity to see each other as multidimensional people—people who share many of the same weaknesses and strengths. As more realistic awareness replaces fantasy and misinformation concerning what to expect from relationships with the opposite sex, anxiety about interaction is declining. Women and men are learning that contact with each other on a friendly basis does not necessarily have to lead to a sexual relationship.

But this new acceptance of opposite-sex friendships is far from universal in American society. While these friendships are gradually becoming more acceptable for singles, married women and men must still contend with the jealousy and insecurity of their spouses. Even the most sophisticated man who acknowledges his wife's need for personal growth feels twinges of uneasiness when she makes friends with another man.

When a married woman develops an opposite-sex friendship, regardless of her friend's marital status, there is suspicion. Society often assumes that the couple either is having an affair or is interested in pursuing one. Opposite-sex platonic friendships between singles are more readily accepted; society assumes the couple is uninterested in each other sexually because they are romantically involved with others, or they are not sexually attracted to each other.

Although more women seem to be open to male friendships, our culture remains divided and confused about this issue, and the number of women who have actually managed such a relationship successfully is still small. Psychologist Joel Block was able to confirm this in a 1980 study involving over 1,000 women. According to those findings, published in *Friendship: How to Give It, How to Get It,* only 18 percent, fewer than two out of ten women, reported male friendships.[1] Interestingly, in our current study, married women, whether employed or not, reported having more male friends than their single counterparts. Apparently, the figure is greater for married women because they can make friends with their mates' male companions. This suggests that men still hold subtle power in determining who their wives' male friends will be. If a man introduces his wife to a male and encourages her friendship with him, he apparently considers the man nonthreatening to his marital relationship.

While a higher number of married women reported having a close male friend, the overall paucity of cross-sex friendships is a striking finding that does not speak well for the relations between the sexes. In point of fact, male-female ties not bound by love, status, or marriage are still rare and precarious; neither women nor men, for the most part, find them easy to establish. It is difficult to give up myths and old insecurities, to work out ways of relating that surmount sexual and sexist issues—the most common friendship complaints that women and men direct toward one another. Yet the desire is there, at least for some women. Many of those we interviewed relate that they would welcome such a relationship.

A forty-year-old secretary put it this way: "I love my women friends. I believe women, more than men, are there for me in a crisis. They know what I feel, and there's no need for competition or judgments or power plays with them. But lately, as I think back to my teenage years and the male friends I had then, and the good times and good humor we shared, I miss having a male friend today. I miss innocent flirtation. Women friends are my basic nourishment, but a male friend would be icing on the cake.''

THE EROTIC ELEMENT: CAN IT BE OVERCOME?

Sexuality presents a formidable barrier to women who desire male friendship. A sexual undercurrent is present in all relationships between heterosexual women and men, whether it is consciously acknowledged or not. Often a woman and a man who want to be friends but who do not want a sexual relationship are painfully aware of their sexual attraction to each other. Indeed, they have been conditioned by society to evaluate each other's sexual attractiveness from the first time they set eyes on each other. The physical attraction may not be obvious initially, but it erupts when the setting is appropriately romantic or when one or the other, because of a recent love affair gone sour or because of sexual boredom or lack of confidence in her or his attractiveness, becomes emotionally needy. Sexual desire, after all, usually has more to do with emotional needs than with lust. Sex promises emotional fulfillment, security, reassurance, and intimacy—even if it doesn't always deliver.

Amanda, a forty-two-year-old actress, felt the need to reassure herself of her desirability and attractiveness after her bitter divorce. Her feelings of rejection combined with secluded, serene surroundings disposed her to consider her platonic friend of over twenty years in romantic terms. "John was my friend from high school—a lifelong friend whom I had never thought of in the sexual sense. He was like a brother to me. But one summer night, not long after my divorce, we spent an evening together on the beach, and giddy from wine and from the stars and the ocean, we started singing show tunes and dancing together, and I said to myself, 'Oh, my God, I'd like to go to bed with him.' "

Amanda did not give in to her desires. She was afraid of ruining her long-term friendship for an impulsive night of passion. Even when strong sexual attraction is evident in opposite-sex friendships, a woman has a choice concerning whether to act on it or not. Popular romantic novels and soap operas tend to convey sexual feelings as so intense that they are uncontrollable. While this characterization panders to our romantic fantasies of being emotionally and uncontrollably enraptured by a true love, real life is much less dramatic. Yes, infatuation is strong, but uncontrollable sexual urges are more the plague of sexual deviates. Granted, it may be hard for a woman to maintain a close platonic friendship with a man who makes her heart beat faster and her palms become sweaty, but if she is of a mind to and if she informs him of her position, should the subject arise, it is manageable. It is only when a woman's motives are unclear to herself or when she is particularly vulnerable that she is liable to act on her sexual desires.

The absence of sex, some women find, allows for a balanced, honest exchange of feelings that sexual involvement might blur. Free from the jealousies, tensions, and restrictions that often surround romantic relationships, barriers are let down, weaknesses are more willingly revealed, and intimate confidences are exchanged. A woman in her mid-forties remarked:

> On those rare occasions when I've met a man who is comfortable with his sexuality and secure in his identity, we have had a very valuable friendship that enriched both our lives. One such relationship has survived a number of involvements and dramatic career changes on his part and a marriage, a child, and a divorce on my part. He has taught me different things about life and about myself; he has broadened my perspective, added to my insight, and challenged me to learn and grow. There has been a greater objectivity between us than usually occurs between lovers. One of the primary virtues of the relationship is that I can say anything to him and he can be completely open with me. That may be a true test of genuine friendship, one that many love affairs would not pass. Sexual/romantic relationships have an obvious excitement and intensity; unfortunately, for me, they also carry with them a pressure to be on my best behavior. With my male friends, I can really let my hair down; I can be completely myself.

Frequently, because of the quandary of sexuality, women choose a male friend with whom they do not have a strong sexual or romantic interest; it is simply easier to maintain a platonic relationship with someone they do not find particularly sexually attractive. However, for some women, a hint of sexual attraction, expressed either indirectly or in a straightforward, nonthreatening way, adds an energy to their opposite-sex friendships.

Janet, a single thirty-three-year-old scientist who has had many platonic friendships, said that she always experiences sexual tension at the beginning of these friendly alliances. "Until things are settled, there is always an element of flirtation. If the subject of sex is approached directly by a friend, I'll laugh it off or treat it lightly. Or if my friend is married, I'll make an effort to get to know his wife. But quite honestly, an undercurrent of at least some mutual sexual attraction, unpressured and kept in perspective, is flattering and energizing, something that I find myself looking forward to."

While some women enjoy flirtation and sexual sparks, others feel strongly about keeping the sexual boundaries well defined. Even a hint of flirtation is offensive. Some of these women react angrily to sexual innuendos; others discourage sexual advances from male friends by retreating from their own sexuality and taking what one traditional woman described as a "ladylike" stance. Still others are able to negotiate a sexual truce by handling requests for sexual involvement with humor, rather than anger. Still, some women are unable to get past the sexual element of an opposite-sex friendship.

For example, Sandra, an attractive, married thirty-eight-year-old businesswoman, said she feared revealing herself to men, because she frequently found they became friendly with her for sexual purposes. She commented: "I know a woman is interested in me as a person when she is my friend. But when a man is friendly to me—open, candid, empathetic—I always wonder if there is a sexual motive underneath. I wonder if his caring is there just so he can score. I've been disappointed a lot of times by men who befriended me and then made a pass at me."

Ironically, some women are disappointed if they do not get a sexual invitation from a male friend. One forty-two-year-old photographer, a woman who had accumulated many male friends over her lifetime, said: "When I broke up with my lover, I let my male friends know. I thought I would be able to have my choice of several possible lovers. But unfortunately—and to my great disappointment—not even one of my male friends asked if I would go to bed with him. The worst myth my mother ever taught me is that men just want one thing: to go to bed with you.''

Indeed, in the aftermath of the sexual revolution, women are finding that men are not the sexual animals they were made out to be. Women and men have similar sexual needs, and sex is not necessarily the first and foremost topic on a man's mind when he meets an attractive woman.

Still, many women who convey their warmth and caring for their women friends by touching them and by openly sharing their emotions are afraid to show this expressive side of themselves to men, for fear it will be interpreted sexually. Reared by the double standard, women still feel uncomfortable interacting with men as friends.

To avoid sexual tension or the embarrassment of an unwanted sexual advance, some women intentionally or unconsciously choose gay men as friends. Women who have male homosexual friends often feel free to express their emotions in the same way they would with female friends. One woman, a forty-five-year-old artist who had many gay male friends, explained: ''We talk about romance. We pour our hearts out together. We find so much in common—for instance, that the straight world can be as lonely and devastating as the gay world. But it's more than that. Many of the gay men I know are very successful businessmen, and they'll offer me good advice and insights concerning my career. And best of all, I can hug and be hugged without giving it a second thought.''

Despite a host of entanglements, temptations, and too few guidelines, a growing minority of women and men are discovering that friendship between the sexes is ultimately more fulfilling than short-term sexual involvements. They are also finding that sex is not nearly as important as we once thought it was in every male-female relationship. Sexual sparks will fly in love relationships, but companionship between the sexes, though not explosive, has its own rewards.

DIFFERENT EXPECTATIONS: WHAT DO WOMEN AND MEN WANT FROM EACH OTHER?

Though women and men interact frequently today, they have considerable ground to cover on their journey toward friendlier relations. Aside from the issue of sexuality, there is social conditioning.

In our society females are supposed to inhibit aggression and sexual urges, to be passive, nurturing, and attractive, and to maintain a poised and friendly posture with others. Males, in contrast, are influenced to be sexually aggressive and independent and to suppress strong emotions, especially anxiety. From Hercules to James Bond, the heroic man is presented as invulnerable. Women are depicted as nothing if not vulnerable.

Just as men have learned that rough and tough is masculine, women have been taught that soft and sweet is feminine. Rather than realizing they are capable of versatile roles, too many women have confined themselves to one dimension: mother, companion, follower, bitch, homemaker, whore, or glamour girl. Limiting views such as these wreak havoc on relationships.

In addition to a very different upbringing, women and men must contend with innate, gender-related differences. There is evidence, for example, that males as a group from birth, are more active and vigorous in movement and more aggressive in their responses than girls. But females, from birth, are more sensitive than males to stimuli of any kind, including visual, auditory, and tactile.

Human behavior, however, is highly malleable, as Margaret Mead, among others, has convincingly demonstrated. Dr. Mead showed that in three New Guinea tribes, there was considerable difference from tribe to tribe in feminine and masculine behavior. In one group, the Arapesh, women and men alike were passive, "maternal," cooperative, and nonaggressive. In the Mundugumor, a tribe in geographic proximity to the Arapesh, women and men alike were fierce, cruel, and aggressive. A third tribe, the Iatmul, showed yet another pattern of sex typing. The men were passive, dependent individuals who spent their time cultivating the arts while the women assumed the more active, assertive role of provider.[2]

When women and men in our society, blinded by sexist expectations, confine themselves to either "masculine" or "feminine" behavior, they are incomplete human beings. The psychologically healthy woman or man, one who is able to develop satisfying, nurturing relationships, must be nonconforming in this respect. She or he needs to take relatively fixed gender expectations and redefine them in the ways that dovetail with her needs. Consequently, she has greater freedom to express and act out a wider range of feelings and behavior.

Typically, for example, women are burdened with the role of nurturer. This allows men to maintain their macho image of independence but interferes with true intimacy between the sexes. In a similar way, if a male friend is treated as the strong protector of his female friend, she may never discover her own strength. Recent studies indicate that the more boys and girls are encouraged to express the traits of the opposite sex, the more effective they will become at all-around problem solving.

Yet stereotypical behavior is still expected of boys and girls. Evidence suggesting that this is the case is presented in a recent study appearing in the *Journal of Clinical Psychology*. Psychologist Sandra Bem found that compassion, eagerness to soothe hurt feelings, tenderness, understanding, sensitivity to the needs of others, and warmth were high on a list of qualities considered desirable for females. In contrast, among the top 5 percent of characteristics considered masculine were aggressiveness, ambition, competitiveness, independence, and self-reliance.[3]

Despite the feminist movement, the picture of the ideal male and female has not varied enough over the last few decades. Ambitious, powerful men are still amply rewarded with money and prestige; these men are still considered prizes for women in the marriage market. Women, more and more, are being rewarded for their ambition, but some part of society still looks askance at the woman who wants power and position at the expense of relinquishing her stereotypical feminine traits. These ambitious, powerful women are generally regarded as a threat to men. Many women still prefer not to show their strengths, whereas men do their best to hide their weaknesses.

Until this rigid thinking changes, friendship between the sexes will suffer. Until women can freely express aggressive or competitive tendencies without society's censure and men can express feelings of tenderness or vulnerability without fear of being judged as weak or effeminate, the sexes will be limited in their friendships with each other.

A recent investigation by researchers Mark Sherman and Adelaide Haas, reported in the June 1984 issue of *Psychology Today,* highlights some difficulties the sexes have in relating. The study showed that not only do women and men talk about different subjects with friends of the same sex, but—more hazardous to friendship between the sexes—the style and function of their conversations is different.

Of 166 women and 110 men interviewed, the researchers found that 60 percent of women and only 27 percent of men reported talking about emotional topics in their same-sex conversations. While men spoke more frequently about current events, sports, and music, women favored such topics as family, health, weight, food, and clothing.[4]

Sherman and Hass did not study which sex more often adapts to the other's communication style. However, it is known that women most often align themselves with male friends who are older and more educated; it is likely that they also defer to their "superior" male companions' style of communication and conversational interests. Women have been trained to do this; they have been taught by their parents, and by society, to put others before themselves.

As one woman reared in a traditional household put it, ''I let the man lead the conversation. I always find out what the man is interested in, and then I grow interested in the subject, so we can talk.''

Concerning the style and goal of conversation, men in the research study said they enjoyed fast-paced talk—conversation that offered humor, playfulness, camaraderie, and practical advice about everyday concerns. Women, on the other hand, more often valued empathy and understanding in their talk with each other. Women felt they needed their conversations with same-sex friends to get along in life, but men more often felt same-sex friendships were a pleasant frill to their everyday lives.

From our own research, it has become evident that women tend to prefer the intrinsic aspects of conversation and friendship—the sharing of emotional experiences. Men value the extrinsic factors, such as discussion and sharing activities together—playing tennis, getting advice, exchanging tips on stocks, and the like. A woman will more often make a lunch date with a friend ''just to get together and talk.'' When a man calls a male friend for a lunch appointment, he will most likely be asked, ''What's up?'' Men need an agenda when they get together.

In conversing with opposite-sex friends, a man may offer advice to a woman when she may simply want someone to listen to her and understand her feelings. When speaking to a woman, who may be prone to listen with empathy rather than offer direct advice, a man may miss a practical analysis of his problem.

Becoming aware of these different styles of interacting, and making some effort to adapt to the style of the opposite sex without losing one's own identity may be what is needed for the sexes to be better friends.

Occasionally, conventional sex roles act to bring the sexes together; in these instances, opposite-sex friendships may flourish despite different styles in communication. At times, for ex-

ample, men value the empathy and nurturance they more readily
obtain from women friends, while women value a man's ability
to separate himself emotionally from a problem.

Some women prefer male friends because they are fearful of
the intensity of a same-sex friendship. These women often unconsciously fear intimacy and seek the safety of a restrained, superficial opposite-sex friendship. Since women have been taught
to view their feelings of dependency and vulnerability as faults,
choosing a male friend, who because of his gender is presumed
to be logical, controlled, and rational, will, they hope, prevent
their "female neediness" from being obvious. While this type
of relationship may appear safe, it is also destined to remain
limited and, ultimately, unsatisfying; it is junk food for the timid.

The fantasy is that an unemotional man will complement an
emotional woman, but the truth is the woman is accepting society's negative view of her expressive nature and viewing the
male's emotional constriction as a strength. The "rational" man,
in reality, fails to exude the warmth and caring that go into the
making of any friendship that is more than superficial. Yet when
the relationship is found lacking, a woman will often blame herself.

The same myth—that men are logical, independent, and rational while women are flaky, dependent, and hysterical—that
draws some women to men acts to repel them from one another.
These women fear they will be emotionally drained by their female friends.

Ironically, contrary to popular opinion, it is not women but
men who are likely to sap a woman's emotions. Typically, a
male's dependency needs are hidden from view because they are
readily met by women, first by his mother and later by his lover
or wife. But a girl eventually has to give up her mother without
getting anyone to replace her. When a woman marries, she becomes the nurturer in the family. Her own dependency needs
remain unmet; hence, they are more visible.

While women and men have a very different experience of
marriage and love relationships, the woman typically being the

emotional giver and the man the receiver, some women still value the male point of view to help them through problems in their love relationships. Sometimes talking to a supportive male friend can release tension, offer a different perspective, or replenish energies that have been drained through dealing with strife in her primary love relationship. A male friend can supplement a marital relationship or other love relationship, but many women have discovered that this kind of comfort from a man may supplant the exchange needed between husband and wife if a failing marriage is to be saved.

Further, when a woman who feels emotionally deprived in her marriage seeks validation of her self-worth from a male friend, she may easily become sexually involved with him. But an affair will usually accomplish the opposite for a woman; her self-image will be further eroded. Besides feeling guilty and anxious about betraying her husband, she may get the message that she is, after all, worthy only as a sex object. In bed with her lover, she again becomes the nurturer, the one who pleases, unless, unlike most women, she can enjoy extramarital sex without emotional entanglement.

When seeking advice, comfort, or understanding from a male friend concerning problems with her primary love relationship, a woman must be clear about her own motives. If she is attempting to escape from a failing relationship—if she is using her male friend to avoid a confrontation with her husband or lover—she may cause the problem in her love relationship to become worse owing to her failure to communicate with her partner.

WOMEN'S UPBRINGING: BRIDGING OR WIDENING THE GAP BETWEEN OPPOSITE-SEX FRIENDS?

In our society girls and boys usually engage in separate activities and seldom play together. Boys are involved in rough-and-tumble play and sports, while girls are considered "good" and "feminine" if they pursue quieter activities.

When the sexes do associate with each other in adolescence, the focus is on dating and romance. The sexual element in adolescent opposite-sex relationships is so important not only because of hormonal changes, which lead to sexual urges, but because our society places great emphasis on the sexual nature of male-female relationships.

Even today, when women are supposed to be able to view themselves positively, with many talents and qualities that are appealing and important aside from their sexuality, adolescent girls who have more male friends than dates are considered odd and lacking in an essential skill: the potential to attract possible marriage partners.

Not all societies teach their children to value sexual or romantic relationships above friendship with the opposite sex. Sociologist Constantina Safilios-Rothschild, for example, in her book *Love, Sex and Sex Roles,* found that girls and boys from the age of fifteen or sixteen in urban Greece and other Mediterranean societies are encouraged to spend time together socially, in groups. Called *parea,* this kind of friendly interaction among Greek youngsters supplements or replaces dating. The consequence of this institution is that, as adults, women and men feel comfortable as friends.[5]

Brought up in a traditional American household, Leslie, a thirty-five-year-old homemaker, regrets her lack of male friends when she was growing up. "It is important to keep girls and boys together in activities they can share," she said, "I regret that my parents separated girls and boys the way they did. And as an adolescent I spent too much energy on romance. Books, movies, and TV stress romance, and I got caught up in it. I was so busy romanticizing relationships that I missed out on simply being friends with boys."

Just as the traditional socialization process stands as a barrier to friendship between the sexes, other, more subtle psychological dynamics increase the complexity of the friendship drama.

The Harvard-based psychologist Carol Gilligan reported in her book *In a Different Voice* that because girls are reared to be like their mothers while boys are taught to be the opposite of their mothers, girls tend to identify with other people's feelings as their own, the way a mother does with her children. Since boys must show they are separate from their mothers, they tend to relate to work and accomplishments more than to the feelings of others. Consequently, men have difficulty becoming intimate, and women may find it difficult to establish their own identity because they experience themselves mainly through personal relationships.[6]

If women and men have these different attitudes, it is no wonder they have such difficulty connecting emotionally as friends. Perhaps if more men were willing to take an active part in child care and other parenting experiences they could influence their children's view of the world and of themselves as whole human beings who are able to experience both intimacy and separation without anxiety. Friendship between the sexes might then be less mired in misunderstandings and mistaken motives.

Even though the concept of active fathering is prevalent, word and deed are far apart. In this sphere, traditional sex-role values are tenacious if not downright entrenched. In 1983, for example, Wenda Brewster-O'Reilly, a researcher at Stanford University, interviewed a dozen dual-career couples and found that, although they claimed to believe in equality of the sexes, wives who had full-time jobs spent an average of 25 percent more time per week on housework and child care than their husbands.[7]

We still live in a patriarchal society in which many parents prefer male children to female children. Though parents may try to hide their disappointment with daughters, children are ultrasensitive to their parents' feelings, and many girls understand, through subtle hints or implication, that boys are more desirable. This may be a devastating realization to a girl, who consequently may reject her own femininity. Later in life, men will be her favorite companions because she has been taught that men are more highly valued. By association with men and by conscious or unconscious rejection of her own sex she hopes to rise above being a woman.

Other women, even though they may not have received any directly sexist messages from their parents, perceive that their father wields the authority and power in their family. Later in life, these women may prefer to associate with the powerful and may value friendships with males more than friendships with their own sex.

Still other women whose fathers were notable for their absence formed a strong bond with their mothers and learned to expect little from men. Ironically, some recall taking a chance and asking for more of an emotional connection from men, only to be thought insatiable and demanding by their male companions.

At the other extreme, some women who have not received the care and attention they needed from their fathers may seek male friends later in life to compensate for that unfulfilled longing.

Some women who have been reared by authoritarian fathers who were emotionally distant purposefully seek out sensitive, caring men as friends. A thirty-three-year-old single architect who is more comfortable with her male friends than her female friends said: "I talk about personal, emotional things with men, but my male friends are very emotional. I was not very close to my father; my mother was the nurturer. I seem to choose male friends who are the complete opposite in personality from my father."

This professionally ambitious woman has followed her successful father's urging to "be anything you want to be." She respected his power in the world and in the family, where her mother was a traditional homemaker. But she still craved the affection and sensitivity of her father, which she was able to get only through friendships with men.

Another factor influencing friendship between the sexes is a woman's relationship with her mother. Since most women are raised to identify with the prototypical nurturing mother, their emotional expectations for themselves and each other may be unrealistically high. If a woman feels misunderstood by another woman, the hurt is greater than if a man misunderstands her. As a result, some women will place their trust only in males as an insurance against being disappointed. These inordinately high expectations placed on women by their same-sex friends is an unfair burden. Idealizing women does not take into account their true character and individuality, just as regarding them as inferior to men does not provide a realistic picture of their actual potential.

In a similar vein, some women feel threatened or smothered by other women—they are repelled by an anticipation of being emotionally invaded. These feelings may stem from a mother who was very critical or overbearing, particularly during adolescence, when both females and males require a degree of privacy. Often these women prefer a male friend, feeling he is less likely to probe their weaknesses because he cannot understand them the way another woman could or that he will excuse her drawbacks, saying, "Women are like that." A man, these women believe, is more likely to appreciate a woman's strengths because they are so different from his own.

Nevertheless, the majority of women feel closer to their women friends, in whom they find empathy and solace. In the wake of consciousness raising, a renewed enthusiasm for the intimacy of sisterhood has brought women closer as friends sharing common goals in the struggle for equality, just as pioneer women banded together in their struggle to maintain the dignity of their civilized world in wild, uncharted territory.

Many more of today's women are self-reliant and do not need male friends to encourage progress in their personal relationships or career, validate their worth, or provide them with power. Growing numbers of contemporary women recognize that women are allies.

If men are to join women in friendship, it is the emotionally secure man who is most apt to succeed. The more confident a man is, the less likely he is to feel threatened by revealing his emotions. Less secure males sometimes develop psychological response sets for rejecting some females; frequently, they are threatened by assertive, self-confident women. In contrast, those men who have begun to share parenting responsibilities, who have been influenced by the women's movement to redefine their roles, and who have become less fiercely competitive and more able to recognize and share their feelings, are candidates for solid cross-sex friendship.

CAN EX-LOVERS
BE FRIENDS?

When the glow of sexual ardor has died and lovers part, whether they can remain friends or not depends on how their relationship began as well as how it ended. Each partner's personality, the jealousy of a spouse or current lover, and their geographical distance from each other also play a part in keeping or breaking an emotional connection with a former lover. When the romance goes out of a relationship or an unresolvable difference in goals emerges and neither partner resents the other's position, some women express a desire to continue the relationship in the form of friendship.

Marcia, a forty-two-year-old copywriter who had a three-year affair with a thirty-four-year-old advertising executive, finally came to realize, about the same time her lover did, that their initial physical attraction was waning. They mutually agreed to end their liaison, which, they had decided, could not lead to marriage because of their different goals in life. Bob, who had never married, wanted a home life with children, but Marcia, divorced when her children were toddlers, was ready to move forward in her career.

Yet they enjoyed each other's company and had come to be best friends. Marcia admitted she still felt close to Bob when they split up as lovers. "I did not want to cut Bob out of my life completely," Marcia said. "After all, how could I completely ignore someone I was so intimate with? I would be ignoring a part of my own existence if I did not respond to him now.''

When Bob eventually found a new love before Marcia started dating seriously again, she felt a few pangs of remorse, but she was ultimately happy about her decision to let love fade into friendship. She was able to remain friends with Bob over the next few years, and eventually, she became friends with his wife. Now she is the godmother for the couple's first child.

Marcia's decision was based on healthy motives. She no longer viewed Bob as a lover would, but she still loved the qualities about him that first attracted her to him: his sense of humor, intelligence, and sensitivity.

It seems to be an idealized image: a relationship of lovers moving from passion and romance through the agony of separation only to be reborn as one of fulfilling friends. In actuality, it is a rare experience that only a small minority of women achieve. For many women, particularly the insecure, hidden feelings of proprietorship interfere with the development of friendship. Being accustomed to the intensity of passion and romance in a love relationship makes it very difficult to shift gears, to give up expectations and settle for what in many people's view is a lesser relationship.

Indeed, some women remain friends with their ex-lovers because of a secret longing to resume the passion and romance they once shared. They are unable to separate from the relationship gracefully. This makes the eventual parting longer and harder. Usually, resolutions to let go are challenged by temptations to call, meet for a drink, and try one more time to ignite a banked fire. One more try may lead to two or more. For most women, gradual withdrawal is far more torturous than cold turkey.

Sometimes, of course, it is the man who feels stripped of his confidence and afloat in a confusing world when a relationship crumbles. More often, though, it is the woman who attempts to cling to her man, since she traditionally has been encouraged to merge her identity with his. In contrast, society esteems men who are independent, encouraging males to strive to maintain an image of self-reliance. These attitudes may explain one recent study that showed that a rejected man was less likely to remain friends with his former lover than a rejected woman. Apparently the threat to pride and self-image, to say nothing of vulnerability, is too much to tolerate for most men.

Besides dealing with her ex-lovers's disinclination to remain friends as well as working through her own anger, jealousy, separation anxiety or dependency needs, a woman may also have to deal with the jealousy of her current lover or spouse if she maintains a friendship with an old flame.

Nancy, a twenty-eight-year-old stewardess, said one of the reasons she was planning to leave the man she had lived with for over a year was his inability to tolerate her male friendships. She explained: "I had several male friends before I started to live with Joe. I have had sexual relationships with some of them, but I don't now. Joe cannot accept the fact that I am only friends with them. Yet he still plays tennis with his women friends; occasionally he will go out to lunch with them. He believes that is his privilege because he is the major provider. I'm very angry at that. That's not the only reason we're splitting up, but it's one of the things about Joe that I could not accept."

Joe's blatantly sexist arrangement cost him his intimacy with Nancy. Ironically, this position, designed to protect the relationship from opposite-sex "intruders," more often results in a prison of boredom, frustration, and resentment from which, as time passes, escape is sought.

"But friends need not be ex-lovers," most spouses or lovers would say. True, but what if that is where the friendship feeling is based? If keeping a relationship with a former lover is too threatening for a woman's current partner, she may be forced to make a choice between that which is most important to her— her current love relationship or her autonomy. When one partner will agree to break off with an ex-lover, does fairness dictate that the other should abide by the same rules? Perhaps so. But what if one person's friendship with an ex-lover is particularly meaningful? How does one place a value on friendship? Even the idea of having to choose can be repugnant. Nor does the dilemma end here. Whether a woman complies unwillingly or rebels unwittingly, a sizable rift is likely to unsettle her love relationship.

True to character, Nancy hoped to remain friends with Joe, just as she had maintained her friendships with several former loves. She admitted, though, that "Joe is too bitter right now. It may take time."

Occasionally, couples find it easier to become friends after a sexual relationship has ended. The former sexual relationship helps to reduce sexual tension and inhibitions between the couple, so that they may communicate more freely.

Deirdre, a twenty-eight-year-old advertising executive, has had the experience of feeling freer, more open in her friendship with a lover after their sexual relationship ended. She said: "David and I went together for two years. We broke up in anger and didn't see or talk to each other for several months after the separation. One day, several months after our split, I called him and told him that I missed some of the things we had enjoyed with each other during our love relationship; we both agreed that we were losing something by not being friends. Neither of us had any desire to continue as lovers—we are not sexually involved with each another—but with two years of trust and a physical bond behind us, we feel free to talk about things we don't discuss with anyone else. It's great."

If the basis for continuing an opposite-sex friendship is primarily for the pleasure of each other's company rather than for sexual pleasure, chances are the couple will remain friends long after their sexual exploration has stopped. But if lovers view each other merely as sex objects, friendship after sex is highly improbable. On the other hand, sometimes the attachment to and affection for the loved one is so great that the rejected lover cannot bear to see or hear his or her former lover. The mourning period takes time, as it did for Deirdre and David.

Sometimes friendship and a sexual relationship end at the

same time, when one partner betrays the other. If one partner ends the relationship by hurting the other, by violating the couple's code of friendship, usually the hurt is too great for the betrayed partner to continue any relationship.

The human spirit can tolerate only a certain amount of pain before it withdraws from the source, but there is no limit to the amount of loving we will accept. And so, when healthy friendship is possible between ex-lovers—friendship that is not possessive but is pursued simply because the friends share warmth and caring and a connection to the past—it is best to cherish it and preserve it.

CAN FRIENDS
BE LOVERS, TOO?

Following tradition, our society expects a steady progression in a relationship between a woman and a man: Strangers become acquaintances, acquaintances become friends, and friends become lovers—romantic, forever-and-always lovers who will share their lives. At any particular step, the relationship may regress or stop. But only recently has the steady progress from the first step to the last been challenged. Those who were still at the age of sexual experimentation during the sexual revolution of the 1960s questioned the "all or nothing" philosophy of the previous generation. Why, enlightened women and men asked, must a sexual relationship lead to a pledge of undying love? Why can't lovers simply be friends, without their relationship progressing to the final romantic step?

Opposite-sex friends who are single sometimes view a sexual relationship with a friend as a possible option, a way to add another dimension to a friendship. Indeed, one divorced woman defending this kind of relationship contended: "Isn't it better to have sex with a friend than a stranger?"

For many, the most satisfying sex occurs between two people who enjoy time together in other areas of life. When a woman and a man are emotionally compatible, when they share interests, activities, and conversation, sex sometimes appears to be the next step in sharing and celebrating their friendship. For a few women and more men—for people who can separate the emotional and physical parts of a relationship—a friend-lover relationship works. For others who become inextricably bound to a sex partner, romance with no promises can only lead to pain and despair.

Andrea, a twenty-eight-year-old dancer, explained that when she got over her adolescent yearning for love and realized she was more in love with the feeling of love than with a person, she was able to enjoy a sexual relationship with a friend:

> I dated Steve in high school twice a week. He made it clear he had only two days a week to see me because he had other girlfriends. I was a virgin when I met him, but after six months, we had intercourse. I thought I was in love with him, and I thought that if I gave myself to him sexually, he would love me more. Instead, he lost interest and dropped me.
>
> I was devastated for six months; then I started to make more friends, both male and female. I went out more, got interested in my life again, and then Steve came back. He told me he missed me. I dated him again on the same basis, twice a week, and we had sex regularly. But I didn't give up my other male friends, even though at the time I was having sex only with Steve. This time it was different; he wasn't my one and only anymore. I was interested in many other friends. I was more mature.
>
> We were friends for five years before Steve told me he was getting married. At the time, I was very happy for him because I was getting seriously involved with someone, too, the man I eventually married. Steve lives in another state now, but if I saw him, I'd be delighted.

Andrea and Steve were both eventually able to enjoy their friendship along with their sexual relationship, but Steve had an easier time of it. The double standard, diluted but still operative, is a factor here. Our society has traditionally allowed men to "sow their wild oats," but, until recently, women were expected to be virgins when they married. Men found sex to be fun and carefree, while women, who had to worry about pregnancy, considered it far from frivolous. To many women today, a sexual relationship is still viewed as a commitment, if not to marriage, at least to a long-term, exclusive relationship.

A forty-three-year-old divorced woman expressed these sentiments when she said she had sexual relationships with her male friends but sometimes got more emotionally involved than she intended. She commented: "I find myself starting to think in terms of cooking his meals, ironing his shirts, and having children with him. I'm not one of the women who can enjoy sex as purely recreational without commitment."

Indeed, psychologist Paula J. Caplan, writing in *Between Women: Lowering the Barriers,* contends that women feel they can gain economic, social, and emotional security from nurturing a man physically through sex, just as they nurture men by cooking, cleaning, and performing what society considers feminine duties. When a woman has been led to expect love and protection in return for sex, she cannot tolerate a man's taking her to bed without telling her she is everything to him.[8]

Aside from social conditioning, recent neurological research indicates that even casual sex between friends releases feelings of affection and tenderness, particularly in women, at orgasm. Even though some men and a few women claim to have had one-night stands without any lingering emotional after effects, there is always a risk of getting more emotionally involved than they anticipated. Certainly, between friends, the line between caring and loving is easily blurred.

While some women and men claim sex can make a friendship stronger and better, for most, the powerful feelings and new expectations aroused when sex becomes part of a relationship will prove destructive. A forty-year-old anthropologist reported that she valued her platonic friendship with a man so much that she was afraid to risk it by having a sexual relationship with him:

> I adore Ross as a person, and I respect him as a professional in my field. I consider myself extremely fortunate to be friends with him. Over the years, I have had fantasies of having sex with him, but once, when we traveled together on business, I had the chance. We were both ready to have sex; I went to the bathroom, bathed, powdered, and perfumed, and I nervously went back to bed. Then I realized I couldn't go through with it. I loved and admired him too much as a friend. I figured if I had sex with him, it might not measure up to our intellectual pairing, our spiritual bond.
>
> We're still friends today, fifteen years later, and I still have my fantasy of what it could have been like in bed. I'm glad it turned out the way it did.

According to a study by Robert Bell described in his book *Worlds of Friendship*, women more often than men fear that sexual involvement will threaten a friendship. Whereas 31 percent of women viewed sexual relations as a threat to friendship with a man, only 20 percent of men thought of it as a threat.[9] Because men depersonalize sex more than women, they may not think it so important a factor in changing the dynamics of a relationship.

While it may be emotionally easier for men than for women to be sexually involved within the confines of friendship, it is socially acceptable only for single women and men to have such relationships. Married women are in quite a different situation. Through the ages, and in most cultures and societies today, there have been rules for the maintenance of the marriage system and proscriptions against breaking those rules. Faithfulness is high on the list of rules—especially for women. The majority of societies that have been studied by social scientists completely prohibit and several punish extramarital sexual relations by women. If a man is the transgressor, predictably, social sanctions are more lenient.

The thought of sexual freedom in marriage may sound progressive and exciting to some, but in real life it rarely works. Most marital partners are too emotionally invested in each other to accept outsiders' sharing sexual intimacies. Jealousy and insecurity cannot be banished, no matter how sophisticated the partners, and setting strict and artificial boundaries on relationships—sex allowed, but no deep emotion—does not take into account the powerful unconscious forces unleashed by sexual interaction. In 1978 anthropologist Nena O'Neill, coauthor of *Open Marriage,* indicated that out of 250 couples she had interviewed, those whose marriages ended within two years were the ones who engaged in premeditated extramarital sex.[10]

When sex enters into friendship one thing is sure: The relationship becomes more complex. If the friends are single and not interested in a long-term, exclusive relationship, the sexual element of the friendship need not be a problem. If either friend is married, or if feelings for each other are unclear and future goals are amorphous, more often than not, severe conflict will damage the relationship.

Again, women and men are likely to react differently. Whereas men often do not identify with the emotional intimacy most women seek in friendship, many women find sexual intimacy makes them particularly vulnerable emotionally. Sharing emotions feels natural to women in the same way physical intimacy feels natural to men. This is not surprising since our society has traditionally rejected women who are able to enjoy sex with many partners, whereas men who do so are envied. Similarly, emotionally warm and nurturing men are still considered odd and may even be shunned by other males.

Some few sexually liberated women are able, much of the time, to separate lust from emotions. One thirty-five-year old real estate agent said she chose an available friend to have sex with when she experienced what she called "the free-floating hots."

She explained: "When I feel sexy, almost any friend I'm attracted to will do in bed."

But even this sexually sophisticated adventurer admitted: "Sometimes I get more involved than the man does, but I just don't express what I feel. I don't want to drive my friends away. Keeping male friends means swallowing a lot of feelings, and keeping them down."

Even though women no longer have to be as concerned as they once were about pregnancy, few can view sex as mere recreation. If friends choose to take the sexual path, they must realize their relationship will change. Whether it will be better or worse is hard to say; so much depends on the individual personalities and the strength of the friendship. Increasingly, women and men are coming to understand that a strong, lasting friendship is more valuable than short-lived sexual pairing.

GUIDELINES FOR
BETTER FRIENDSHIPS
BETWEEN THE SEXES

A good same-sex friend is hard to find, but a lasting opposite-sex friendship is an extraordinary achievement, since society's lack of acceptance of such relationships is so pervasive. Overcoming sexist attitudes and the highly charged nature of sexuality as well as genuine male-female differences in communication styles is difficult. As if these deterrents were not enough to discourage opposite-sex friendships, contending with jealous spouses or lovers can make opposite-sex friendship too complex, too risky, or too demanding for many people.

For mavericks who would not consider letting gossip or sexism ruin their relationships with the opposite sex and who by their integrity and honest communication are able to overcome jealousy, the rewards of opposite-sex friendships are emotional nourishment, pride in forging a relationship against the odds set by society, and joy—the simple but unique and irreplaceable joy that comes only from a genuine sharing of feelings between two individuals. It is a spiritual connection as much as an emotional and intellectual bond. And with a friend of the opposite sex, a hint of sexuality, especially if it is never acted upon, can heighten and intensify these feelings.

If you are interested in pursuing opposite-sex friendships or improving the ones you have already, the following guidelines may ease the often rough and circuitous path to and through such friendships:

1. *Resist thinking in terms of sex stereotypes.* Do not automatically assume your male friend will always be strong, aggressive, and unemotional. Instead, encourage authenticity of feelings and expressions of individuality in your opposite-sex friend by setting an example and by responding positively when your friend's responses are genuine. Question your own gender-learned responses, and perhaps your friend will question some of his own.

2. *Be honest about what you want from your relationship with your opposite-sex friend.* Try not to kid yourself about your motives. It is unfair to initiate a friendship for the purpose of later seducing your friend.

3. *If you are married, discuss your feelings about opposite-sex friendships with your spouse, and take his feelings into account.* Sometimes a spouse's jealousy or anxiety about a platonic friend can be overcome if you introduce your opposite-sex friend to him. Include your friend in family outings, if your spouse is amenable.

4. *While a marital partner is due consideration, select your opposite-sex friends on the basis of how well you get along with them rather than what your spouse thinks of them.* Women with strong identities and secure marriages should be able to choose their friends by themselves without guilt, anxiety, or doubt.

5. *Initiating a sexual relationship with your friend is likely to put a strain on your friendship.* Carefully consider the possible consequences if you decide to become sexually involved with your friend. Discuss them with him.

6. *If you do have a sexual relationship with your male friend and do not wish a full romantic involvement, resist society's pressure to conform in this manner.*

7. *Do not rush a friendship.* If you are interested in getting to know a man who is reticent, resist the urge to reveal all your secrets at your first meeting. Your candor may scare him. Most lasting, intimate friendships are developed gradually over many years.

8. *Keep your friendship and work relationships separate if you are friends with your boss, coworker, or employee.* Women and men who work together are more often becoming friends today, but mixing work and friendship is not advantageous for your job or your friendship. You need not treat your friend like a stranger at work or avoid making friends through work, but you should treat your friend at work with the decorum and respect he is due in his position. Social expectations should be kept separate from work expectations, or confused or hurt feelings may result.

9. *Do not overburden your opposite-sex friends with your problems and anxieties.* To be a mature and responsible friend, a woman must feel she wants rather than needs to be friends with a male. Do not fall into the trap of allowing your male friend to protect you against the world's indignities. Some discussion of negative feelings and anxieties is acceptable with your male friend; no human being is always full of positive thoughts and fearless confidence. But, as one woman who enjoys sports and camping trips with her male friends said, "I always carry my own gear." Emotionally, make sure you carry your share of the load.

10. *Do not let gender differences hinder conflict resolution with your opposite-sex friends.* For example, a disagreement over where to go Saturday night—to his friend's party or to her friend's dinner—may lead a male to become critical, overly analytical, openly angry, or overbearing, whereas a woman may cry, feel helpless, or blame herself for the problem. These reactions are stereotypical. Certainly, men do not always become angry and

women do not always feel helpless. However, since many of us are still victims of a biased socialization process, it is not uncommon to react in these ways. To make matters worse, these reactions may cause further discord; he may indict her for crying, she may feel helpless in the face of his anger. And the couple may digress from the issue under discussion and move further from resolution.

To overcome these gender-related traps, women and men need to be appreciative of the negative effects of sexist upbringing. In this manner a woman is less likely to feel victimized by her male friend's anger, and a man is less likely to react in a critical or overbearing way. By becoming aware of our sexist reactions, solutions will become easier and friendships stronger.

6

IS THERE
FRIENDSHIP
AFTER
MARRIAGE?

Marriage is certainly a watershed experience, and traditionally, it has had a more pervasive impact on women than men. It sets in motion the kaleidoscope of change that alters all of a woman's relationships, including friendships. There are often abrupt geographical changes as well as the social and emotional changes that accompany the change in marital status. Suddenly she is "Sadie, Sadie, Married Lady" even if she has kept her own last name; there are the financial changes that accompany the instant merger of two lives. And there is the need to absorb family and friends that formerly belonged to one or the other into the constellation of the couple, as well as the forming of new friendships as a couple. Finally, the maintenance of the couple's friendship with each other, after the courtship and honeymoon have ended, is sometimes a surprisingly difficult task.

The prevailing notion is that women, in order to fulfill their emotional needs and dependencies, require marriage more than men. But recent studies, including our own, have revealed the opposite to be true; women, more than men, retain separate friendships after marriage. While men usually choose their wife as their confidant, women generally turn to each other to confide their innermost feelings, their joys, miseries, and problems. More than men, women lead separate emotional lives after marriage.

Social scientist Lillian B. Rubin reported in her book *Intimate Strangers: Men and Women Together* that when she asked women and men if they would remarry if their present coupling ended through death or divorce, the majority of men answered yes unequivocally, but almost half the women questioned said they would not want to marry again, especially those who had been wed for a long time.[1] For many women, marriage has not been what it was promised to be. Instead of offering protection, it has offered subjugation; instead of fulfilling their emotional needs, it has drained women of their emotional reserves; instead of providing friendship, it has placed them in a servile role; instead of bolstering their identity, it has blurred their self-image.

As we have seen, if women are seeking intimacy and the experience of equality, it is with each other that they are most likely to find satisfaction. Sometimes, of course, the experience is found with men, but this is seldom the case; more often men's empathetic abilities are found wanting. A forty-eight-year-old medical technician who acknowledged that she needed women friends throughout her long marriage explained:

> My women friends are even more important to me now than before I got married twenty-eight years ago. If I need support of any kind—whether it's because of a problem with my children, a difficulty at work, or most recently, because of my anxiety upon finding a lump in my breast—I turn to my women friends for support. My husband tried to understand my point of view, but he just doesn't provide me with the perspective I need. Maybe he is too emotionally involved in my problems, or he just doesn't understand the woman's point of view. He'll listen to my problems, but he'll either get gloomy over them, or he'll get angry and tell me to stop feeling sorry for myself and pull myself together. Anyway, I usually discuss my everyday problems with my hus-

band, but the "I think I'm going to die" problems I share with my women friends. And when I talk to them, it's like a breath of fresh air.

Despite the understanding and nurturance married women friends provide for each other, their relationships are not often encouraged by their husbands or by society. The current view of marriage includes the ideal that a woman and her husband are supposed to be best friends, and other close relationships may threaten that primary bond. A husband's jealousy, possessiveness, and fears concerning marital confidentiality are often evoked by his wife's friendship circle. These difficulties often create ambivalence in married women concerning their friendships. Anne, age thirty, explained how her husband's feelings made her indecisive about how strongly she would pursue a friendship: "He gets a little jealous about my feelings for Sylvia, and I'm caught in a tug-of-war. Sometimes I think I have to drop her to please him; sometimes I think the friendship is more important."

Even if a couple's marital bond is strong, conflicts and misgivings concerning friendships can loosen their marital knot, at least temporarily. To avoid misunderstandings, it is best for a couple to consider together what their friendships mean to them before they marry. Will Bill expect Alice to stay home with him every weekend? Will she require that he give up his drinking buddies for a home life? Will they share their friends with each other? Who, primarily, will be the friend maker in the family, the social secretary? What does the couple expect from their married social life?

Most couples discuss each partner's financial responsibilities; they discuss where they will live, whether they will have children or not, even how often they will see their in-laws. But few couples about to be married ever consider how pervasively their friends will affect their lives after marriage. Perhaps in the initial romantic excitement and absorption in each other relationships with friends pall by comparison, but later, romance generally fades in favor of friendship, both within the marriage and outside it. While premarital friendship agreements are too formal a way to oversee relationships, an informal mutual understanding of what friendships mean in each other's lives and how each partner's friendships are expected to change after marriage should be part of every couple's premarital dialogue.

WOMAN AND HUSBAND: INTIMATE FRIENDS OR DISTANT INTIMATES?

The idea that marriage is supposed to provide fulfillment for each partner's emotional needs is relatively new. In the preindustrial era, American marriages were made purely for the purposes of economic survival, sexual satisfaction, and procreation. Friendship was outside the realm of marriage. If men wished to have a companion to share leisure hours, they chose a male friend, or if they wished to confide in someone, they chose a mistress; if women wanted friendship, they sought it in other women.

Today, of all the ties holding couples together—shared parenting roles, finances, a home and property—marriage is likely to succeed in proportion to the degree of companionship it provides. And, in fact, with divorce the decision of more than one couple in three, friendship in marriage is a goal accomplished by too few. Even with romantic feelings, compatible sexuality, and a successful division of family responsibilities, a marriage lacking in companionship may still leave a woman or man frustrated and empty.

One woman, Susan, described the beginning of her marriage as a "feeling of having taken out an option on a partnership." She and her husband were confidants. As open and emotional as the early phase of their relationship was, it didn't succeed. Little by little, they bottled up their feelings of both love and resentment until the passion was drained from their union. As Susan explained:

> The friendship has disappeared from our marriage. We had interests in common once, and we made it a point

to spend time together. But, somehow, life interfered. The children came along, and my time was consumed with them, while Herb, more and more, escaped to his study to work. Our interests diverged without us ever realizing it, and little by little, we started to lead our own lives. If I attempted to inquire about Herb's feelings, he just clammed up. As for myself, I guess I didn't respond to him anymore because of my disappointment and hurt. I never expected marriage to be perfect, but I expected more than talking about the weather, the children's report cards, and the price of food. It's supposed to be more than a business arrangement.

Both women and men marry dreaming of love, the romantic and erotic components in a relationship. Nonetheless, a large part of the daily emotional nourishment in marriage springs not from romance but from friendship. Performing whatever duties are called for in a marriage as provider, parent, and sex partner is enough to make the relationship functional. It's not enough to assure satisfaction. For that, companionship must be added to the marital stew.

If companionship is so highly valued in marriage, the corresponding issue arises: How is it achieved? Herein lies a major conflict in marital life. Enduring friendship requires that individuals supply one another with a great deal of pertinent information. In many marriages, though, an opposite process, one of noncommunication, occurs: "What he doesn't know won't hurt him." "The best thing may be not to tell her. Why bother my spouse with problems she (or he) really doesn't understand?"

Certain subjects may become forbidden topics of discussion in some marital relationships, building walls against further communication or friendship. For instance, disagreements over child rearing, career aspirations, money problems, or past or current infidelities, spouses know, are potential firecrackers. Once they have been lit in heated discussion, the resulting explosions may be too damaging. Many couples feel it is best to avoid futile arguments. And yet, when not faced, difficulties are never resolved. They are added to a list of conscious or unconscious resentments.

One thirty-eight-year-old woman who had been married for fifteen years said her husband "talked" to her but that their talk was of "mundane things—what we're having for dinner, what's on TV, where we'll find the money to repair the car. We don't share feelings," she continued. "I don't think my husband is capable of that. And I'm not interested in that anymore either, because I seem to hit against a stone wall when I try to tell him anything about what I really feel or want. Our interests are so different, and our days together are all the same. Our relationship is just no fun anymore. If it weren't for the few women friends I have whom I can share my feelings with, I would have considered an affair a long time ago."

It is not surprising that many letters to the advice-giving sages in the daily press deal with problems of this kind. There is an impressive research literature documenting the association of good communication between spouses and satisfying marriages. It shows rather conclusively that openness of communication is an excellent source of marital friendship.

Despite its proven value, one reason open marital communication is so hard to establish is that the companionable marriage is a relatively new phenomenon. Very little in our education has prepared us for it. It is difficult to imagine how revolutionary the idea is that wives and husbands should be friends with each other. Women and men have always been sexually attracted to each other, but there is only very recently an emphasis on good social relations between the sexes in marriage. Most middle-aged adults today grew up in a household in which friendship between their parents was not even considered as a goal. Against the pleas for openness between wife and husband are pitted the long-standing social facts of life. "If you talk too much, you give yourself away; you give her (him) something to use against you." Deceptions and lies are almost institutionalized standard operating procedures between the sexes. As a result, rather than sharing the closeness of a friendship, many wives and husbands live in their very separate emotional worlds. There may be any number of reasons for this plight: If reared in an uncommunicative family, an individual may not have developed adequate verbal skills. Some people are shy; they may lack self-confidence ("Why should anyone want to listen to me? I have nothing important to say"). Some become intimidated, while others are hostile and do not communicate in order not to antagonize. Still others are suspicious, self-protective, and hence secretive. Sometimes communication, especially for men, emphasizes actions or gestures rather than verbiage.

One thirty-five-year-old housewife, understanding her husband's inhibitions against expressing his tender feelings, appreciated that his presence was all he could give her in a crisis. She explained:

> When my mother died, I really needed someone to talk to who would understand how I felt, someone who would offer me a kind of nurturing, I guess. My husband, I found, was not capable of it, so I went to my women friends to get the understanding I needed. I was able to get all my feelings out with them. I would cry and they'd cry with me. My husband would just get uncomfortable when I cried. But, in fairness, I must say my husband was there with me when I needed him. He stayed home with me when I was very depressed, he held my hand at the funeral, and he did everything he could for me in a practical sense. And I noticed that when his best friend's wife died of cancer, he did the same thing for him. He went to visit his friend often after the funeral. He'd spend a lot of time doing things with him, even though the two of them were never very talkative. But somehow his presence was enough.

Communication, even if nonverbal, is not the only factor that affects the quality of a marriage. Time also plays a role. Predictably, most wives and husbands report the kind of relationship in their early married years that typifies close friends—the exploring and mutual discussion of beliefs, inner feelings, likes and dislikes, and plans for the future. But as the relationship grows more complex with the coming of children, the acquisition of a home, more time-consuming duties, and increased career involvement, the amount of companionship and the intensity of satisfaction it yields diminishes dramatically. In striking contrast to the enthusiasm of courtship, conversation becomes painfully strained.

Sheila and Harold have been married for four years. For the first three years of their marriage, they both worked—Harold as a pharmacist, Sheila as a teacher. During those three years, Harold and Sheila had a common goal, purchasing a home, which they accomplished. At the end of their third year of marriage, two things happened: Sheila gave birth and Harold opened his own pharmacy. As a result of these events, Sheila left her teaching position and was at home all day caring for the child; Harold was home less because of his increased responsibility. When Harold returned home, he was sometimes irritable and usually quite fatigued. Often he was greeted by a wife who felt equally out of sorts. To prepare himself for the unpleasant news and growing friction at home, Harold began to stop for a drink after work. Sheila, disgusted with the unpredictability of his arrival home, stopped preparing meals. Harold, in turn, began eating out more frequently. They became more and more distant.

As Harold described their situation: "It used to be that we sat down, had cocktails and a leisurely meal together. We would discuss our day and enjoy each other's company. Then I came home and the house was a mess, the meal was lousy, and I was greeted by a tiger ready to lunge at me."

Sheila stated: "I felt Harold no longer had any interest in me. He seemed to have more interest in his business. When he came home, all he wanted to do was eat quickly, watch TV, and go to sleep. When I suggested that we go out together after the baby went to sleep, he constantly refused because he was tired.

Well, I was tired also, but I desperately needed his companionship."

Harold commented: "We seem to have been unprepared for the extreme change in our lives. Our son added fulfillment to our lives, but he also extracted a price."

A price indeed. A large-scale research effort conducted through Cornell University revealed that average parents of preschool children talk to each other only about half as much per day as they did in the intimacy of their first years of marriage. This in itself is not necessarily corrosive; the dwindling quantity is minor compared to the painful change in quality. Researchers found conversations once spiced with exchanges about books, ideas, and personal relationships were almost entirely concerned with routine affairs: "What did you do today, dear?" "Oh, nothing much. What did you do?" "Was there anything in the mail?" "The plumber came to fix the sink."

For some wives and husbands the gap developed during the early parenting years becomes too wide, and the companionship lost is never regained; there is a lack of both the motivation and the skill necessary to reconstruct the original connection. Frequently, their aloneness with each other surfaces after somewhere between eight and ten years of marriage. This corresponds to the period when divorce rates are very high; it is a time when the parenting function is not quite as consuming, the career is launched, and the relationship is reevaluated. It is a time when many people feel they no longer have anything in common and, consequently, no reason to remain married.

Of course, the strain of preschool children on marriage does not always contribute to the dissolution of the relationship, nor does it necessarily have to weaken it; with the burden of parenthood comes a supply of equivalent or even greater joys. However, the companionship aspect of the marital relationship almost always suffers. As numerous parents of young children can testify, it is an uphill battle to obtain the time in which to be companionable. Some couples may feed the children early so that they may enjoy a late dinner alone; others may make a purposeful decision to cram one or two evenings with household duties so that the remaining nights afford relaxation and time together. Still others plan to go out to dinner regularly, leaving children and responsibilities behind. Though these strategies are useful, they are far from perfect because fatigue, interminable childhood demands, and the limits of emotional resources may undermine the best attempts at privacy, and the disagreeable fact remains that until children are of school age, marital friendship often sinks into remission.

Then, as the children grow more self-sufficient—usually in the second decade of marriage—for some couples, marital friendship is renewed; like a blossoming plant it shines with life and fresh color. With more time for each other, the conversation may return to shared experiences of importance. Listen to one woman with two children, ages eight and ten, who began to work part-time two years ago:

> When the children were small, Herb and I were in separate worlds. I had my tales of woe concerning the misdeeds of one of the children, and he had triumphs to tell from his day's activities. We both listened dutifully and pretended to be very interested, but we were bored and didn't really appreciate what the other was talking about. Neither of us was fooled by what was happening and, after a while, conversation decreased sharply. Now that we have more time and are less hemmed in than in the past, we are more tolerant listeners, and we have things of value to say in return. Our lives are less pressured, and consequently we are more able to be sympathetic to each other's triumphs and failures. It's beautiful. We go out together, do many things jointly, and talk more; we have the time to understand each other. We're involved; our marriage is companionable again. It's like renewing a long-lost friendship.

What accounts for the difference? Why is there a recovery of companionship in some marriages and not in others? Aside from personality factors, which enter into any complex human interaction, the most common answer has been that couples who are not companionable when time allows were probably never really companionable. These marriages, it is reasoned, were based primarily on temporary infatuation and had no true basis for closeness. Undeniably, some people's choice of a mate rests on ready availability rather than sound judgment. They may think themselves in the grip of a special and unduplicated passion but, out of insecurity, neurotic deprivation, or overwhelming pressure from family and friends, they choose unwisely. Yet this is not always the case. In discussions psychologist Joel Block has had with hundreds of the formerly married, it was evident that many couples who initially were well matched became unmatched with the passage of time due to major differences in their personal growth and development.

A particularly common aspect of this unmatching process is found most frequently in couples operating within the framework of what might be described as a "traditional" marriage: She takes primary responsibility for the children, prepares the meals, and cleans the house. He provides the income, makes household repairs, and is second in command with the children on weekends. By the assignment of career exclusively to the husband and homemaking exclusively to the wife, the disparity of intellectual worldliness between the couple is likely to deepen, and consequently, the basis for marital friendship is severely limited.

In contrast to this pitfall (and occasionally despite it), some individuals manage to grow along with each other. These are the couples who stand a far better chance of renewing and intensifying their marital friendship. In this regard we have observed the following trends in our research: Wives who work, even part-time, more often consider their husbands to be friends than do homemakers. Women who were college students are similarly more likely to report their marriage as having friendship qualities. It appears that having independent, stimulating outside interests is a very important factor in keeping a marital friendship alive and vital. Combine the stimulation factor with skillful communication, mutual respect, and a good deal of tolerance and you have the basis for a solid friendship.

COUPLE FRIENDSHIPS: TOGETHERNESS FOUND, INTIMACY LOST

A century ago, few married couples socialized. The idea of sharing friends with spouses either was considered highly unusual or was not considered at all. Men would get together with their male friends, usually in a tavern or other local gathering place, and women would remain at home where, on occasion, they would enjoy the company of other women.

In more recent years, particularly in the last half century, the belief that women and men could be socially compatible emerged, and couple friendships became more common. According to Joel Block's research reported in *Friendship,* to be coupled in our society means keeping company with other couples primarily; 68 percent of married people in his investigation saw friends only in a couple context. Marital partners, it was found, seldom got together with friends separately. In these few instances, it was more often the women than the men who saw each other on a one-to-one basis.[2] In our updated study, couple-to-couple friendships continue to be the greatest source of socializing by married people; however, in contrast to the earlier report, the great majority of women interviewed maintained their individual friendships.

Previous studies have found that most couple friendships were initiated by men; from our interviews with women, it now appears that men's dominance in making the first introductions in mutual friendships is diminishing. Of the women we interviewed, about one third said they most often initiated couple friendships, another third said their husbands did so most frequently, and a final third said each marital partner had about equal input in forming these friendships.

In the past, men assumed the traditional homemaker could easily form friendships with other traditional wives, based on their similar life-styles. Presently, as more women enter the job market and more actively pursue their own interests, they want and need more control in determining who their own friends will be. Many women today no longer settle for socializing with the wife of their husband's friend, if they have nothing in common other than marital status and children.

Although the couple-to-couple relationship is the most common friendship vehicle among the married, it is not without frustration. Even if each partner in a marital pair had equal input in the formation of the foursome, the chances are that the eight relationships shared by four people will not proceed smoothly. Often one pair of friends, usually the two who originally met, will enjoy the relationship most, and the other two will attempt to be friendly in a forced way. Although socializing between couples promotes marital sharing, it often does not provide the privacy, trust, and total communion needed for true intimacy. "Two may talk and one may hear," Emerson wrote in an essay on friendship, "but three cannot take part in a conversation of the most sincere and searching sort." Not to mention four or six or eight.

If a couple's motives for socializing are purely recreational, if they simply would like compatible dinner companions or tennis partners and they don't necessarily wish to discuss their problems or feelings, couple relationships are ideal. If couples do genuinely like each other, it is a lucky accident that can promote marital solidarity as well as mutual friendship. There is a balance achieved in these relationships that does not usually provoke the jealousy of a spouse; after all, the spouse is there to witness what is going on in the friendship at all times. Even fantasies about another person's mate may be openly admitted and joked about; so long as the friendship is couple-based and four (or more) people are interacting, the erotic elements seem to be downplayed. However, if a relationship is formed with an opposite-sex partner outside the marital pairing, once again, it is frequently considered suspicious and is actively or covertly discouraged.

The implicit rule of couple relationships is that each sex usually converses most with each other, although the four partners will share some conversation. While flirting between the couples is sometimes tolerated, outright sexual advances usually mean the end of the friendship. Mate swapping, or swinging, is still considered deviant in American culture, and when it is engaged in, the couples involved do not generally view each other as friends. The taboo against emotional involvement and inter-dependency in the creed of swingers is so strong that they will stop having sex with any couple who becomes friends. Friendship and sex, in two-couple contexts, do not mix.

Regardless of sexual taboos in couple friendships, jealousies do arise. As women and men develop more similar interests in today's world of greater equality between the sexes, chances are increased that the wife of one spouse and the husband of the other may become just as friendly or friendlier than they were with the partner of the same sex who introduced them. Even if there are no sexual overtones to the unexpected friendship, feelings of envy or possessiveness may overcome the left-out spouse. It is, after all, a severe blow to the ego to consider that *your friend* likes your spouse better than he or she likes you. Add to that the fear that *your spouse* may like your friend better than you, and anxiety levels reach the outer limits of tolerance.

Another factor that affects the course of couple relationships is equivalent social status. Unless the four members of two couples have similar economic, social, and work backgrounds, an imbalance in the relationship, and feelings of inferiority on the part of the person of lower status, may cut the couple friendship short. A forty-year-old secretary whose husband initiated most of their mutual friendships through his work, complained that she "could not relate" to his friends:

> They are all in the scientific field, even the wives, or at least the wives have academic careers of their own, and I feel left out. Actually I sometimes feel inferior. It wasn't until one couple we were seeing got divorced that I came to understand that I was appreciated. Jill kept up her friendship with Mel on a casual basis, after she was divorced, since they both worked together. Mel and I would have her over for dinner occasionally. But one time she stopped by to see me; I didn't think we'd have much to say because I thought she was basically Mel's friend. But she told me she hardly knew my husband at all, that they just talked about work together, or superficial things. She said she related to me on a more emotional level, and she hoped we could be friends. I was surprised and very pleased.

When a married person does develop an individual friendship outside of coupledom, it is least likely to be someone who is unmarried, the example of Jill's friend notwithstanding. It is evident from our research that we are all on the way to developing two distinct kinds of social life, each of which categorically excludes a large segment of the population. Many married couples seek out other couples exclusively, and if one member, usually the woman, develops an individual friendship, it is likely to be with one half of the couple—predictably, the same-sex half. At social gatherings, there is likely to be an even number of women and men with no extras—no unattached women or men to complicate the situation.

The net result of this exclusivity—one way of living for marrieds, particularly those bringing up children, and another way for singles—is loss. For those who are married, family life becomes increasingly narrow and humdrum; singles, in contrast, miss exposure to families that could potentially contribute to a sense of wholeness in their lives. Children, too, would benefit by an assortment of different types of people in their lives. A married couple who socializes with unmarried friends of different ages, both sexes, and varied interests offer their youngsters an opportunity to increase their knowledge of life-styles and of people generally.

Clearly, couple friendships have limitations, most notably, lack of variety and diversity of life-styles. There are, however, potential benefits of couple friendships: They enable married members of the opposite sex to mingle socially, and perhaps become friends, when, in a sense, their spouses act as chaperones. Since social taboos against opposite-sex friends for married women are so strong, for some women, particularly those who are not employed, couple friendships represent their best opportunity to interact with men in a friendly way. If women are receptive to these friendships and if their spouses are not threatened, it is possible to get beyond ritualistic social exchanges and move toward real closeness. In fact, these social couplings could be the next best alternative to one-to-one friendships between the sexes.

PROCLAIMING SEPARATE
FRIENDS: A CAUSE
FOR MARITAL CONFLICT?

Modern marriage has been described as one of the saviors of Western civilization; it promises a unique combination of romantic passion, loving friendship, and economic partnership. The satisfaction of romantic passion and economic partnership is left for other investigations. As for loving friendship, the promise is most often mightier than the reality. Many marriages don't work or don't work for very long. It is likely that a goodly percentage collapses from mere overload. For many couples the extreme demand for marital togetherness sanctioned by our society contributes to a feeling of bondage rather than bonding. Like Siamese twins, spouses feel obligated to always appear as a couple. No other society, to our knowledge, expects as much from marriage, which is regarded as the source of all emotional satisfaction.

Commonly, each spouse expects the other to put her or his emotional needs above everyone else's. A problem arises with these expectations when one partner receives the emotional attention and nourishment desired and the other doesn't. Most couples are aware of this; they acknowledge that even at its best, marriage cannot meet all the needs of both spouses all the time. In practice, though, this fundamental truth is frequently ignored. How many couples in our society freely allow each other individual friendships outside marriage? Very few indeed.

For women, even same-sex friendship is likely to cause vague discomfort, if not outright conflict, because that relationship often threatens a husband's position of being first and best in fulfilling his wife's needs. If the traditional expectation of modern marriage is the standard by which spouses judge their relationship, then friendship outside marriage may be construed as evidence of a personal failure to satisfy a spouse. Again, perhaps one of the reasons the divorce rate is soaring today is the widespread belief in these utterly impossible expectations.

The majority of women we interviewed acknowledged that they had female friends with whom they associated. Most felt, rightly, that one person could not totally fulfill their needs, and if the ideal of a perfect marriage was that each partner could be totally satisfied through the other, then there is no perfect marriage, not even a nearly perfect one. Yet, because of society's impossible ideal, many women felt guilty about seeing friends when their husbands were alone, and others had to wage minor battles with their husbands to preserve their separate friendships.

Liza stayed home to rear her children then went back to school to earn her M.B.A. Eventually, she rose in the corporate world to an executive position. She went along with society's unwritten rule that women friends should not interfere with the marital relationship, but eventually she found it arbitrary and contrary to her needs:

> I had been the traditional suburban woman for fifteen years. My women friends were only lunchtime friends, or kaffeeklatsch friends. My socializing on weekends and in the evenings was done only with my husband and his friends. A group of couples he knew from work would go out with us. But somehow I felt empty, left out. I decided that I needed friends of my own, not just casual daytime acquaintances but friends I could rely on. What I did was really an act of desperation. I put an ad in the local newspaper. I actually advertised for friendship. I forget the exact words, but I said something like: "If you feel lonely or isolated and want to join a women's group for discussion of current or personal issues, contact this number." And I gave my phone number. You wouldn't believe it, but sixty women responded to the ad. We met in my living room; it was packed, and the excitement was flowing. I gained what I felt was missing in my life—the ability to make my own friends, to establish my own social identity. I did not want to cling to my husband and his friends like some half-wit who can't talk for herself.
>
> Out of that first meeting, which took place twelve years ago, I now have six very close, very dear friends, and we have formed a women's center in town, where we have a wider network of acquaintances. Now I don't feel as though there is something wrong with me if I see my women friends alone, even when I leave my husband alone to do so. And there is nothing wrong with my marriage if I choose the companionship of women

over my husband's company at times. After all, my
husband and I are two different people. His idea of having a good time is going sailing, or windsurfing, or
playing cards. My favorite things are going to plays and
art shows and to restaurants. I enjoy doing these things
with my women friends. At first I thought there would
be a price to pay, but you know what? After some initial griping, my husband enjoyed his new freedom, too.
When I went out, he would sometimes play poker with
his buddies or go sailing with friends who enjoyed the
water. We were never secretive about where we went.
And we each had more fun than if we had forced each
other to do things that we really didn't care for. I figure,
if he does one thing, and I do one thing, then we have
two things to share together later.

Many women similar to Liza, constantly surrounded by a spouse
and children who depend on her for their daily existence, have
learned that spending time away from the family, whether it is
by themselves or in the company of friends, is refreshing and
replenishing. Friendship between marital partners, just as
friendship between same-sex partners, can become stifling and
boring if two friends see each other continually to the exclusion
of other friends. Judith, a thirty-six-year-old teacher who considers her marriage "strong" and her husband a "good friend,"
has come to realize that she relies on her women friends to regain her perspective when she and her husband are in the midst
of a fight that seems to drag on interminably, or when she has
become weary of domestic life.

"Sometimes I need my women friends just to let off steam,"
Judith said. "If Fred and I are having a fight that we can't seem
to resolve, I'll talk to my best friend, Ellie, about it. Sometimes
she'll just commiserate with me, and usually that's all I need.
Occasionally, she'll help me see the problem in a different light,
and that helps me resolve it. At other times, when the kids are

whining and my husband is complaining, I'll escape to Ellie's, and an hour later, I'll come back home feeling refreshed. And the kids and my husband will usually show me more respect. When I leave for a while, they miss me.''

Of course, if either spouse repeatedly ducks out of marital arguments by escaping to the comfort and support of a friend, little or no progress will be made in seeking a truce at home. Escape works well as an emotional safety valve only if it is temporary; problems must eventually be faced. Occasionally, though, supportive friends give us strength to renew the struggle, and we may return to the fray with more hope and greater insight. Any seasoned writer or artist knows that if she or he is stuck, if the creative juices won't flow, a brief period away from the task at hand relieves stress and helps the unconscious to generate new ideas. Similarly, a discussion of problems or a restorative time spent with friends can generate new solutions to difficulties in relationships. This is not to suggest that a woman ask her friend to act as a marriage counselor on a continuing basis; but occasionally, every woman will benefit from a friend who will listen to her and offer her support when her spouse can't or won't.

Yet friendships in which marital problems are shared are traditionally frowned upon; marital privacy is supposed to supersede friendship bonds. Marital disputes are to be settled privately between spouses without interference from outsiders, whether they are friends or relatives. Indeed, the "interfering mother-in-law" and the "nosy friend" are shunned and ridiculed. According to the norms of Western society, friends cannot be of any help in solving marital disputes; they are likely to complicate the situation, or make it worse. Only professionals schooled in marriage counseling who will guarantee complete confidentiality to the couple are regarded as helpful in solving marital problems.

Certainly, in some instances, professional counseling is the best course for a couple sinking into the quicksand of marital despair. But surely, in other instances, friends can be helpful.

However, loyalty to a spouse, a reticence concerning weaknesses or faults, is often the norm. Women are strongly socialized to perpetuate the myth of male independence and superiority. Guilt over betraying their spouse's secret vulnerabilities prevents many women from sharing their marital frustrations with each other.

Often the marital disagreements caused by a wife's friendships reflect underlying problems in the marriage. For example, a husband who is highly dependent on his wife emotionally but who is loath to admit it because he wishes to maintain his masculine image may actually encourage her to see her women friends. But, in an indirect way, he may sabotage her efforts to maintain her friendships by "forgetting" to tell her, for instance, that he had to work late and couldn't stay with the children so that his wife would have to cancel a dinner appointment with her friend.

Dora, a forty-four-year-old court clerk, said her husband, Jim, voiced no objections to her leaving him alone several evenings a month so that she could visit her friends. But regardless of where she went with her women friends, whether it was to a League of Women Voters meeting or to dinner at a favorite restaurant, he would find an excuse to call her.

"Once when I was dining with friends, the waitress went to each table asking for me. When she finally found me in the crowded restaurant, she said someone was on the phone for me, and the person calling said he had to speak to me about an emergency. Of course, it was my husband, and his emergency was that he forgot to tell me that we needed gas in the car. Did I notice it? he asked. I could have screamed. He treats me like a child."

Jim may feel neglected and left out. He may feel jealous, thinking his wife prefers the company of her women friends. Or he may feel he should serve as his wife's protector, as he has been socialized to do. Either consciously or unconsciously, he may distrust his wife. How many men have told their wives they are going out with a male friend and ended up in bed with a woman?

Jim may not realize he is insulting his wife by checking on her. Yet his seemingly benevolent gesture represents his own dependency needs. A male's dependency on his wife may hark back to his dependency on his mother in childhood; if his mother was not there when he needed her, he felt abandoned. If his wife leaves him for the company of others, he may experience the same sense of abandonment.

A wife's friendships may dredge up the hidden insecurity and dependency of her husband; they may also overturn roadblocks set up to protect the status quo in a marriage that maintains male dominance. This inevitably causes conflict. Patti, a housewife and mother, had expressed no discontent with her traditional role until she met Dawn. Patti admired Dawn because, like herself, she was a conscientious mother, but in addition to performing her wifely and motherly duties, Dawn had gone back to college to study architecture. Soon after Dawn went back to school, Patti, who had quit college after she married, told her husband she would like to obtain her degree. Greg felt a wife "should stay home with the kids while they're small." He blamed Dawn for Patti's "rebelliousness." Actually, Patti had been discontent with her domestic role for a long time, but she had been afraid to voice her boredom and frustration to her husband. Although Dawn encouraged Patti to pursue her new ambition, she was not responsible for her friend's conflict with her husband. No friend can influence another for better or worse unless she is already ripe for change.

Nevertheless, Dawn was the catalyst that precipitated major changes in Patti's marriage. Following Dawn's lead, Patti learned to be more assertive in expressing her needs to her husband and others. She eventually earned her master's degree in education. Subsequently, Patti's husband expressed gratitude to Dawn for "instigating the change that brought a new bounce to my wife's step." Patti learned to express her own needs, while her family, instead of suffering from her new attitude of independence, found her excitement to be contagious.

Husbands are likely to be more jealous than their wives concerning separate friendships because men seldom understand the need for them. Married men do not usually have intimate friends in the same way that women do because their need for intimacy is satisfied by their wives. One married man confessed, "It's like a slap in the face if my wife chooses to go out for the evening with a woman friend instead of me. It's as if she's saying, 'I enjoy her company more than yours.' "

The man's wife, Megan, not only was distressed by her husband's view that her friend was a competitor for her time and affection, but she was also disturbed that her husband relied solely on her to meet his every need or whim. As she explained, "I wish I could find my husband a good friend. I know he's lonely. There's nobody he calls up to say hello to or just chat. It's always a business conversation. He turns to me exclusively for comforting. I am his only confidant. Perhaps if he had friends he would be more sympathetic to my friendship network."

Some women have fully accepted the prevailing norm of putting their husband's needs before their own and have thus cut themselves off from friendships. A study reported in *Social Forces* indicated that in both middle- and working-class marriages, about 40 percent of women said they did not spend evenings with friends away from their husbands.[3]

Today, we believe, women's notions of friendship and marriage are changing. When divorce takes its toll in an alarming number of marriages, when even happily married women are realizing that men aren't their sole or even primary reason for living if they are to derive from life everything that it promises, women are increasingly turning to women friends to supplement their marital relationship. In doing so, they are making their marital relationship stronger, not weaker. When women acknowledge that they are individuals with many complex needs that one person will never completely fulfill, rather than clinging to the romantic fallacy that they have only one need—the love of a man—they are freeing not only themselves but also their men from a quagmire of impossible demands.

MARRIED WOMEN, SINGLE WOMEN: CAN THEY BE FRIENDS?

When marriage vows are exchanged, vows of friendship between the bride and her single friends are sometimes broken. Even if old friendships between women are maintained, they are seldom on the same intimate level after marriage claims one's attentions. There is no formal dissolution, just as there is no formal agreement between friends to love each other "until death do us part." Most often a spouse's needs and the responsibilities of making a new home take precedence over a friend's needs. When the bond between a woman and her husband has become official, initially, at least, time spent with each other seems more important than pursuing any other relationship.

Speaking of their married friends, many of the single women we interviewed felt abandoned. Nursing feelings of hurt and rejection, they complained that their married friends were "swallowed up" by their husbands. In fact, numerous married women confirmed this, as noted earlier. "I find myself under a great deal of pressure from my husband," declared one woman, echoing the sentiments of many. "I make an appointment with a girlfriend for an evening and he demands that I spend the evening with him. 'Who's more important?' is how he puts it. I try to explain importance has nothing to do with it, but to no avail."

Considering that the task of making marriage work is formidable because it takes more than love but a willingness to share time, thoughts, and feelings, it is beneficial for a newly married couple to seclude themselves from others for a while. Certainly their romantic feelings for each other make it easy to do so. But completely neglecting former friendships is a serious mistake; if a woman's friends were supportive and fun to be with before marriage, there is no reason why they won't be as valuable during marriage. Granted, some of the interests they shared as singles may not last; however, if the relationship between the two women was solid to begin with, a change in marital status need not destroy it.

Sometimes a couple socializes with a single woman friend as a threesome, but even if she was the wife's friend originally, jealousy on the part of the wife may be aroused. Especially if there is some insecurity in the marital relationship, a husband's friendship with his wife's female friend may cause a cooling off of the friendship between the women. Naturally, if a woman's friend is open and empathic to her friend's husband, it does not mean she is trying to seduce him. She may simply be displaying the same qualities that attracted his wife. There is a distinct difference between seductiveness and friendliness, although some wives may find the boundaries blurry.

Even if the intent of friendly overtures is sexual, some women can forgive flirtatiousness in a friend. Charlotte, thirty-four years old and married for five years, did not let her friend Vanessa's flirtatiousness spoil their long, intimate friendship. Charlotte commented: "My friend Vanessa was always a flirt. I remember she was able to attract men much more readily than I, when we were both single, because she was so aggressive. She would introduce herself to a guy whose looks she liked without any qualms, while I'd sooner crawl into a hole than make the first advance. I guess that's why I'm not too surprised that she flirts with my husband. She seems to thrive on male attention. At any rate, I discussed it with my husband, and he assured me that Vanessa isn't his type."

Charlotte pursued a wise course. She understood that flirtatiousness was second nature to Vanessa and that expressing misgivings about it to her might cause embarrassment and hurt feelings while doing little to change her friend's basic nature. Instead, Charlotte had a frank discussion with her husband. By confronting her husband with her feelings, she was able to be reassured while still maintaining her friendship with Vanessa.

Envy is another factor that could come between a married woman and a single friend. This is most likely to occur when a single woman is unhappy about not being married, a feeling that may be exacerbated by society's pressure to marry (there is still pressure to marry by a certain age) or when her friend's marriage seems like a personal affront. She may very easily feel left out, left behind, and unwanted.

Coming to terms with feelings of envy may be necessary if the friendship is to remain intact. Sometimes confronting it head-on may be the way to deal with it, particularly if that has been their pattern of interaction in the past. "I wish I were in your position" or "I envy you" are difficult words to say, but once they're said, the feelings behind them can be discussed and defused.

Sometimes single women are surprised by friends who say they feel lonelier after marriage than when they were single. Life with a spouse who won't share his feelings can make a woman feel desperately isolated. But often wives who find their husbands noncommunicative don't confide their discontent; they seek relief from loneliness through a woman friend's company. If they share marital difficulties at all, it is often with other married female friends who they feel are more able to understand.

Yet it is often a single woman who provides a friend with a different perspective on her marital difficulties that may enable her to solve them or at least accept them more gracefully. Maureen, a thirty-three-year-old homemaker and mother, credited her single friend, Sherry, with helping her realize how she had contributed to a lack of intimacy with her husband and children. She explained:

Sherry, an old college friend, had come to spend the weekend with us. After I married and had two kids, Sherry was still a full-time career woman; she took her work very seriously, and she is now a senior editor for a major woman's magazine. I really admire her.

The evening she arrived, my husband and I did our best to be sociable over dinner, but we were both very tired from our respective work week at home and at the office, and the kids were coming down with colds. They were whining, and the youngest, Jeremy, wanted to sit on my lap. I said, "No, not now. I'm too tired," but Sherry said, "You can sit on my lap, Jeremy," and she held him for a while, and I noticed how much she relished it.

Later, when the kids were in bed, Sherry and my husband started talking about politics. They both love the subject. I'm usually too tired to discuss anything more complicated than the weather after dinner, so I didn't say much. I was a little annoyed at my husband for being so interested in Sherry's ideas, because he never listened to mine so intently, but then it hit me: I hardly ever listen to him with total attention when he talks to me. And I did the same thing with my children. I often took them for granted, or pushed them away, figuratively speaking. But Sherry, alone most of the time, was delighted with my family.

Later in the weekend, when Sherry talked about her ten-hour-a-day, six-day work week, about not coming home to her empty apartment until she was exhausted because she hated to face the emptiness, I understood how lucky I was. I think she told the story partly to remind me of my good fortune, and I'm grateful. I've resolved to listen to my husband talk about disarmament or inflation, or whatever he wants to talk about, and to hug my kids whenever they want to be hugged. But, of course, they'll have to listen to me, and hug me, too.

While married women may neglect their single friends as a result of jealousy, protecting their marriage against the possibility of unwanted romantic invasion, in some cases it is the single woman who rejects the now married friend. On occasion, envy of her friend's new marital status may be a divisive factor. In other instances, just the opposite may occur: A single woman may find that her married friend's new status has limited her time and her interests.

Jessica, age 23, fresh out of Columbia University with a master's degree in journalism, worked as an editorial assistant at a major publishing company in Manhattan. Absorbed in her career, and in her busy social life of late-night parties, dates, and weekends at the shore, Jessica initially kept in close touch with her college friend, Maggie, but later found their relationship strained.

> Maggie and I were best friends at college. We roomed together, read the same books, and talked endlessly about our hopes and our plans. We both wanted to be famous writers. But Maggie sold out. She married a medical student, and she became the doctor's good wife. She gave lots of dinner parties, helped in charitable organizations, played tennis, and joined lots of groups. But her career went down the drain, while mine, as far as I was concerned, was just starting.
>
> I had lunch with Maggie a few times, but she was a different person than the one I knew in college. She was talking about the garden club; I was still talking about getting published. We drifted apart. I haven't seen her in six months and I don't miss her.

While a difference in values might cause the loss of old friendships, deference to a spouse also causes friendship to fade between married and single women. In some cases, it is the husband who doesn't appreciate his spouse's friends. For example, Sharon, in her mid-thirties, realized that seeing her single friends alone was the best course for her. She reflected on the early phase of her courtship and marriage and how she came to terms with the marital conflicts that emerged over her friendships. Her story is typical of the friendship issues many women face in marriage:

> When Edward and I started to see each other, we pretty much cut ourselves off from friends. Evenings, weekends, and holidays were spent in romantic isolation— long walks in the woods, drives down to the beach, dinner at his apartment or mine, just the two of us together. We kept in touch with our friends during the day either by phone or at an occasional lunch. This went on for a few months, and then gradually we ventured out with other couples; we started to open the doors to the dowry of friends each of us brought to the relationship. That we remained single through our twenties is a factor here; we both had a fairly large circle of friends. Each time there was excitement but also an underlying suspense and tension: Will he like my friends? Will they like him? What will his friends think of me?
>
> I knew all my friends since childhood and, in Edward's view, the only thing we had in common was a shared history. To some extent this was true; there were differences in interests, occupations, and sometimes values. Yet we shared something indefinable, perhaps, but a bond nonetheless; these were attachments I was loath to break. Edward couldn't understand why I still clung to them, and I couldn't understand or accept his forceful criticism of my friends. One time when we went out to dinner with a friend of mine and her date, the whole night was spent talking about old times. Edward got stuck listening to this man's business problems and was bored to death. Oh, did I ever pay for that! I didn't hear the end of it for months.

Following this incident, Edward declined to have anything to do with Sharon's friends. This caused "quite a rift," as Sharon expressed it. Sharon felt Edward's rejection of her friends was a personal affront. Edward contended that he had married her, not her friends. Sharon disagreed strongly, but she resigned herself to seeing her friends alone. This worked for a time, but Edward soon tired of Sharon's abandoning him in favor of her "private world." At this point, Sharon stood firm. She acknowledged that it was unrealistic to insist that Edward like her friends, but she was not willing to break off her relations with them. Sharon drew several conclusions from her experience:

> As I think back to the early part of our relationship—that seclusive phase—I'm glad we didn't rush to inspect each other's worlds immediately. That time gave us a chance to solidify as a couple, to get to know each other better and form a strong communication network before we moved into an area that turned out to be surprisingly sensitive. As difficult as this issue was, it would have been worse if we hadn't taken time for ourselves initially. Also, I realize that by pushing my friends on Edward, I made things miserable for both of us. My dictum "You must like my friends" alienated him. Lastly, I'm pleased, despite Edward's disapproval, that I did not follow the pattern of many women and give up my old friends. We're married seven years now and I believe that Edward actually respected my decision of several years ago.

In keeping her friends despite opposition from her husband, Sharon made a courageous choice, one that caused bickering and heated arguments with her husband. However, Edward resigned himself, and she gained immeasurable comfort and support from her old friends.

Sometimes a woman who maintains her friendship with a single woman despite her spouse's initial objections finds that eventually he actually comes to enjoy the friend or at least accept her. Even though society is suspicious of three-way friendships, couples do find their variety stimulating. Josephine, a forty-two-year-old sculptor married for twenty years, spoke of one such friendship with obvious affection: "Our friend Serena is like a part of our family, like a dear aunt to our children. She enriches our life immeasurably by providing a different point of view about things, and she has a sense of humor and intellect that both my husband and I enjoy. I guess we get a kind of vicarious excitement when we listen to her tales of dating and romantic single life that we otherwise would have forgotten about long ago. And I suppose she gets something important from her relationship with us. We provide her with a family life she doesn't have.''

HAVING CHILDREN: A BARRIER TO FRIENDSHIP?

Just as marriage is likely to strain the relationship with single friends, the birth of a child may widen the friendship gap between a married woman and her childless peers. For many women, friendships with singles and childless married couples are once again endangered owing to lack of time (especially if the new mother is employed outside the home) and sometimes lack of money (particularly if the new mother gave up employment to care for the baby full-time) and divergent interests.

Filling the friendship void, new mothers tend to flock together, to share each other's company. Indeed, these women with common needs and experiences find sustenance in each other. Despite society's adulation of motherhood, it is often a boring, tiring, and frustrating job. Rearing infants and toddlers can be a severe strain on a woman's time and sheer endurance. Friendship with other women who are experiencing the same trials of motherhood is almost a necessity for survival.

Valerie, a forty-two-year-old mother of four, recalled her woman-dependent existence of several years earlier: "When I was a young mother, I'd start talking to other women with babies almost anywhere I saw them—at the pediatrician's office, the supermarket, the park. I needed adult companionship and understanding desperately, and I needed it from women who were in my own situation. When my husband came home from work, he did not want to hear about all my problems or about how tired I was. He said he had enough of his own problems at the office. My women friends provided me with the listening and understanding I needed.''

Indeed, a woman must experience motherhood to understand how supremely joyful, excruciatingly painful, and absurdly maddening it can be. The intensity of the mother-child relationship appears to magnify all emotions. One young mother told us how desperate she felt one day when her friend, who also had two young children, rescued her from feeling overwhelmed:

I was babysitting for my friend Dottie's two children, ages three and five, while taking care of my own, also the same ages. I didn't realize it would be too much for me. The kids did everything they could to make me angry that day. They spilled milk all over the freshly cleaned living-room rug, climbed on the dining-room table, and got crayon marks all over the bedroom wall. When Dottie returned at the end of the day, I was sitting on the stairs with the vacuum cleaner in one hand and a tissue in the other, sobbing. The kids were going wild upstairs. I couldn't take it anymore.

Well, she didn't think I was going crazy, even though I was convinced that I was. She said she had days like that, too. Feeling overwhelmed once in a while didn't make me a terrible mother—just a normal one. She made me a cup of tea, and she went upstairs and told the kids to calm down in a very stern voice, and they must have known she meant business, because we didn't hear a sound after that. I felt understood and relieved.

Tears and tantrums, along with caresses and sharing confidences, are the stuff of intimacy. In dealing with the uninhibited feelings of children, a mother's own raw feelings tend to emerge, too. These spontaneous feelings, shared by mothers in dealing with their children, build the friendship bond.

Once again, while shared experience is important, exclusivity is limiting. Single friends or childless married friends are sometimes not only neglected by new parents but made to feel different, left out, no longer a member of their coveted membership club. Said a thirty-two-year-old woman married for six years: "Most couples my husband and I socialize with have kids now, and they're not as available to spend evenings with us as they used to be. We understand that, but when we do see them, they'll talk about their kids practically all evening, or sensing that we are bored, they'll say, 'Let's not talk about kids because Holly and Martin are here.' Somehow, although they mean to be polite, that makes us feel different, uncomfortable; the conversation is no longer spontaneous."

Regrettably, this experience is not uncommon. Women who are secure in their marriages and identities, however, are not afraid to explore the worlds of others. When a woman has a serendipitous assortment of friends—young and old, married and single, parents and childless, male and female—she is reflecting a need to learn and expand herself as well as an ability to accept and love others in spite of their differences. Such a woman is likely to have not only a richly varied circle of stimulating friends but also a solid marriage.

CHAPTER

7

FRIENDS AND THE FORMERLY MARRIED WOMAN: TILL DEATH OR DIVORCE DO THEM PART?

Miriam, married fourteen years, had only recently sensed that her marriage was breaking up. When her husband confronted her with his unhappiness, she was unprepared for the reality of separation.

I was thrown by the attitude people had toward me as a woman alone. Some so-called friends dropped me socially. It was as if they thought it were unsafe for me to be in the proximity of their husbands. I realize that divorce is increasing, but is it also contagious? The loneliness was horrid. Hours on the phone or sitting in front of the television were a poor substitute for companionship; there was no one to laugh with or make comments to. I tried reading but found myself turning pages and not remembering what I had read. One night, at bedtime, I came across one of his shirts, left in his haste to get out; how long, I wondered, will it be before all traces of his being here will be erased? How long will it be before my life returns to normal? Who among my friends can I still count on? Who will offer support and a shoulder to cry on? For a while, pressed by these questions, I slept day and night, I savored sleep like a fine wine; it was my only true sanctuary.

Betty, fifty-seven, a widow for four years recalled:

The first few months after George's death were hell. I didn't want to go out; I was depressed, anxious, angry. The flood of emotions overwhelmed me. Then, when I started to get out, I didn't want to go back home; the silence was menacing, the air seemed heavy. It was like having hot and cold chills; first I didn't want to go out and then I would do anything to avoid going back home. I would go to lousy movies, sit in the library, make busy-work for myself. Anything to avoid the solitude. I would go any place where I could be near other bodies, other faces, other voices.

As is apparent from the experiences of Miriam and Betty, if ever there is a time a woman needs true friends, it is when she is faced with divorce or widowhood. If she is not employed, the experience is even more traumatic. Not only does she lose a husband, often the most intimate person in her life, but she also loses her "job," in the sense that her husband, home, and family were her job. Yet, except during the very initial stage of these two wrenching experiences, women sometimes find old friends abandoning them like the geese leaving New England with the frost.

Often the women who must face this double loss—the loss of their friends along with the loss of a spouse—are those who have relied heavily on the couple friendships their spouse brought to the marriage. Couple friendships, as we have seen in the previous chapter, are often based on activities, or cocktail party chatter, rather than one-to-one conversations and personal disclosure. It is often the case that the term "friend" is applied loosely among couples. More accurately, when couples speak of such friendships, they are usually referring to social acquaintances, not true intimates. Consequently, it is not a surprise that those couples do not continue their relationship in a time of crisis; it is simply an extension of the general tone of the relationship.

Some couples may not want to socialize with a single person after they have known her as part of a couple—"it's embarrassing," or "she just doesn't fit in," they claim. If it was the husband who initiated the friendship, the couple may feel an allegiance to him, pursue his friendship only, and leave the former wife to fend for herself. In some cases, the wives in couple friendships may feel threatened by the newly single woman, especially if she is very attractive, or if they feel insecure within their own marriage; in these instances, they may gently redirect their husband's social life.

When women have cultivated their own women friends, they tend to receive the emotional and practical support they need to get through the crisis of divorce or widowhood—a time of turmoil, tears, and sometimes, terror. One 38-year-old homemaker who had, with considerable effort, forged a social life separate from her husband's "to find some emotional connectedness to other adults," found her close women friends were caring, nonjudgmental, and simply "there" when she needed them. "I don't know how I would have gotten through the last years of my marriage, or the divorce, without my friends," she said.

Contemporary divorcées and widows share a similar social status in most communities, in contrast to the turn of the century when divorce was a rare occurrence, considered either an indulgence of the rich and eccentric or a desperate act of the inhumanly abused. Indeed, as recently as the 1950s, in some strongly religious or conservative social circles, divorced women were considered unfit company for married women. A divorced woman was regarded as morally corrupt by certain segments of society; she was thought to be lacking in character and somehow tainted, even though the divorce might have been her husband's decision.

While widows have always been considered worthy of concern and sympathy rather than scorn, like divorcées, problems of loneliness abound; they too rely increasingly on friends in a society where independence and mobility are prized, and where the extended family has given way to many widowed women living alone.

Friends often relieve a woman's stress and loneliness and ease feelings of guilt and depression during her transition to single life. The large majority of women we interviewed confided in their close friends concerning their marital difficulties. Those women who were widowed also tended to share their fears and concerns with friends. In some cases, marriages that were on shaky ground were steadied for a while by a woman's friends; the emotional contact she did not receive from her spouse, she got readily from her friends. A divorced friend might help a woman through the painful process of divorce.

Ginger, a thirty-five-year-old journalist, said her friend's divorce and subsequent growth as an individual helped her to face the shortcomings of her own marriage. "When Stacey got a divorce, she was still envious of my marriage, but I was envious of her autonomy. More and more, I began to see how our lives moved in separate directions, hers in exciting, new ways—she eventually continued her education and became a rabbi—and mine remained stale, dull, restricted, I felt, due to my husband's insecurities and jealousies, as well as my own. When I finally separated, Stacey thought it was a good move. She helped me through it. I don't believe I could have done it without her example."

When a woman's marital status changes, her friendship needs change, too. Some fortunate women gain sustenance from old friends, and they search for new friends to fill the gap created by the loss of their spouse; others, rejected by former friends, must start afresh to form a whole new network of relationships. In either case, many women have found the period after divorce or widowhood a time not only of reorganization and anguish but of tremendous personal growth and renewal. For many, women friends were the bulwark that helped them withstand tumultuous changes and not only survive but flourish. For others, however, friends' negative reactions to their changed marital status wrought pain, disappointment, and bitterness.

FOR BETTER OR WORSE: FRIENDS' REACTIONS TO DIVORCE AND WIDOWHOOD

Despite some continued friendships, many among the divorced and widowed lose access to the network of married friends to which they formerly belonged. The resulting social isolation, combined with the emotional trauma of marital dissolution, gives rise to a form of loneliness that can be especially tormenting. Bereft of community, the formerly married react in a variety of ways to this loneliness. Some bury themselves in activity—social service, politics, college classes, and self-improvement regimens. Others, those who must avoid loneliness at any cost, may rush into another romantic relationship almost immediately. Still others, particularly when they feel panicky, clutch at the telephone for companionship. Suddenly this impersonal electronic device takes on a new meaning; it becomes a lifeline to the world. Friends may be called endlessly on any pretext: "I hope I'm not disturbing you, but I wanted to know if the PTA meeting is still scheduled for Thursday evening." The underlying hope is that an offer will be made to get together or a question asked to unlock feelings. Of course, subtlety is not a universal preference; many individuals choose to dispense with pretense and be direct: "Can I stop by this evening? I really don't want to be alone."

The reactions of friends to these requests, whether masked or overt, vary. Some withdraw; others respond quickly with a desire to help. In some measure, the difference in response corresponds to the basis of the friendship. If affection and mutual loyalty are fundamental to the bond, if the friends share segments of their personal lives with each other, the relationship is less likely to be dramatically altered by the change in marital status. In contrast, if marriage provided the main basis for the friendship, divorce or widowhood is almost sure to weaken it.

Of course, the way friends respond to divorce or widowhood depends on their own needs as much as it involves the nature of a woman's friendship. How a woman views divorce—whether she sees it as a "giving up," a failure, or the freedom to solve problems and to start a new life—will reflect in her reaction to her friend's separation.

The initial response of friends is often followed by awkwardness. Some friends continue to be supportive; others begin to feel burdened by the weight of the complaints being aired. Still others seem frightened of the divorced or widowed woman and act as if she had a communicable disease. Often at the root of such an anxiety response, when it concerns divorce, is a friend's unsatisfactory marriage. Divorce is a dramatic act having the power to stir those surrounding it, if only momentarily, to take another look at their own marriages. As Helen, married twelve years, disclosed:

> Mainly, I was unsure of how to behave. Should I inquire into the gory details? Or pretend to ignore the whole matter and talk normally about other things as if nothing happened? As it turned out, the first time I spoke with Deirdre after hearing of her breakup, I mumbled some regrets about her situation—it felt like the awkwardness you experience in offering condolences at a funeral—and waited for her to take the initiative. We talked of politics, children, and mutual friends while I wondered if she would bring up the subject of what went wrong and how she feels these days. Finally, she did let me know what happened, but she didn't offer a full explanation; apparently, her nerve endings were too raw to discharge all her feelings, grievances, and fears.
>
> Soon after Deirdre left I found myself in deep thought about our meeting. I wondered again why Deirdre didn't

speak more openly to me. I suppose she was too proud
or maybe too ashamed. She seemed ambivalent, wanting to be touched but not able to be vulnerable. I realized also that the need to have her say more was for reassurance—mine! I wanted to hear that there was a
problem that was remote, unique, unrelated to anything
going on in my marriage. Deirdre's separation, I had to
admit, scared me. If it could happen to her—she seemed
to have a sound marriage, I never suspected there was a
problem—could it happen to me?

The conflicts engendered by a woman's early separation experiences add another dimension to her reaction. For example, if
a woman never came to terms with the divorce of her parents
when she was a child, she may become extremely distressed or
preoccupied with her friend's divorce, or she may be critical of
her friend, finding her separation "unjustifiable." Or if a friend's
father died when she was very young, causing severe and extended financial and emotional hardship for her family, she may
react to her friend's spouse's death as though it were a disaster
from which recovery is impossible.

The awkwardness and confusion felt by women receiving the
news of a friend's divorce are shared and magnified in the divorcée. Hearing the news causes strains, but the chore of deliv-
ering it is worse, as Vivian, a thirty-six-year-old nurse, reported:

During that last year our marital situation grew worse
by leaps and bounds. It was as if a cancer had come out
of remission with a renewed ambition to destroy everything in its path. Up to that point, I hadn't said very much
in private; in public the most that William and I exposed
was an exchange of sarcastic tones. Now it could no
longer be contained; I felt obliged to say something. I
visited an old married friend. After the initial greetings
and a bit of small talk, I simply blurted out, "William

and I are separating." After a few mumbled regrets, Jean waited for me to take the initiative, to explain what happened. This was a moment of pure anguish for me. I had come for human warmth, I needed support, but I was ashamed and embarrassed by my plight. I felt an overwhelming sense of failure, of having screwed up a significant segment of my life.

I didn't want to appear to her as a whiner, a weakling begging for sympathy. I was hesitant, apprehensive. Finally, with my heart pounding and my brain racing at superspeed, trying to sort out my ambivalence, I started to open up. I had reached the point of no return; whatever penalties I envisioned for spilling my guts couldn't be worse than the pain of holding everything in. Out it came, in a gush as unceasing as a waterfall: anger, grief, and guilt. I needed that release and I'm glad it occurred, but I hardly see Jean anymore; we've drawn away from each other.

Apparently, the reactions of women hearing of a marital breakup and the women conveying the news have a common element: fear. Few women have marriages so stable that they are not shaken upon hearing of a friend's separation, and nearly all those who have formed a marital bond are concerned about being judged a failure at its dissolution. However, facing the fear, rather than withdrawing from it or giving up a friendship, is a more beneficial manner of coping and offers greater promise of much-needed support. In fact, whatever the potential drawbacks of broaching the subject of a recent loss—embarrassment, rejection, or shame— practically all of those interviewed agreed that it is an important step to take. Acknowledging the separation personally and reinforcing it publicly is the first step toward independence and a critical event in the reorganization of one's life.

Sometimes a woman who has lost the intimacy of marriage through divorce or death seeks to make up for it in her friendship with one woman. Day and night, she will call her close friend and willing listener to discuss her problems, allay her fears, and relieve her loneliness. When the emotional dependence is one-sided, the friend may draw away and the relationship will dissolve.

Newly single women must realize that it is unrealistic to expect a married friend to respond to their needs at all hours. Actually, in discussing problems with any friend in any situation, a balance must be established. Unless relationships are reciprocal in terms of emotional give-and-take, they are not on firm ground. A friend who feels "put-upon" will sometimes withdraw completely unless she is assertive enough to state her limits.

Indeed, while some women take flight from their peers, our research, as well as the findings of other studies, shows that more than men, women appear to be able to respond openly and intimately to each other in these crisis situations. We found that practically all women revealed some details of their troubled marriage to at least one close friend. Correspondingly, women also shared their grief and loneliness with other women friends after a spouse's death. Women are able to be more vulnerable than men in each other's presence, partly because society allows them to be and partly because they usually will solicit the expected response of nonjudgmental listening and comforting from each other.

While men more frequently face the traumatic events of terminal illness, death, or divorce alone, women often find solace and support during these times. Said one sixty-five-year-old widow: "When my husband was critically ill, many of the women from the married couple friendships we had would visit us both often, but they made flimsy excuses for their husbands not showing up. And yet my husband had been good friends with many of these men. I think men have great difficulty facing weakness and powerlessness. Women are used to it, though, and they get through the pain of it by facing it together."

One report of women who filed for divorce in Cleveland's metropolitan area found that most woman-to-woman friendships did not change, but their friendships with males were likely to worsen.[1] In our study, most women reported that their close friendships with other women remained intact, regardless of the friends' marital status, if the friends were on intimate terms before divorce or widowhood.

Some women were able to maintain friendships with men, but most often these relationships took on decidedly sexual overtones. Frequently, divorced and widowed women are the target of sexual advances of married men, often the spouses of their friends. These men assume that a woman who was accustomed to an active sex life may be amenable to a few afternoons of unfettered sexual pleasure. They do not realize that although the divorcée or widow may be especially vulnerable during the period immediately after her trauma, a married man's advances are usually considered at best an embarrassment and at worst an insult.

The divorced woman's sexual needs are indeed important, but for most women, sex is not a need set apart from other needs of closeness, intimacy, and some sense of emotional security. Even if a woman could morally justify an affair with a married man, many women would not risk a friendship for sexual pleasure.

But there are exceptions. When the sexual attraction is combined with a close friendship developed over years, the change of a woman's status from married to single may be the spark that is needed to set off the firecracker: a passionate affair with a friend's husband. Shirley Eskapa in *Woman versus Woman* explains that "the easy familiarity between the husband and his wife's friend means that a certain intimacy has already been established. Long before their sexual connection, they are trusted friends. Their subterranean or informal courtship, then, is founded on mutual trust as well as chemistry. Their sexual connection is an extension of friendship and trust. It is this friendship and trust that makes the sexual connection not only more instantaneously important but far safer than the sort of casual sex that is also, and often, the result of sexual boredom."[2]

Some wives, sensitive to the possibility that their spouse may develop a sudden libidinous interest in a divorced woman and offer to become "surrogate husband," purposely discourage friendly relations.

Tina, a thirty-eight-year-old saleswoman, explained that she had enjoyed a friendship with a divorced woman, Mickey, whom she regarded as "a lot of fun" but also "sexually promiscuous." Tina found vicarious excitement in her friend's ability to "toss caution to the wind," but when her friend started to become "too chummy" with her husband, she became furious.

> One weekend, I took a trip from our Long Island home to visit a friend in Connecticut. My husband encouraged me to go; he said I'd have a good time. Well, when I got back home, I found that my so-called friend Mickey had flown over to Martha's Vineyard with my husband. They had spent the day there with her kids and our kids. I don't mind that they went; my husband loves to fly and loves company when he does—I'm very fearful of flying. But they could have told me! The fact that they kept it a secret till afterward really bothered me. After that, I not only shared my disappointment and concern with my husband, but I cooled my friendship with Mickey.

Divorced and widowed women may, in fact, be regarded as more of a sexual threat to married women than single women. After all, married women are sexually experienced. They are generally considered by their married counterparts to be more sexually active than single women, and they do have some connection with their friends' husbands, even if it was only a casual friendship.

The experience reported by Audrey, a high school teacher separated nearly a year, draws attention to the painful contrasts in the reactions of her married friends:

A couple of my friends have really been supportive. They've called frequently, offered to help me with various odds and ends, listened to my woes, and generally given me the feeling that they're with me, that I'm not completely alone. One friend in particular, Wendy, spent an entire night with me; I was suffering through an acute "crisis of confidence"; suddenly I felt unattractive, unworthy, discarded. It was a night of terror, suicide crossed my mind, not just once, but several times. Wendy stayed with me; she refused to leave my side. I talked myself out and she listened without praise or blame; she was there for me, I felt calmed by her strong presence. Finally, she put me to bed, exhausted, near dawn. I don't think it too dramatic to venture that she saved my life.

That's the good news about a friend being there for me. The bad news is that for several of my other married friends I've become a leper. As long as I was married, I was half a couple—safe. As a separated woman, suddenly I've become threatening to their marriages. All but Wendy and one other friend dropped me. Even friends that I spent countless evenings with as part of a couple no longer talk to me. What really rocked me, though, more than a cold shoulder, were the unjust sexual rumors circulated about me which I learned about from one of my loyal friends. The sad irony is that the rumors were initiated by friends whom I regarded as solid. This really threw me off balance for a while. In fact, it was reminiscent of the loss and mourning I experienced, as well as the burning resentment, when my husband left.

Widows are not immune from suspicion either, regardless of the amount of remorse they show over their husband's death. Most widows are older and probably have been married longer and more happily than their divorced counterparts. In addition, their initiation into the world of the formerly married is usually abrupt;

they are thrust rather than eased into this unfamiliar terrain by their loss. Consequently, it is not unusual to feel like "half a couple." Perhaps because they are threatening to wives, widows are more often cast aside by couple friends than widowers. Charlotte, widowed nearly a year, found she was unwanted as a dinner guest by some of her friends:

> You know, when a man's wife dies he gets invited out to dinner all the time. There's this "Oh, poor thing, we can't let him stay home and try to cook for himself" feeling. Nobody seems to feel that way about widows. It's unfair. So, if a married friend won't take the initiative, should I? I feel insecure about that; maybe I'm not wanted. Maybe I'll be dull company without my husband. And, of course, there's my married friend's vigilance about her husband's faithfulness. Rule number one for a woman brought up traditionally is: Avoid showing interest in another woman's husband. It seems ridiculous but this is still an issue, and it inhibits me from taking a social initiative with married friends.

Sometimes a woman may experience a disturbing ambivalence in relation to a friend's loss. While a friend may sympathize with the suffering and pain of the divorced, ironically, she may also experience pleasure. This is more likely to occur when envy, which may have loomed silently in the background of the relationship, suddenly surfaces. Perhaps the divorced or widowed woman is favored with wealth or unusual talent or a highly desired position; the failure of her marriage or the death of her spouse may be deemed to balance the scales. Maxine, for instance, frequently contrasted her own precarious financial position with her friend's affluence. Janice had been married to an extremely successful businessman for seventeen years; she was able to buy many luxuries and afford many comforts. Maxine, whose husband's business had recently gone bankrupt, had difficulty paying for the basic amenities of life. When Janice announced her impending divorce, Maxine could barely hide her glee. Janice noticed how intently interested Maxine was in the messy details of the divorce, particularly the financial arrangements.

A year later, Maxine separated from her husband. She told Janice afterward that she had been preoccupied with dissecting her divorce because Maxine was thinking of leaving her own husband at the time. "But to even things out," she confided to Janice, "I wanted you to think I was happy with Mike. After all, our lives had been so different all those years, or at least I thought so. You had everything, I thought: the right man, money, social position. But it turned out that we're both pretty equal right now."

And so they were, financially and socially. Janice's wealthy husband, now living with a woman fifteen years younger, managed to hide many of his assets when his business was evaluated by Janice's attorney, so that the court ordered him to pay his wife and children maintenance and support that amounted to a small fraction of what he could afford. Maxine, who had secretarial skills, managed to find a fairly well-paying job as an administrative assistant to a top executive.

Divorce, for many women, means at least temporary and sometimes long-term poverty. According to sociologist Lenore Weitzman, a woman's standard of living generally decreases by 73 percent the year after her divorce, while a man's rises by 42 percent.[3] Some lawyers actually advise women that they should not expect a fair share of their husband's wealth under equitable distribution law; many lawyers contend that women are lucky if they receive 30 percent of their spouses' assets. Divorced women, and often widows, will have considerably less funds than their married friends. This may form a barrier to friendship in a practical sense; newly single women will not be able to afford to return many invitations to dinner, parties, or a night at the theater, for instance. Even if a married couple insists on "treating" all the time, the inequity may become embarrassing.

Fairly affluent women may turn away from a financially

desperate friend as though her poverty were her own fault. When her husband became physically violent, Josephine, a twenty-nine-year-old homemaker, "ran away" from her husband, taking her two preschool children with her. She had one friend she had known since high school who at first "felt sorry" for her. Mary helped Josephine both financially and emotionally while she struggled for financial independence.

"I stayed with Mary for three weeks, until I found an apartment and a job," Josephine explained. "She and her husband were very good to me; they took care of my children and me as though we were family. Then, when I got a job, I thought I could make it on my own, and they did, too. But the kids started to become behavior problems; the babysitter said they were uncontrollable during the day, and since a good deal of my pay was going to the babysitter anyway, I quit and got public assistance. After I did that, Mary and her husband would no longer talk to me."

Mary felt Josephine "should have buckled down and helped herself." Having never experienced single motherhood herself, she did not understand Josephine's conflicting feelings about leaving her children to go to work. Josephine said: "I felt as though I were torn down the middle."

Honest, open communication of feelings is crucial if friendship is to last during the crisis period of divorce or widowhood. If women can allow themselves to be vulnerable at a time when they often feel wounded and unprotected, they are taking a difficult step but one that will be of utmost importance in aiding their recovery. And if the female friends of a divorcée or widow overcome their own insecurities and fears by sharing them with their newly single friend, they will gain greater self-confidence and a more realistic understanding of their own anxieties. In the process, the friendship will be renewed.

Sally, a twenty-nine-year-old college administrator, explained that a few close women friends gave her a feeling of security during her bitter divorce. In retrospect, she said:

I still love my former husband, but I love the person I am becoming more. I believe friends can support growth more than a spouse can. Growth can be too threatening to a spouse. But friends can accept it because they have their own lives; they are not completely dependent on you. And women friends don't seem to have the fragile egos that men married to ambitious women seem to have.

I've earned my doctorate since I separated from my husband four years ago—something I've always wanted but could not do when I was married. My women friends encouraged me to keep on trying even when I wanted to quit school. I have a few relationships with men, sexual and platonic. But during the transition from married woman to single woman, my women friends helped me the most. Even now, friendship is more important to me than it ever was. I would never give up my friendships for marriage. I have four very close female friends and two very close male friends. Even though I'd like someone to be there when I come home every night, someone to rub my back, or even just to watch TV with, I feel fortunate because I have six relationships to depend on now, rather than one.

While helping a woman through the rough spots in the often difficult journey from marriage to single life, friends must understand that they can only offer assistance; they can't show her the way or complete the journey for her. If the newly single woman is pushed toward independence too soon or is coddled too long, her own growth will be stunted. Solicitousness or unasked-for advice only hinders growth and friendship. The friends of a divorcée or widow must be encouraging and supportive without being smothering or pushy. Such friendship is hard to come by.

Yet many women find it in each other. The majority of women keep their close friends through their divorce or the death of their husband and long afterward. Some believed that going through the crisis together made them closer friends and stronger individuals. The friendship of women, during these times of upheaval, created a new strength and confidence in their own abilities. It allowed them to discover their hidden strengths and overcome their paralyzing fears. These women, by relating to each other with empathy, were able to tap inner resources that had remained dormant in their marriages and previously untested friendships.

REASSESSING FRIENDSHIPS: THE FORMERLY MARRIED WOMAN'S REACTIONS

When the friendships of a once married woman fade, it is often as much her doing as her friends' choice. A divorcée or widow is totally free to choose her own friends; she need no longer consider her spouse's preferences. When friendships no longer satisfy, they may be dropped from the newly independent woman's social circle. This breaking away may occur over several years, or it may happen quite deliberately and suddenly as the formerly married woman makes an effort to disconnect herself from her old way of life and old friends, which for some women bring forth painful memories and uncomfortable feelings.

On occasion, in order to avoid the embarrassment and pain of being dropped from the social circle of married women with whom they have associated, a woman may choose to make the break first. One woman, a fifty-eight-year-old widow who sensed the beginning of a strain in her interaction with married friends, took such a tack:

> My husband had cancer and he was ill for nearly three years. By the end of the second year of his illness, it became evident that he was going to die. This was a bittersweet year. We were close, almost self-contained; our immediate family became one. Although Ted, my hus-

band, was weakening, his spirit remained strong until the end. During the final year of Ted's life I started to really solidify as a single person. This was a paradox of experience: Ted and I were closer than ever, and yet a part of me, "woman alone," was being born. This was a particularly wrenching experience—at first I felt guilty feeling single while Ted was still alive. In fact, it was a widow who comforted me in my conflict, who helped me accept my dual feelings.

I knew then, during the third year of Ted's illness, that I would not continue my friendships with married women on the same basis as before. I felt too different; suddenly we had less in common. I didn't want to feel like a fifth wheel. This is not to say that my friends would have openly rejected me. I can't imagine that. I do feel, though, that I would be uncomfortable with their kindness—too close to pity for my taste—and I could not stand the inevitable, slow drifting apart. So, with a great deal of difficulty, I decided to strike out on my own, to take control of my own friendship fate.

Sometimes keeping married friends is too depressing for some formerly married women because in their presence they are reminded of the marital intimacy they once had and now achingly miss; they are painfully reminded that they are "half a couple." Others feel uncomfortable, as Phyllis, thirty years old, who had been separated for six months, revealed: "I've been invited to dinner by a few of the couples my husband and I had seen together, and although I felt awkward, I was close friends with the wife in each instance, so I didn't feel too out of place. But I've returned their invitations by just inviting the wife to lunch or occasionally to join me to see a movie. I can't seem to bring myself to have a dinner party for couples, the way Jason and I used to, because I believe people would want me to have a man there, and I'm not ready for a new relationship with a man yet. Perhaps when I'm dating again, I'll do that."

In a similar vein, some divorcées and widows reject the company of women during certain social occasions that are traditionally attended by couples; these usually are tradition-bound women who believe that it is "demeaning" for women to dine alone or in all-female groups in restaurants or go to dances or formal occasions without an escort. Esther, a sixty-two-year-old woman widowed nearly a year, said she was "too proud" to socialize with widowed women in groups in many public places. She expressed it this way: "I'll go out with one woman friend at a time, but I've been invited several times to join a group of eight women—all widows—for lunch at a restaurant, and I have refused. I don't want to belong to a group of women who never enjoy the company of men. Even at a dance, all these women flock together, as if they were afraid of men. I think their attitude is defeatist. They're saying, 'This is it. We're going to be alone for the rest of our lives.' They've resigned themselves to going out together."

Whether a woman retains her old friendships or not depends, to a large extent, on how she feels about herself during the time of her divorce or her husband's death and immediately after. If she feels she has nothing very worthwhile to contribute to friends because previously she allowed her husband to keep the social ball rolling and failed to develop her own social skills, she may indeed find herself without companionship. Friends and acquaintances may sense her reluctance to socialize, and rather than understand that she is going through a period of lowered self-esteem and uncertainty about her social skills, they may believe her withdrawal is a sign of rejection.

But if a woman considers herself friendly and socially adept, she will more readily retain old friends and make new ones. If she views herself as a capable, independent person who can overcome her loneliness, she has come a long way in her healing journey. A forty-five-year-old woman who had been twice divorced and who retained her close friendships throughout her three marriages, said: "I'm a very outgoing person. I've never been lonely because I've made it a point to have my own friends, independent from my husband's friends. Whenever I feel low, I call on my friends to cheer me up, and it seldom fails: They pick up my spirits. Especially after each of my divorces, I needed my women friends more than ever. I had one, in particular, Anne, whom I could call any time—even in the middle of the night—and she would listen to me. When she eventually got divorced, I helped her pull through, too.''

Sometimes anger at a spouse, a natural reaction after his separation or death, will interfere with a formerly married woman's ability to make or keep friends. Colin M. Parkes, in his book *Bereavement,* found that widows who expressed extreme anger over their husbands' death were more socially isolated than those who were able to overcome their anger or express it less strongly.[4] Either they created the isolation themselves, preferring to be alone to deal with their extreme feelings, or their friends declined to put up with their unsettling emotions. In either case, the angrier widows were more isolated.

While some former spouses remain on friendly terms after divorce, most harbor hostile feelings toward each other. In all too many instances, divorce is a grim process including the breakup of the home, disputes over the division of property, and a fierce struggle to win over the children. Strong feelings of hostility and rancor in a separating couple are common. For friends, this may lead to a conflict over allegiances. With whom does the friend side? Some friends will ally themselves with husband or wife, some will try to maintain a strict neutrality, and others will be primarily concerned with the welfare of the children. In the more amiable separations—a fortunate but infrequent occurrence—taking sides is a minor issue. In the most bitter uncouplings, those that involve the discovery of an extramarital affair, the urge to destroy the sexual wanderer sometimes becomes overwhelming. Formerly gentle spouses can turn into seething monsters, taking out and exposing family skeletons in order to "teach the son of a bitch a lesson." Inevitably, friends figure in the wrath: "If you're friends with my ex-spouse, you can't be friends with me" is an all-too-common dictate. Demanding 100 percent loyalty in this way can hamper friendships severely. Often the dictate backfires, and the friend chooses the spouse who is less demanding and less possessive as more worthy of friendship, or withdraws from both.

While some of the formerly married alienate their friends by embroiling them in their postmarital conflict, others turn to family in addition to friends. This is particularly true of women who are newly separated. However, although a woman's family may provide her with financial help once her divorce is underway, they may also be more critical of her than her friends. A woman's parents may still regard her as "their little girl" in need of protection and guidance; hence, they offer advice and criticism. If parents help the divorcing woman financially, they are even more likely to feel entitled to make judgments about her life. Consequently, many women find greater acceptance for their feelings and new life-style, particularly if it is unconventional, among friends rather than kin.

Most women find the postmarital healing process agonizingly slow, despite help from family and friends. Catherine Napolitane and Victoria Pellegrino, in their book *Living and Loving after Divorce,* say that one to five years after her divorce, a woman will go through what they call a "yahoo" phase. During this time, she is more concerned with personal growth and achievement than with being dependent on men or hoping for remarriage.[5] It appears from our research that widows go through a similar phase. After mourning and making a frantic effort to renew their old way of life, many widows have to accept that women will comprise their most intimate contacts since fewer than 5 percent of women who have been widowed after age fifty-five remarry. Women who have been socialized to think that they need a man in order to be happy will have to reevaluate their ideas about women's status along with their social expectations. So long as they believe that they are social inferiors to men, women who socialize solely with other women will feel as though they are "settling." Whether women socialize in groups or one-to-one is a matter of personal preference, but women must get over the notion that they "have lost all their social value along with their husband," as one woman put it, if they are to maintain satisfying friendships.

For some women—those who married in order to avoid loneliness, the insecure, and those who are afraid to meet others—the chances of social rehabilitation are seriously impeded. To become an individual requires learning to live without somebody to lean on. Some women have forgotten how; others have never learned. In either case, being single not only presents a new friendship challenge but calls for a massive psychological reorientation. Inevitably, a shifting of friendships will occur, and losing some friends along the way is common. To avoid disappointment, guilt, or self-blame, the newly single woman must not hold on to the misconception that true friends are "friends forever." Naturally, every effort should be made to keep a friendship that is satisfying, but if the friendship's hurts are greater than its joys, or the effort put into it is considerably more than the friend is making, letting go may be the best course.

WHEN IT'S TIME
TO MOVE ON:
MAKING NEW FRIENDS

Without doubt, the end of a marriage strains the ties of camaraderie between the formerly married and their friends. It is in this context of a tenuous social network, feeling quite alone, that newly single women face the major task of reshaping their lives. Postmarital loneliness can be especially tormenting. No longer is the companionship of the marriage available; however, with all the bitterness that surrounds divorce, it is easy to forget that nearly all those who have formed a marital bond have shared countless intimacies. The relationship may have been stormy and painful, but there was caring. The dissolution of the marriage, even for those who keenly desired its end, leaves a void to be filled.

As the women we interviewed described their situation, they

spoke of having a different set of needs for friendship, not the least of which was for basic companionship. Both divorcées and widows needed someone to have supper with on a Tuesday night or to go to a matinee with on Sunday; they needed new friends to fill time blocks when their married friends were involved with their spouses. Thus, many women in transition found themselves, at thirty, forty, fifty, or, in the case of widows, sometimes sixty or older, searching for a new set of friends.

As noted previously, there are a multitude of reasons for the melting away of relationships with married friends. In addition to psychological factors—disruptive emotional reactions, conflicts of loyalty, and growing differences in life-style—there are practical matters. That is, changing one's friends is not entirely the result of being rejected by them or even of having decided to reject them. The change may occur merely because getting together has become more problematic: The separated woman very often may begin paid employment and consequently have less time for socializing. As a forty-two-year-old woman explained:

> After our separation it was mandatory for me to return to work. Without working I could never afford to keep the house, and my sons would only suffer another dramatic change. So, rather than move, I chose to take a full-time job. Now I had full responsibility for the house—cooking, cleaning, shopping, and laundry—and I didn't return home until six in the evening. After supper I didn't know where to start; going over homework, housework, giving the boys attention. It was exhausting. On top of it all, I was desperately lonely, but when my friends called I hardly had time to talk with them, much less see them. It was very, very frustrating.

Although making new friends may at first seem formidable, most women are able to do so once they get over the initial shock and hurt of separation. Although women who return to work after they are divorced or widowed have less time for neighborhood relations, many find friendships through coworkers. Women who are joiners have a variety of singles' groups and women's groups to attend where meeting new friends is probable. It appears that friendship is a priority for most formerly married women, since most singles' groups, such as Parents without Partners, are dominated by women. According to Robert S. Weiss, in his book *Loneliness,* women, in contrast to men, found Parents without Partners a valuable group for establishing same-sex friendships. New friendships tended to be between women of similar age and socioeconomic status.[6]

Women's centers frequently sponsor "women in transition" groups where divorced or widowed women can share their fears, hopes, and practical concerns—like finding a job or a babysitter. "My concerns," a recently separated woman remarked, "are the problems of being a single parent, difficulties with loneliness and dating. These matters are foreign to my married friends. I want friends who have something to say about these pressing problems. I'm restless with what I now regard as the small talk of my married friends."

While support groups can be most helpful for women who wish to recover from grief or from the damage to their self-esteem and emotional equilibrium following a divorce, they are not suitable for every woman. Some shy or solitary women may not be ready for the self-revelation these groups encourage. Each woman must understand and accept her own nature; if she would rather not discuss the intimacies of marriage in a group but would like companionship, perhaps joining a special-interest group, taking a class, or pursuing a hobby or sport with other women will enable her to find the friends that she needs to discuss feelings on a one-to-one basis.

Still other women prefer to find new friends in their neighborhood or through their married friends. Many widows, in particular, find solace and a social life through religious activities sponsored by their church or synagogue. For some women, the religious community may serve as a family substitute; it may provide a sense of belonging when they feel alienated from old friends and the community at large. Brenda, a widow in her mid-thirties, found this sense of belonging through a widows' group sponsored by her church. She made new discoveries concerning her ability to enjoy herself, without her husband, as a member of her church's widows' group. She put it this way:

> When my husband was ill, I was traveling back and forth to and from the hospital every day for months. He had leukemia. The final stages of his illness were so painful to witness that it took everything out of me. I was emotionally wrung out. After his death, the women at the church helped me to start enjoying life again. Today, three years after my husband's death, I'm happy to say that I think life is wonderful again. Just last year, a group of women from the church went on an opera tour of Europe. I decided to go along; it was something that really interested me. My husband was not interested in opera, so I had never gotten the chance to indulge myself before.

Some women go through a period of self-imposed isolation after divorce or widowhood; the need to be alone to sort out their memories, and their lives, is necessary for healing. But for others, isolation may be imposed by geographical location. More than any other circumstantial factor, living in a small town appears to be a handicap. Decidedly, those women we interviewed who succeeded at rebuilding their friendship network most rapidly usually resided in large metropolitan areas. A metropolitan area offers the most opportunity for interaction with other singles; the wide variety of groups and activities is unmatched by the more subdued suburbs. The suburbs, many formerly married women said, were strictly married-couple territory, with their PTA meetings and dinner parties for couples. And today, when so many women have returned to work, suburban neighborhoods appear much like ghost towns during weekdays.

For older widows, retirement communities appear to be ideal for maintaining an active social life. Marge, a sixty-year-old widow, had moved to a retirement village with her husband, Richard, a year before he died. During that time, the two enjoyed many couple friendships. After Richard's sudden death from a heart attack, Marge said most couples did not abandon her; they invited her for dinner, card playing, or golf even more frequently.

Also, she discovered, there was a community of widows. As she put it:

> The retirement community is open to couples over age fifty-five, but 10 percent of the 500 homes here are occupied by widows or single women. The women who had lost their husbands, these women whom I hadn't even noticed before, formed a protective circle around me when my husband died. That's what it felt like—protective and warm. Many of them said, "If you're lonely, come on over." And rather than face each day alone, I took them up on it. Now I socialize with a group of ten widows here, and one or two I see regularly. I believe that if my husband and I had stayed in our old home in the suburbs, I would have been much more lonely after he died. There were two widows on our block that I knew of, but there were some families I didn't even know, and a few were young couples that recently moved in. I really had nothing in common with them.

An important factor here is the woman's willingness to participate in an environment of unattached people. One woman in her early forties described her experience:

> When I was married we lived in a stuffy family community. It seemed that our entire neighborhood was in bed by eleven. On weekends after an evening of bridge, dinner out, or a movie, lights went out about midnight.

When my marriage broke up, I found myself to be the object of my friends' pity and, sometimes, their suspicion. After a while their reactions to me and the lack of opportunity to meet new people convinced me to move closer to the city. I thought a fresh start in a new but not totally unfamiliar place would do me a world of good. Dana, my daughter, was reluctant at first, but finally she agreed. After we got settled in our new place, I began going to public events and joining organizations. I pursued all kinds of social opportunities. Dana made friends quickly at school. She adjusted beautifully. I deliberately became involved with groups of other unattached people such as Parents without Partners. Some of the people I met at PWP were not easy to relate to. Their conversations were so predictable it was tiresome: Horror stories of divorce, problems with children, and tales of financial woe were not exactly my idea of an evening out. But despite some real losers, I met some very nice people.

There are two people I met with whom I feel particularly close. One is Gail, a delight to talk to. She comes to the house and we really confide in each other and give each other support. We're each other's psychologists. She tells me how terrific I am and I tell her how terrific she is. There is something very fine and sturdy about Gail. She's a woman who has been through an awful lot and not only survived but prospered. I have really learned something about womanhood from her. Mary Alice is another gem. I met her at a singles' tennis evening. Over a period of several months we've gotten together quite often. One night, very late, she called me in obvious distress. She had found out she was pregnant and was having a very difficult time dealing with the prospect of abortion. Her "boyfriend" didn't want to take time off from work to accompany her to the clinic, so I went instead. It was a very trying time, but I'm glad I came through for her; we're still very close even though we both have steady men in our lives now.

NEW LOVES, OLD LOVES, AND FRIENDS

In addition to finding new same-sex friends, some formerly married women form opposite-sex friendships for the first time in many years. At a time when memories of a disappointing marital experience or one suddenly halted by death are still at issue, opposite-sex friends can be a useful element in the healing process. When emotions are wounded, as with a broken limb, there is a period of knitting during which isolation is required; but if the limb is to grow strong again, it must be tested. Feelings operate in similar fashion: We need to try them out, exercise them, even if cautiously at first, in order that they may return, in time, to full functioning. Aside from companionship and stability in a world where one-night stands are not uncommon, a relationship with someone of the other sex in which there is no romantic interest can provide a bridge, an emotionally safe step toward developing new romantic associations.

As Joel Block found in his study of remarriage *To Marry Again,* six out of seven divorced persons remarry.[7] What is more, young widows have about the same chance of remarrying as divorcées, but for older widows, the choice of eligible men is markedly reduced; there are far fewer widowers after age fifty-five, and those who are available frequently marry younger women.

Dating, for all the fears of rejection and questions of intimacy the term provokes, is a necessary element in the healing process. Just as a patient's first steps are shaky after a long illness and confinement to bed, the initial dating experience for most uncoupled women is unsettling. Even the word *dating* sounds awkward and unnatural; the term seems more fitting for adolescents.

Despite the initial uneasiness with both term and practice,

dating remains the most popular method of developing new romantic associations and evaluating the desirability of a continuing relationship. For these reasons, the great majority of women begin going out within the first year after the termination of their marriage. For some the experience is mildly pleasant; for others it is distressing—evenings of straining to make conversation, of trying to conceal boredom, grief, or anxiety, of plotting how to disappear without offending.

Often a formerly married woman, as well as her family and friends, will be more concerned about the social, educational, and economic status of her love partner than they were the first time around. Divorcées and widows have often established a lifestyle and social circle based on their former husband's status; most women wish to maintain that position, or better it, when they remarry. While marrying for love is certainly prevalent the second time, romantic feelings do not preclude taking into account more practical considerations. One forty-year-old divorcée who had been married to a physician stated: "I won't embarrass myself or my friends by going out with anyone who I feel is unsuitable. A man, at this stage of my life, must be successful to attract me. Sexual attraction alone certainly isn't enough to hold my interest; after all, I'm not a teenager."

When friends do not wholeheartedly accept a woman's new partner, there may be a variety of reasons for their lack of enthusiasm. If he is very different from themselves in socioeconomic status or in age, the discrepancy may be a barrier to friendship. Inevitably, friends will compare a woman's new love to her spouse, and if he is found lacking or unworthy, the friendship between the women may be cooled. Sometimes a formerly married woman seems to go out of her way to choose someone most of her friends consider inappropriate. In these instances, the newly single woman often asserts that she is in the grip of a special and unduplicated passion. However, close examination usually reveals considerably less than an ideal romance; rather than being controlled by the power of love, she may be choosing a partner out of insecurity—the fear of being alone. In other words, a choice that actually rests on ready availability and the willingness of a man is temporarily rationalized as a grand passion.

Occasionally, married couples are able to remain friends with both formerly married partners after they divorce. But when one or the other brings a new love into the social arena, the friends' loyalties may be realigned. Social inequities based on sex may come into play. For example, if a woman starts to date a man much younger than herself and much less educated than her former husband, while her former partner dates a woman who is younger and less educated than his former wife, the friends may reject the woman's new love but find the man's date perfectly acceptable. Men are allowed and often encouraged to have love partners who are much younger and educationally inferior, but it is considered demeaning for a woman to do so.

Often a formerly married woman will wait until the relationship with her new man becomes "steady," or exclusive, before she introduces him to her friends. At this time, couple relationships that the woman enjoyed while she was married may resume with the addition of the new man. The four people in this new quadrangle will have to like each other, and again, chances for intimacy are low, compared to one-to-one friendships. On the other hand, a woman may find that her unattached friends become angry or jealous when she begins dating. One woman, a widow, felt an undercurrent of distress in her friendship as she developed a new male attachment:

> My husband and I had been friendly with Sam and Bea, the couple who lived next door to us, for ten years. Sam's wife died one month before my husband died. Afterward, we would occasionally see each other outside in our gardens, and we'd chat. Three or four months after my husband died, I couldn't bear my loneliness any longer, and I asked Sam over for lunch. Even though I had no particular attraction to him in the past, I felt I would like his companionship. It turned out that he was

just as lonely, and we started seeing each other regularly. We found an attraction for each other that we never realized before.

My married friends were happy for me. They invited Sam and me over for dinner just the way they had invited both my husband and me over. We all got along very well. It is only with my single and widowed friends that I sense a hint of disapproval. They never tell me outright that they think my seeing Sam is wrong, but they never mention that they are happy for me either. I know a lot of them are lonely and frustrated at not finding eligible men, so part of their reaction may be jealousy.

It is not unusual for friends who used to share complaints about the lack of male companionship to feel jealous when one of them starts to date. To overcome these feelings, it is best to acknowledge them rather than harbor them secretly. June, a thirty-six-year-old divorcée, confided that when she actually discussed her feelings of envy with her friend concerning her ability to find a man, her friend was not offended but was touched by her honesty. Pamela reassured June that no one, not even her new love, could ever replace the deep friendship they shared, and she made a greater effort to spend more time with June.

Divorce or widowhood need not be the signal that life has come to a halt. Many women have succeeded in the face of broken marriages, despite the almost universal feeling among the divorced and widowed that rebuilding one's life is a hopeless task. Gradually, out of necessity, most lives will move toward coherence and order. With most women, though, the process of recovery is not likely to proceed without setbacks. Some problems may be resolved smoothly; others, such as developing a new social network, may not be solved for months. Some emotional issues may take much longer: Strong feelings toward the former mate, feelings of injustice, and fear of making it alone and of new emotional involvements stubbornly refuse to vanish.

If a woman pursues her goals and interests, she will be surprised to discover that she can find joy in her own accomplishments. Actually, the more self-sufficient and content she is with herself, the easier it will be for her to make friends—both male and female.

CHAPTER

8

THE MENTOR-
PROTÉGÉE
RELATIONSHIP:
FROM BUSINESS
FORMALITY
TO FRIENDSHIP

Although it is only in the last two decades that the term *mentor* has become a commonplace expression for any career woman who is worth her M.B.A., the word originated thousands of years ago in Greek mythology. When Odysseus left home on his journey, he entrusted his son, Telemachus, to his adviser and friend, Mentor. The mentor of today also acts as a devoted substitute parent: powerful, protective, caring, encouraging, willing to share advice, skills, and knowledge with the protégée, but also willing to let go. To be successful, a mentor-protégée relationship must end as the protégée becomes a peer to the mentor. However, in some instances, a strong and lasting friendship may develop between the two.

In the initial stages of their relationship, the mentor and protégée are not usually friends because they are not equals; the relationship most often occurs between an older man and a younger woman. Although female mentors are becoming more prevalent as women reach positions of power in business, the vast majority of mentors are still men. The mentor is often admired as someone who has accomplished what the woman aspires to; he has been where the younger woman wants to go and is able to offer direction, recognition of her ability, and visibility; if he so chooses, he will initiate her into the professional and social world she desires to enter.

Numerous studies indicate that having a mentor can give anyone's career a boost, but women, in particular, need mentors to overcome the still prevalent sexism in business. Gail Sheehy, in a *New York* magazine article, "The Mentor Connection: The Secret Link in the Successful Woman's Life," found, with a few exceptions, that women who gained recognition in their careers had mentors.[1] Linda Phillips-Jones studied 332 successful women in business and industrial settings and found that two-thirds of them had mentors to guide them at various stages in their careers.[2] In a study by Nancy W. Collins of over 400 executive and professional women who had mentors at some point in their careers, over half the women said their mentors were "very valuable" to their career, and more than a quarter believed their mentors had "some value"; no one responded that her mentor had "no value" to her career.[3]

A study of 1,250 executives by Gerald R. Roche of Heidrick and Struggles, an international management consulting firm, found that two-thirds of the respondents had at least one mentor; those who benefited from mentors earned more at a younger age and were better educated, more apt to follow a career plan, and more likely to act as mentors themselves than those without mentors. In addition, those executives who had mentors derived greater pleasure from their work and were more satisfied with their career progress than the executives who did not. Although women executives comprised a very small percentage of the sample, they all reported having mentors.[4]

Of 100 top businesswomen studied by Agnes K. Missirian, 85 had mentors. Only 60 percent of the women who did not have mentors reached the level of vice president compared with 100 percent of the women who had mentors at some time in their careers. Eighty percent of the women who had mentors earned at least $50,000 per year, as opposed to only 20 percent of the group without mentors. Most striking in this study was the difference in emotional qualities of the women who had mentors and those who did not. Coworkers perceived the women without mentors as "cold and emotionally distant." Missirian perceived "a bitterness, a hostility and a discontent in the demeanor of these women which was in sharp contrast to the mentor group."[5] The women who had mentors believed the world was mostly full of exciting possibilities and that people, in general, were helpful and supportive.

Did the women with mentors find them because of their positive, friendly attitude? Or were they so enthusiastic and positive about life because they had someone to provide help and support? The answer, probably, is both: A positive attitude often brings forth the success and friendship that more negative people find lacking, and success and friendship breed still more positive feelings and even greater success.

HOW A MENTOR CAN HELP A WOMAN IN HER CAREER AND IN HER LIFE

A mentor is, at first, usually less than a friend but more than a teacher. Psychologist Daniel J. Levinson, in his study of male adult development, *The Seasons of a Man's Life,* likened the mentor-protégée relationship "to the intense love relationships between parents and grown offspring, or between sexual lovers or spouses." Most mentor relationships, he reported, last two to three years, at the most ten years. According to Levinson, protégées are usually eight to fifteen years younger than their mentors.[6]

From our study, we have concluded that women often stay with their mentors longer than men. Also, the age difference of a mentor and his protégée varies considerably when the protégée is a woman; usually a mentor is older, but women's mentors may be the same age, or even younger than the protégée. Since women's careers are often delayed or interrupted due to childbearing, more older women than older men are in need of mentors.

Levinson described the functions of a mentor as teacher, sponsor, host, guide, exemplar, and counsel.[7] Teaching necessary business skills, using his power to help a protégée up the career ladder, acquainting her with a new social and business world and familiarizing her with its values, acting as a role model, and offering support and encouragement are all part of what a mentor can give a protégée.

A formal education is a prerequisite for upwardly mobile career women today, but just as important, if not more so, are the skills of dealing with people and everyday problems obtained on the job—the valuable skills a mentor can provide. These skills include technical training, too, in business, science, the arts, or any field.

Men and women in the upper echelons of business appreciate that skill, hard work, and persistence count in getting ahead, but they also understand that more is required if you are aiming to occupy the top-floor executive suite. Personal style, a knowledge of the corporation hierarchy, and knowing how to play the game of office politics are the power-packed business tools that are indispensable for the climb to the top. Women, who are often excluded from men's inside information at the office, can learn the nuances of the business hierarchy and the intricacies of office politics from a male mentor.

Helene, a thirty-three-year-old single woman who had been dedicated to her career from the first day at her job, could not understand why she was receiving no promotions and only minimal raises despite her high productivity. She had been assistant regional sales manager of a large cosmetics firm for six years. When she finally asked her boss for what she thought was a well-deserved raise, he not only refused but informed her the "division was being redesigned" and her job was in jeopardy. He advised her to look for other employment, and he suggested that if she left before the end of the year—six months hence—she would get three months' severance pay. Otherwise, she would get nothing but a pink slip.

Helene was stunned, hurt, and puzzled. She had done her best, had performed better than most other employees in her position, and yet soon she would be without a job. She wanted to know why she was being dumped, but she had no one to talk to. Other management-level employees were all close-mouthed men, and she had never had a mentor. But she recalled a manager of another division she had met some time ago at a company conference. Lowell had been with the company for fifteen years, and he seemed to get along with everyone, particularly the bosses. He had chatted with her at some length when they met and had appeared to have a genuine interest in her work. Out of desperation, she called him, explained her difficulty briefly, and asked if he could offer any insight.

Over lunch the next day, Lowell informed Helene that the head of her division was known to make sexist remarks at all-male meetings and was a dictator in terms of leadership. Further, Mr. C. had "pet projects" that he expected his employees to pursue diligently; lack of enthusiasm for his ideas was akin to treason.

Helene confided to Lowell that she had returned to Mr. C. a few sales schemes that seemed impractical to her, with her own comments showing how they could be made more workable. She admitted she was annoyed when they were returned to her with instructions to carry through with the original plan regardless of her misgivings.

Over the next half year, Lowell and Helene met frequently for lunch to discuss business and socialize. They soon became friends, and Lowell introduced Helene to his wife and children, who also became fond of her. Rumors spread at work that Helene and Lowell were having an affair, but they both understood that office gossip was the rule rather than the exception when women and men became friends on the job. They did their best to downplay their visibility.

Helene and Lowell had long discussions about Helene's career goals. At first, Helene intended to file a complaint with the Equal Rights Commission in an attempt to keep her job, but as the pressure on her from higher-ups increased, her work atmosphere became intolerable. Lowell supported her in her decision to leave. He gave her recommendations, and Helene soon found another job with a more innovative firm where her superiors welcomed her creative ideas and advanced her career at a satisfactory pace.

Three years later, Helene was still in contact with Lowell, although they lived several hundred miles apart. They still shared business and social news and remained friends.

Lowell had acted as teacher, sponsor, and guide to Helene. In addition, he gave her the encouragement and support she needed to boost her self-esteem when it was at a low ebb. She commented: "I only wish I had found a mentor sooner, so that I would have understood the politics of the business world; I was so unsophisticated. But I'm happier in my new job, and Lowell helped me to make the right decision—to move on."

Sponsoring a protégée means that a mentor is willing to use his power and influence to help a woman he believes is deserving, because of her exceptional ability and hard work, to advance in her career. In order to gain greater visibility for her, he may give her increasingly difficult assignments to test the extent of her ability. He will allow her to stretch, to grow to the extent she is capable of, and when she is ready for new challenges, he will point to her accomplishments and recommend her for a promotion.

Becoming a mentor to a woman is more risky than finding a promising male to mentor. Office gossip concerning a possible sexual liaison must often be dealt with. Mentors must sometimes fight against sex discrimination for a protégée and occasionally endanger their own career advancement by challenging the status quo. Men who mentor women are frequently mavericks; they are secure enough in their career and marriage to take calculated risks. Martha, a forty-two-year-old businesswoman, expressed appreciation of her mentor, who had helped her overcome sexism to climb to a high position:

> I've worked for Albert for twenty years. He was my sales manager in my first job, fresh out of the University of Michigan. I was twenty-two and he was forty-six; his daughter, now a close friend of mine, was seventeen at the time. I was like a second daughter; both Albert and his wife, Rosa, treated me like family. Albert saw to it that I moved right along with him, up the corporate ladder. He has guided my career and has extended himself to promote my advancement.
>
> Remember now, we are going back a number of years, before the resurgence of feminism. Women were patronized at best and, more often, regarded with contempt in the corporate world. I recall one instance about twelve years ago when Albert nominated me among several other regional sales managers for a ten-day business seminar out west. Several of his nominees were selected. I was not. I happened to be sitting in his office when the company president called and implied that he wanted *the men* to have this opportunity, which in all likelihood would lead to advancement. In a very polite and forceful manner, Albert told the president I was going; he contended that based on merit, I was number one, period. As you might imagine, my road to becoming vice president of a mid-sized corporation has been paved with such incidents—and Albert stood behind me in every instance.

As a role model, a mentor can be extremely important in shaping a woman's work style, but unfortunately, since the number of women who act as mentors are few, opportunities for identification with successful women are limited. Identification involves having affection and admiration for someone, then emulating the admired person in ways that suit you. It is more than imitation; identification is a selective process in which only certain traits or habits are copied. Finally, it is a process of letting go as new behavior learned from the role model becomes internalized.

Only 6 percent of all top management positions are held by women. The few women who might serve as mentors are often too beset by the stress of survival in an arena dominated by men to provide help or support for younger women. Some, particularly older women who have not had the benefit of a mentor themselves, show a resentment toward those who haven't equaled their achievements:

"The handful of women who are now in their fifties and sixties who were terribly successful," writer Nora Ephron said in an interview in *Mademoiselle,* "had a kind of 'I made it and I have no affiliation with anyone who hasn't . . . I have no feelings at all for a person who can't get it together and be where I am' attitude. My mother [a screenwriter] had that air of superiority." [8]

The "Queen Bee" syndrome described by Ephron is, fortunately, less widespread than it is publicized. All the women we interviewed, whether they had mentors or not, said they were not only willing but enthusiastic about one day becoming a mentor to an inspiring and aspiring protégée.

One thirty-eight-year-old woman, Alicia, now the publisher of a chain of weekly newspapers, remembered her first mentor, a woman, saying, "She was the first person who gave me a chance. She had faith in me. She's an editor to the bone. She taught me how to write—how to get to the point, how to find a unique lead. And that reflects how I think. She shaped the way I look at things.

"Gerry and I are friends now. I don't need her as a mentor anymore. But what I'd like to do is give some young woman what she has given me—faith in herself, encouragement, and the needed skills to make it as a journalist. I really feel it's my debt. I've been quite successful, and I owe it to the world to help by becoming a mentor myself.''

Women mentors can act as role models for their protégées in their personal lives as well as their professional lives. Alicia revealed: "When Gerry became pregnant and left the newspaper where I worked as a reporter and she was a senior editor, I missed her a lot, and I thought about how happy she must have been at home with her baby. When I saw her newborn—how cute he was—I decided I had to have one of my own. I told her that, and she thought I was kidding, but I definitely was serious. I became pregnant a few months later. Of course, my husband and I were thinking about having a child for some time, but the fact that Gerry did it first spurred me on to become a mother, too.''

There probably was some unconscious competitiveness at work in Alicia's decision, even though she denied any feelings of envy. Rivalry, competition, hostility—all of these negative feelings are part of the process of identification, along with affection and admiration.

Harry Levinson, in his book *The Exceptional Executive,* suggested that since women in business are still working in a predominantly male world, they need the guidance of male as well as female mentors, to help them better understand male psychology and thereby gain an advantage in business.[9] This may be true, but if the values of a protégée and her potential mentor are vastly different, their relationship will not develop. Jessica, a thirty-six-year-old lawyer, explained: "Actually, there were two lawyers in the firm where I first worked who had the power to help my career and who expressed a personal interest in me. One was a man, the other a woman. I chose the woman to be my mentor; her values were so much more like mine. Mr. A., on the other hand, used a lot of dirty tricks as well as foul language and bullying to get ahead of the other guy, to win his case. To him, winning was everything. I had different values. Although he was a very successful lawyer, I never respected him.''

A mentor, like any effective parent or caring friend, will offer advice and encouragement to a protégée. At times of crisis or self-doubt, the mentor will be a source of support to keep the protégée afloat. Ideally, a mentor promotes her protégée's growth by expressing confidence in her ability. The theory of self-fulfilling prophecy is at work in most mentor-protégée relationships: If a person you respect believes you will do a difficult job well, even though you initially have doubts about it, you may gain the momentum and confidence in yourself that are needed to complete the job. A thirty-year-old woman in advertising said: "Doris just piled on the work, and she'd give me some very difficult assignments. Whenever I hinted that I thought the work might be too hard, she'd say, 'That's why I gave it to you. I know you can handle it.' And somehow her faith in me kept me going. I never disappointed her."

While the effective mentor freely criticizes a protégée's work and even her style of interacting with coworkers and superiors, she is quick to defend her if others are critical of her. Her mentor is willing to stand by her work if it is questioned, and if she has made a genuine mistake, a mentor will not lose confidence in her. Like a true friend, a mentor does not let unintentional blunders ruin a relationship; the commitment and trust shared by mentor and protégée is too strong to be disassembled by accusations or errors.

The true mentor-protégée relationship goes beyond career usefulness; it is a caring relationship as well. Because it would not have started unless there existed some chemistry between the two, it is possible that it will deepen into friendship, barring conflicts and betrayal. It appears from our research that the mentor-protégée relationship grows in the same way as a friendship or a love affair. Intimacy breeds vulnerability and highly charged feelings, so that when the relationship has grown into a meaningful friendship, it is also experienced as more explosive and variable; more ups and downs are likely to be experienced, more anger along with more joy, greater frustration along with jubilation. A lasting friendship is the added bonus of a mentor-protégée relationship.

A TWO-WAY STREET:
HOW MENTORS BENEFIT
FROM PROTÉGÉES

Mentors are not altruistic saints; they are ambitious executives and professionals who know that spending time and energy teaching a smart, young protégée is a solid business investment. When a mentor is able to spot a rising star and help develop her potential, she not only derives pleasure from her skill at bringing out her protégée's talent and associating with her but also enhances her own status. Higher-ups will notice the fine taste and keen judgment of the mentor in choosing a young wonder, and if they don't, the mentor will call attention to her, and indirectly to herself.

Julia, a forty-three-year-old public relations director, explained:

> I certainly did not spend ten or fifteen hours more than my usual forty-five or fifty hours per week teaching Fay everything I know out of the sheer goodness of my heart. I knew she had tremendous potential, and I knew that if I trained her well—taught her the things you don't learn in college—she would be a tremendous help to me in getting new clients. Her personality is particularly appealing to me; she's got purpose, drive, enthusiasm, and native intelligence. There are some employees I've taught who had more education than Fay, and many with more experience, but I never met anyone else with so much raw talent and drive. She has a natural writing ability; she knows how to write and speak so that people stop what they're doing and pay attention. It's turning out that the price I paid to train her, to give her everything I've

got and everything she deserves, has been repaid hand-
somely. She does better work than anyone else here, and
she's attracted several big clients for me, which has
earned me, as well as Fay, some well-deserved recognition and financial reward.

Often, people who are in a position to be mentors are not only
successful and accomplished in their field but also very busy.
They will, therefore, often take on a protégée to help with their
growing work load. A lawyer, a physician, an architect, or almost any professional, for instance, may hire a young assistant
to help ease the strain of overwork and, witnessing the new
trainee's potential, provide her with greater responsibilities and
more advice and attention than was originally intended.

Some mentors believe they owe a debt to others; often when
a successful woman has had the benefit of a mentor, for instance, she feels she ought to help other young women who are
struggling the way she did. She will follow the role model of
her mentor by becoming a mentor herself. Some men will avoid
the risk of becoming a mentor to a woman, because they do not
feel women take their careers as seriously as men. Many women,
in contrast, understand the hardships and ultimate determination
of a woman who succeeds in the career world; those women with
less stamina and less motivation are left behind.

When a man is a mentor to a woman, he has moved beyond
sexism. But again, even the kind godfather type of mentor is not
completely altruistic. There often is an undercurrent of sexual
desire in cross-gender mentoring. Frequently, it is sexual attraction in addition to talent, but never a substitute for it, that mo-
tivates a mentor to groom a protégée. This attraction, however,
often remains hidden, and only in a minority of instances is it
acted upon. Instead, the increased sexual energy is diverted to
work.

A wise mentor understands that a well-selected protégée will
eventually become his equal or surpass him. If he is a secure

person, he will not be threatened by the inevitable turn of events that will cause him to be viewed as mortal and fallible by a once adoring protégée. Rather, he will understand that he has developed a resource that may be of great usefulness to him.

An English professor who was a prolific author published by academic presses took a particular interest in Miranda, a graduate student who he felt had exceptional writing talent. He spent more time than usual criticizing her assignments, and when she completed his course, he gave her an A and promptly asked her to be his teaching assistant. She proved to be an invaluable source of help, not only with the more mundane chores of marking tests but also by providing him with fresh insights for his own writing. Eventually, Miranda became an influential editor and was able to facilitate the acceptance of her former professor's manuscripts at a large publishing house.

Some mentors may feel a stagnation in their own careers, and to relieve their restlessness and boredom, and possibly for the pleasure of vicarious achievement, they may decide to place their undirected energy in refining young talent. Occasionally a mentor who is blocked from further advancement in his own career invests his time and redirects his goals, centering them on his protégée. If she manages to get where he originally wanted to go, he may also experience a sense of fulfillment.

The motivation to become a mentor is similar to the yearning to become a parent. There is a need to nurture, to extend the self beyond one's own boundaries, to prolong one's influence, and to ensure that one's memory and work will be continued. Psychoanalyst Eric Erikson theorized that generativity, the nurturing of other's capabilities, is a necessary stage of life and that if adults don't interact to produce generativity, they stagnate and cannot reach their full level of maturity.

Indeed, fathers with influence often serve as their successful daughters' mentors or role models. Margaret Hennig, in her Harvard doctoral study of twenty-five women who held the position of president or vice president of a large corporation, found that each of the women as young girls had identified with her father rather than her mother. Their fathers had encouraged the girls to pursue their interests and talents in whatever direction they wished; they did not downplay the girls' femininity, but they emphasized the importance of skills. In their careers, each of these women found a male mentor to guide her as her father had done.[10]

Claudia, the first-born child in a family of four children, at age thirty-nine is the managing editor of a metropolitan newspaper. She explained that her father was her inspiration and guide in both her life and her career:

Dad was a newspaper editor, but he never encouraged me to follow in his footsteps, because he felt the pay was low and the hours long. Yet he loved his work, and frequently the news was part of the family's dinner conversation. My mother was a free-lance writer, part-time, but I was never as interested in what she did as I was in my father's world. I was interested in the ideas and events my father covered: politics, sports, headlines. His enthusiasm about work was catching. When he saw how interested I was, he helped me get a summer job at his paper. I loved it. From the first summer I worked there, I knew that I wanted to be a reporter, and whatever else happened in my life, happened. I didn't think about getting married or having children. I just knew I wanted to get my degree in journalism and go to work.

I did exactly that, and when I was working full-time at my first job on a small weekly, which I found myself, independent of my father, I often called him to ask his advice about certain news stories. My dad was always interested in what I did, and he had no doubt that I could do what I wanted to do. He taught me the skills I needed, and he gave me confidence in using them. I didn't want him to use his influence to get me a job, so he didn't. I felt I had to prove myself. I guess it was the way he did things, his attitude about life, that gave me my drive. To him and to my mother, education was the most important thing in life, and working was a privilege. That's the way I feel, too.

Gail Sheehy, in *The Mentor Connection,* said a father can choose an ambitious daughter as a favorite because, unlike a son, she is not his rival.[11] In a similar vein, mentors may sometimes choose women protégées because they do not view them as competitors in the same way as men would be. Also, some men may prefer women as protégées because they can relate to them on a more emotional level. Indeed, although it is seldom the motivating factor for starting the relationship, at least on a conscious level, the need for intimacy is sometimes the reason why a mentor-protégée relationship will continue for many years.

As the mentor and protégée reveal themselves to each other, learn to trust each other and depend on each other, share failures and victories, and laugh and commiserate together, they form an attachment that is separate from work. This is the factor that makes the mentor more than a teacher and enables him or her to wield an influence over a protégée as strong as a beloved parent's, spouse's, or friend's. Actually, a mentor's influence may be more powerful than any of these others; a mentor may counteract, for instance, the ambivalence of a spouse's feelings about his wife's career.

This intimacy is also a strong incentive for the mentor to pursue the relationship with a protégée as a friend, after she has learned the necessary skills and risen to a position to which she has aspired. Judith, a thirty-nine-year-old bank vice president, recalled with obvious pleasure the words of her fifty-six-year-old mentor, who is still her friend. He told her one hectic day when they were both under pressure to complete a quarterly report and prepare for a meeting with the board of directors: "You are my inspiration, Judith. Somehow, you bring out the best in me. Next to being a bank president, the most important thing I've done in my life was help you to become vice president.''

GETTING A HEAD START ON YOUR CAREER WHILE SEARCHING FOR A MENTOR

As with the relationship to a friend, the relationship between a mentor and protégée can't be forced. It must happen spontaneously, and in order for it to take root and grow, the two must have compatible temperaments, values, humor, and intellects; they must experience the compelling attraction to each other that is often called chemistry.

Trying to find a mentor through direct questioning of potential candidates will be as unrewarding as searching for diamonds in a coal mine. Just as the naive question ''Won't you be my friend?'' will evoke embarrassed expressions or fumbling reassurances of your likable personal qualities from anyone over twelve years old, asking a likely candidate directly, ''Will you be my mentor, please?'' will earn you the reputation of being unsophisticated, lacking in business acumen, and a poor risk as a protégée. Ironically, the women who least appear to need mentors are the ones who find them.

But any ambitious woman knows that she can't sit back and wait to be found, either. There are less obvious approaches that may attract the mentor you've been wishing for. Just as there are ways to improve your chances of meeting friends, there are ways to make the conditions favorable for finding a mentor.

First, pay attention to your work. Don't be so intent on finding the right connections that you neglect putting 100 percent of your effort into your job. The best way to attract a mentor is to be outstanding at what you do; that takes hard work as well as ability. By following a standard of excellence, you will be getting a head start in your career, and a head start in finding a mentor.

But hard work is not enough to get ahead in your career or to find a mentor. You must be visible; you must let coworkers and, most importantly, the superiors who have the power to advance your career know that you are extremely accomplished at what you do and that you are ready for new challenges. Well-bred women have been taught not to brag, but there are ways of letting others know about your accomplishments without being branded as a braggart. When bosses or coworkers ask, "How are you?" respond by telling them about your latest success at work. Mention that you have just landed a new account or have found a new way to increase efficiency and cut costs. Or, when the office gossip approaches your desk, don't duck away; give him some tantalizing rumors about how well your work is going.

Business is no place for modesty concerning your ability. If you have won an award, it is not gauche to display it on your desk. If there is a common problem you and other workers share, it is not pushy to offer to head a committee to resolve it, since you have thought of a number of solutions. If you have thought of suggestions to help your company save money, it is not presumptuous to send them, with a polite note, to the company president. In business, making yourself stand out by touting your successes shows that you have abundant self-interest and ambition—qualities that mentors admire.

But even if you are the best in your field, regarding yourself as emotionally invulnerable, completely independent, and immune from mistakes will send potential mentors scurrying in the opposite direction—to a woman who asks her superiors for assistance with tough problems, follows through with their suggestions, and is appreciative of their advice. The woman who attracts mentors also thanks her bosses for their criticism of her work; she is judicious about arguing with them and avoids being defensive. If she feels the criticism is valid, she will do her best to improve; if not, she seeks to resolve the differences amicably or move on.

If you can arrange to meet your potential mentor in a social situation, you're a giant leap ahead in getting her or him interested in you as a protégée. In most instances, your mentor will move in different social circles, but if you know anyone peripherally in a potential mentor's circle, perhaps an introduction can be arranged. Before meeting the mentor of your dreams, it is helpful to do some background research: Does she or he like tennis, sailing, skiing? Antiques, sculpture, or classical music? Fine wine or aged Scotch? If you have similar interests, your chances of finding that elusive chemistry are greater.

Once you have met your potential mentor, don't be afraid to express your admiration. Listen attentively; graciously offer a few honest compliments, but don't overdo it. Flattery can backfire. In her book *Blackberry Winter,* Margaret Mead said she enrolled as a student in anthropologist Franz Boas's class and nodded each time he asked a rhetorical question. She attracted his attention, and with his help as a mentor, she launched her career as an internationally renowned anthropologist.[12]

There are a few guidelines about whom not to choose as your potential mentor. Don't choose your direct boss, don't choose anyone you don't like as a person, no matter how powerful a position that individual holds, and don't choose a man simply because you are personally or sexually attracted to him. He must possess the skills and power you need to get on the career fast track. Common values and personalities that comfortably mesh are more important than the gender of a mentor.

Many successful women have chosen their direct boss as their mentor, but it is better to find a mentor who is at least two levels above you. Often your immediate boss will have little influence over advancing your career, and if you prove to be a fast learner and hard worker, it is tempting for your boss to keep you in your current position as a valued employee rather than advance your career. Also, choosing someone higher in the organization than your immediate boss allows you to discuss boss-employee relations with your mentor—an important part of learning office politics and business decorum.

Although admiration aids the process of identification, falling in love with a mentor is not a prerequisite for business success; actually, this less-than-professional situation can be a hindrance to your work. Nancy W. Collins, in her book *Professional Women and Their Mentors,* warned women that searching for a mentor is not like searching for a husband.[13] The mentor-protégée relationship is temporary and primarily business-related; under no circumstances should a woman rely on it as her primary source of emotional satisfaction.

To preclude the possibility of depending solely on one person for feedback on your work, you might try to find two or more mentors to help you with different aspects of your career simultaneously. Gaining different perspectives on your work is a smart business move, and by not placing all your emotional and business eggs in one basket, you're providing yourself with extra career security. However, some women prefer one mentor at a time because of the intensely committed relationship they can develop and maintain. This must be an individual decision based on your business and emotional needs.

If, after you've done everything reasonably possible to make yourself visible without becoming an outrageous show-off or nuisance and if you have performed your job duties conscientiously, you still don't attract a mentor, your career is not necessarily hampered. Mentors may hold the career ladder for a woman, but the responsibility of climbing it is hers. If a potential mentor is not attracted to you, don't be discouraged. Lack of interest doesn't automatically mean that you are not smart enough or personally and socially attractive enough to be a protégée. Many individuals in a position to mentor are too busy to take on the responsibility of a protégée. Some may not recognize your talent because of shortsightedness; others simply may not have the temperament to mentor.

When Sybil, a manager in the retail industry, decided she was serious about her career, she used every ploy she could to interest a mentor, to no avail. She eventually decided to give up her search, and she has found, to her surprise, that she is doing well, in terms of salary and promotions, on her own. She confided:

I had made a clear decision that I wanted a career; being successful was definitely a priority. My decision came after being in the job market for a number of years. I had been coasting up to that point. In order to get the right type of experience and make the connections I needed, I even took a lower-paying job that had career advantages. I measured immediate income against potential future income and felt the payback was considerable. In effect, I invested in job experience. My career path was critical; income and convenience became secondary.

I eventually got to the mid-management stage and began to look for a coach, a mentor, someone in a more senior position who could teach me, advise me, and support me. This turned out to be a major barrier. As one man, a vice president, told me, 'To interest a sponsor, you must have promise, you must present yourself as someone worth investing in, and your advocate will expect a return on the help he offers.' Unfortunately, this VP's contention proved only too true. Male mentors did not feel I would be able to make it to the top and were reluctant to invest in me. Women in a position to guide my career were practically nonexistent. It now appears that I will not have the advantage of a mentor. However, I have every reason to assume that I will become successful enough on my own to offer the mentor advantage to a younger woman.

MENTOR, PROTÉGÉE, AND SEX: A DISASTROUS CAREER COMBINATION?

Because the mentor-protégée relationship develops into a close emotional liaison, the boundaries between work, friendship, and sexual involvement can become blurred. If emotional intimacy between a mentor and his protégée creates the spark that ignites motivation and creativity at work, can sexual involvement provide a similar impetus?

The answer we received from protégées was unanimous. It was a resounding "no." Sexual involvement with a mentor, the women said, never helped anyone's career, and in some instances it hindered or seriously harmed a woman's career. Nancy W. Collins, in her study *Professional Women and Their Mentors,* evoked a similar response when she asked over 400 women the question: "If you have had sex with your mentor, do you advise it?" About one fifth of the women said they had a sexual relationship with their mentor, but all of them regretted it.[14] The evidence clearly suggests that if a woman is headed toward the boardroom, she is unwise to spend time with her mentor in the bedroom. While a man may be able to have a discreet affair with his protégée and not suffer serious consequences, the woman is not protected by a position of power. She is in a vulnerable position as a protégée, and she is open to criticism and derision from coworkers due to the still-in-effect double standard. "She slept her way to the top" and "See what happens when women are allowed to work with men" are familiar comments. The protégée and mentor who dare to pursue a sexual and a business relationship simultaneously are in danger of losing their credibility. Their judgment and morality may be questioned, and the woman's ability may be suspect.

More damaging than office gossip for a protégée is her own uncertainty about her ability. Once she is involved in a sexual liaison, she may not know herself whether she is moving ahead in her career because her work is first-rate or because her mentor feels grateful for her sexual favors or guilty over his relationship with her, particularly if he is married. Reassurances from the mentor concerning her capability at work will be more difficult to interpret when the protégée knows he has his own emotional and sexual interests to protect. In the face of such uncertainty concerning her ability, a woman is bound to lose some measure of confidence and self-esteem, the very qualities that are needed in abundance to advance her career.

Monica, twenty-four years old, naively thought a sexual liaison with her mentor would not hurt her career. In retrospect, she would never have consented to the affair if she had realized the consequences ahead of time. Monica arrived fresh from graduate school to work as an administrative assistant for an executive at a management consulting firm. After six months on the job, she caught the attention of the company's vice president at a meeting she attended with her boss. When she was introduced to Charles Warwick, she mentioned a few ideas she had for improving the efficiency of her department. Charles was amenable to them and asked her to prepare a memo with her suggestions. A week later, he asked her to lunch.

Monica readily accepted the invitation, and she found that the vice president appreciated workers like her with creative initiative. He not only used her suggestions but promoted her to assistant manager, a position in which she could work more closely with him. Their mentor-protégée relationship developed quickly and naturally. Charles taught Monica the skills and style of effective managers.

Although Charles was eighteen years her senior and was married, Monica was attracted to him. She discerned, by the frequency of their lunches and by the way he looked at her, that the attraction was mutual. One morning, while Monica was working on a report with Charles, he kissed her. A full-blown affair, which lasted for two years, ensued.

Even though they tried to be discreet, office gossip was rampant. And despite Charles's warning Monica from the start that he did not want to divorce his wife, she was resentful when he wanted to end the affair. Monica was transferred to another department soon after Charles made his decision to discontinue their trysts. He felt they were getting "dangerously involved" and feared that both his career and his marriage might be destroyed if they continued. So that they could "forget each other," Charles felt it was best that Monica and he no longer work so closely. At first Monica thought the move to a different department would be best for her, too, but she found a resentment among her coworkers that made her working atmosphere intolerable. Apparently, the women viewed her as a seducer who for her own career goals had almost ruined the mild-mannered, well-liked vice president's credibility. The men, on the other hand, felt that since the boss had "dumped" her, Monica was fair game sexually. After six months of trying to regain her former reputation as a hard worker and a winner, Monica found her position hopeless, and she looked for work elsewhere. Although Charles gave her a recommendation, she had to start over, in a new company, to regain confidence in her ability to get along on her own. Emotionally, she licked her wounds for two years before she met a single man at her new job whom she eventually married.

If both mentor and protégée are unattached, there may still be career repercussions for both of them, but particularly for the woman, if they become romantically involved. Career decisions may be seriously compromised; attention may be diverted away from work to the romantic relationship. Credibility, again, is often marred. And if the protégée marries her mentor, she may be stifled in her career; promoting a protégée is considered good business practice, but promoting a spouse is frowned upon as a form of nepotism.

Despite the ease with which a mentor-protégée relationship can slip into a sexual relationship, it is by no means inevitable. Just as women who are friends with men can control whether or not an attraction will turn sexual, so, too, a protégée can honestly discuss her feelings with her mentor and tactfully turn down sex while keeping her business relationship with him intact. If the mentor at this point wishes to discontinue the relationship, she can assume that the motive for his initiating the relationship was sexual rather than career-oriented and that she is better off without such a mentor.

Unless the subject of sex is brought up by her mentor, however, it is best for a woman not to broach it. If a protégée initiated a discussion about her sexual or romantic feelings with her mentor in an effort to set limits, her remarks would probably be taken as a sexual invitation rather than a discouragement. Once the topic of sexual involvement has been introduced, an intimacy is established that can't easily be banished. Indeed, a woman's hint of attraction to him may influence a mentor to view her differently—more as a woman than as a protégée.

Yet we do not recommend that mentor and protégée attempt to remain distant and unemotional; it is by revealing their caring and admiration for each other that their relationship can best benefit their careers. Research indicates that the mentor who is able to form a closeness with subordinates has a more powerful effect on their learning than the one who is more formal and distant. According to James G. Clawson and Kathy E. Kram in "Managing Cross-Gender Mentoring," a balance must be struck between intimacy and business in the mentor-protégée relationship to ensure that work will proceed uninterrupted and with the greatest efficiency.[15] Each must be attuned to the other so that when one crosses an intimacy boundary which might endanger the working relationship, the other will step back.

Clawson and Kram suggest that it is important for women and men who work together to understand the difference between "personal" and "private" matters. For instance, your health and how you cope with pressure at home and on the job are personal matters, but they are acceptable topics of conversation between a mentor and protégée since they are areas that may affect one's work. But marital difficulties or fantasies, sexual or otherwise, are private topics that do not make for a successful mentor-protégée relationship.[16]

It is often damaging to your career if coworkers suspect you are having a sexual relationship with your mentor, whether you have one or not. This means not working late alone with your mentor. Avoid touching each other, even if only innocently on the shoulder or hand, don't routinely lunch together alone, and avoid business trips together, if you can.

Romantic partners often share inside jokes or expressions, and they tend to interact spontaneously. Mentors and protégées would be wise to let others in on their private jokes or inside expressions, and they would do well to let others know of their respective schedules well in advance. Naturally, a protégée's work should be of top quality, and it should be highly visible, so that gossip concerning her sexual-vs-work ability never gets a chance to start. She should never let anyone, including herself, doubt her business skills.

Some women may protest that these restrictions are unfair and even harsh—and they are! However, along with technical competence, no other factor is as critical to a woman's career as the personal image she projects. Recall the scandal and subsequent fate of Mary Cunningham as documented in her book *Power Play: What Really Happened at Bendix.* Sexual gossip about her and her mentor, William Agee, president of Bendix Corporation, forced Cunningham to leave her high-level position.

When a mentor and protégée enjoy a productive relationship without crossing sexual boundaries, there are immeasurable rewards: career advancement minus office gossip concerning why the protégée was promoted, self-respect at maintaining standards of morality if one or both parties are married, a confidence in one's own business ability, freedom from guilt or embarrassment, and possibly a lasting friendship. If you are ever tempted to indulge your sexual fantasies with your mentor, first think carefully about the benefits of not doing so.

BEWARE:
MENTORS ARE FALLIBLE

It is easy for a protégée to idolize her mentor, to believe that he is the knight in shining armor who will save her from the hard work and drudgery of making it on her own. She may fantasize that he is the one who will save her from the oblivion of the secretarial pool or the poverty of the undiscovered artist; he will show the world how worthwhile she is. In reality, a mentor rescues no one. In fact, he may make his protégée work harder and longer than she ever has before. He is no more than a person who can help a protégée to do what she was always able to do on her own but somehow lacked the initiative or power to do by herself. He may ease the path of success for her, but he never will be able to rescue her from her own weaknesses or inadequacies: A mentor is no more than a catalyst; he is not the instrument of success himself.

If a protégée does not make these distinctions, she will be destined to be forever dependent on her mentor. She will never understand that she is the moving force in her success, that she can make her own decisions and evaluate her own work. A mentor who does not allow her to take credit for her own victories or who must have a say in all her decisions will ultimately hinder, rather than help, her career.

To avoid overdependency in a mentor-protégée relationship, try to keep a realistic perspective; remember that you, as a protégée, are contributing as much to the relationship as your mentor and that he has as much to gain from it as you. This may be particularly difficult for women to do, because they have been socialized to denigrate their talents and take a passive role, but it is essential for career success to take credit for your work.

Make sure you maintain other friends and business contacts and, if you have the emotional energy and time it requires, other mentors. Accept your mentor's input, but don't be afraid to make your own decisions or to challenge your mentor if you feel it is warranted.

Just as relying on only one friend to fulfill all your emotional needs is both unrealistic and risky, relying totally on your mentor to enable you to fulfill your career ambitions can be dangerous. Betty Harragan, author of *Games Mother Never Taught You,* was quoted in *Savvy* as saying: "It's easy to bet on the wrong horse. It's no longer safe to assume that a powerful man will move up in a straight line in one corporation, as was common in business once."[17]

If your mentor's career topples, your ambitions are also frequently cut short. A protégée's career reputation often reflects her mentor's until she sets out on her own. Lois, a thirty-one-year-old accountant, had been closely tied to a senior accountant in her division as his protégée when funds he was responsible for were reported missing. She explained: "He was never proven guilty of embezzlement—there wasn't even enough evidence to go to court—but he was fired, and three of his top accountants went along with him, including me. It was difficult for me to find another job with the same prestige and pay, since the company would not give any of us recommendations, and my mentor's reputation was shot. So linking myself with him was a hindrance rather than an advantage for me. His career had, in effect, been killed, and mine had been seriously injured. I trusted him. I really don't think he was guilty, but our superiors did, and that's what mattered."

Jealousy, which is occasionally present in any close relationship, will almost inevitably play a part in any mentor-protégée relationship. Sometimes a protégée's success may be threatening to a mentor, and at other times the mentor's status and prestige may evoke envy in his protégée. Women in particular often have to work longer and harder than men to gain the same position in the career world, and women often do not receive equivalent pay. Inequities related to sex may be especially grating to a protégée who has a male mentor, but she will have to remember that he is not personally responsible for them. A mentor who accepts the risks involved in grooming a protégée is probably doing all that he can to help deserving women get ahead in business.

Sometimes a mentor will overwhelm a protégée with hard work and long hours while he seems to be relaxing—and collecting all the prestige and praise. This situation quite naturally causes jealousy. But, for a time, a protégée may have to swallow her ego and accept it; she will have to understand that her mentor went through the same difficult training period she is struggling with and that, in time, she will become totally independent of him. Then she can bask in the prestige and praise that she earns on her own.

Perhaps even harder to deal with than mentor-protégée jealousies is the jealousy of others directed toward them. If coworkers reveal their envy, try to minimize the importance of your
relationship with your mentor. Don't brag about being chosen
as a protégée; instead, emphasize your envious coworkers' strong
points. Attempt to spend more time with your neglected office
friends if they express jealousy or resentment over the time you
spend with your mentor. Sometimes discussing feelings of jealousy directly with office friends defuses the situation.

Jealousy may also surface in a protégée's spouse, especially
if the mentor is male. When a married woman has a close emotional relationship with a man other than her husband and that
male is the object of her admiration and daily work life, it is
difficult to deny his importance. But she must, if she is to keep
a lid on her husband's jealousy. When she is with her spouse,
she must focus on him, just as when she is with her mentor, she
must devote her full attention to him.

If there is no stoking of the fires of jealousy on her part, a
married protégée need not feel guilty about her ambitions or her
business relationships. Just as many women have decided to keep
their own friends despite their husband's preferences or jealousies, many have chosen to retain their mentors despite their husband's initial misgivings. Often, with time, a woman will find
that as she pursues her work with serious determination, she will
win over an ambivalent husband. As he begins to understand the
importance of her career to her, he will start to admire her ability and spirit. If he doesn't, a serious discussion of her goals
and his is in order.

If a protégée feels that she is being taken advantage of or
being manipulated by her mentor to satisfy his own needs while
hers are being neglected, she should express her dissatisfaction
in a nonaccusatory manner. If she is overburdened with work,
for instance, she might explain the situation; perhaps her skills
are not yet up to par, or she is simply lacking confidence. If she
feels her mentor is heading in the wrong direction—if their goals

and work style are divergent—only open, honest communication can resolve these basic differences. If they can't be resolved and if she continues to be at odds with her mentor for some time, perhaps she had better move on.

GOODBYE, MENTOR;
HELLO, FRIEND

Mentors and protégées must understand from the beginning that theirs is a temporary connection. Any effective mentor understands that the ability of the protégée to strike out on her own is the ultimate test of the success of their interaction. As one mentor of many women and men, a writing instructor, put it, "A good mentor eventually makes himself obsolete."

Yet parting is never easy. Just as parents and children feel ambivalent about "letting go," mentors and protégées are often loath to sever their ties. The protégée feels anxious about striking out on her own, even though her mentor has taught her everything she needs to know to be independent, and she may feel guilty for leaving him. Women in particular are prone to guilt at parting, since they have been taught from earliest childhood to please others, to hang on to others, and to protect others from emotional pain. Finally, some women may fear surpassing their mentor, especially if he is a male. Women are sometimes unsure of how their career success will be viewed by those close to them; mentors, like many spouses, may not look kindly on being surpassed by a woman at work, even if they trained and nurtured that woman.

Research suggests that women, more than men, have difficulty letting go of their mentors. Nancy W. Collins, in her study of 440 professional women cited earlier, found that women's relationships with mentors usually last longer than men's—sometimes longer than is beneficial to their careers. When the relationship does dissolve, it is often due to geographic relocation, a job change, or a gradual drifting apart. Sometimes it ends bitterly as the protégée seeks to liberate herself in a manner reminiscent of a child-parent independence struggle. Occasionally, there may be an initial cooling off as the mentor and protégée become equals; this may be followed by a warm, moderately close friendship. For instance, thirty-three-year-old Pia, a physician, continued her friendship with her former mentor for several years. She described the course of their relationship this way:

> Sheila gave me tremendous support and encouragement. I was very close to her—enormously and deeply affected by her, in fact. She really taught me how to doctor, how to pick up subtle diagnostic signals in a patient, how to conduct a practice, and how to be cognizant of the politics of medicine. We saw each other socially and played tennis together, but medicine was the foundation of our relationship. She had an unusual commitment to medicine and was very willing to give of herself. I realized later that this quality was offered only as long as I remained a novice. As the balance of giving and receiving became more equal, our relationship became more distant. Our friendship is more mutual now. I'm as likely to give her advice as she is me. But I no longer experience the intimacy we once shared.

Sometimes a mentor fosters dependency in order to feel needed, powerful, or useful and when the protégée becomes more independent wants nothing more to do with her. If a friendship lasts, it will be a casual one, no longer as intense as the mentor-protégée relationship. But this is not always so. The subsequent friendships between mentors and their protégées are as varied as their personalities and their emotional and career needs. Women, perhaps because they value the intimacy of friendship so highly or because they are not afraid to admit their dependency needs, more often attempt to retain their friendly ties with their mentors. Men, taught to be independent, are more likely to move on without looking back.

Even if a man forms a close attachment to his mentor, the

relationship is likely to be secondary to his career progress. In order to deny his dependency on his mentor, a man may consciously or unconsciously distance himself by causing a rift, by creating disagreements. A woman, however, is often loath to cause such confrontations.

Yet, according to Gail Sheehy, a woman must not hold on to her mentor beyond the time he is useful to her in her career. In order to succeed, she must become independent. In *The Mentor Connection,* Sheehy said: "From the female case histories I have collected, it is my observation that women in business who remain reliant cannot advance to the top position and are likely to become a millstone to their mentors, who usually, in the end, discard them." [18]

When is the time right to leave your mentor? Each woman must answer that question for herself, and each, if she is honest with herself, will know when she no longer needs her mentor's expertise. An article in *Savvy,* "50 Ways to Leave Your Mentor" by Marcia Stamell suggested that the optimal time to terminate the mentor-protégée relationship is after two to three years, when differences of opinion surface often, when you no longer want your name linked with your mentor's, or finally—and this point we feel is the most important—when you know you can make it on your own. [19]

Frequently, leave taking is not final and dramatic. It happens in gradual stages, just as a child grows independent of her parents in slow, almost imperceptible stages. This makes the final parting easier to bear, although sadness and anxiety are a natural part of separation. Yet the sadness is tinged with joy and pride as the protégée eagerly embarks on new challenges and new relationships, while the mentor takes note of her ambition and independence with pleasure; after all, these are the qualities he nurtured in her.

Sometimes leave taking is more drastic. Because of geographical relocation, conflict, illness, or death, the mentor-protégée relationship may be severed suddenly. If it had previously developed into an emotionally close relationship, a time of mourning is to be expected. Losing a mentor can be as devastating as losing a member of the family or a close friend. One's career, as well as one's emotional life, is affected.

But many women we interviewed gradually shifted their status from protégée to friend easily and naturally. They were able to develop lasting friendships with both female and male mentors when geographical distance or career moves did not interfere. In these instances, the emotional part of the mentor-protégée relationship had become as important as the aid that each gave the other in her or his career. A new social equality between mentor and protégée often led to a greater appreciation of each other's personal qualities, with less emphasis given to their respective careers. The social and professional distance that made friendship difficult, if not impossible, in the beginning of the relationship gave way to increasing closeness. When the mentor and the protégée had grown close, without infringing on each other's independence, they were free to be friends.

CHAPTER

9

CRIMES OF
THE HEART:
DESTRUCTIVE
FRIENDSHIPS

Indisputably, friendship can provide the psychological nutrients so important for optimal enjoyment of life. However, like all interpersonal relationships, friendship is potentially harmful. Thus, as in parent-child, teacher-student, or doctor-patient relationships, the consequences of interaction may be constructive or debilitating. Consider the myth that students need only have knowledgeable teachers to grow intellectually. When the data are examined, we find that teachers who provide a sound emotional relationship with their pupils elicit as much as five times the achievement over the course of a year as those who coldly pursue intellectual development. Documentation of similar relationship issues, most notably the psychotherapy relationship, is growing. The direct implication is that the quality of an interpersonal relationship may retard or advance an individual's psychological and intellectual development.

As a result of friendship, some women have been influenced not only to think differently about superficial matters but to transform their attitudes about life profoundly. In one investigation, improvement was greater on several psychological indexes when a troubled individual consulted with a friend who understood her than when she saw a professional psychotherapist. There is some evidence that appearance can change and that physical health is improved by some relationships. Many physicians who have become alert to interpersonal sources of stress have been able to prove that for some patients asthma, skin eruptions, hypertension, and other physical symptoms disappeared with the development of more satisfying relationships.

While constructive friendships help us to feel and function at our best, destructive friendships, those that involve unresolved or hidden conflict, envy, invasion of privacy, or other negative consequences, can cause us to feel and act miserably. Being obliged to remain in close contact with someone on whom we are dependent may, if this person is obnoxious and overly demanding, literally give rise to a "pain in the neck," headache, digestive upsets, and other psychosomatic maladies. The experience of those in the psychological professions, for example, has amply demonstrated that the relationship of parents to their children, especially when parents make excessive or contradictory demands, can be an influential factor in the development of neurotic or psychotic symptoms.

While friends don't normally drive us into psychotic episodes, they can affect us in powerful ways. One woman, distressed over an argument with a friend, explained how a close relationship that went sour changed her beliefs: "I was so angry and so upset about the falling out with my friend that I never went to church afterward—and I had always been a religious person. I had actually convinced my former friend to go to church earlier in our relationship, but when I saw how hypocritical she was, I refused to be there with her."

We think of the ending of love affairs as evoking a period of mourning, but we hardly ever think of friendship difficulties as causing serious disruptions in our lives. The ending of a friendship that was once sustaining might result in a period of mourning similar to the grief one encounters after a divorce or the death of a close family member.

THE DARK SIDE
OF INTIMACY

Women's friendships are influenced by their first female-to-female experience, the mother-daughter bond; consequently, many powerful transference issues come into play in female friendships. Women often make demands on each other that they wouldn't think of making on men, just as a daughter demands her mother's nurturance in a traditional household while her father often remains relatively aloof. Because women's friendships are characterized by intimacy, vulnerability, and emotional dependence, they are often rife with unfulfilled expectations and subsequent hurt.

One thirty-four-year-old woman, an illustrator, mused about the differences between women's and men's friendships: "Men can easily gain a sense of camaraderie with other men. But women are constantly judging themselves and each other. It seems men can separate things more clearly—love from sex, friendship from business, their feelings from their intellect—but women are likely to get the lines blurred. I think men are more accepting of each other than women, but then, it may be because they can compartmentalize their relationships more, and thus, a man won't be disappointed if a friend can't be everything to him as a friend. It might be that men's relationships with each other are based on lower expectations than women's, too."

If lowered expectations breed male camaraderie, then intimacy, the intimacy that women friends often share, is born of intense caring, enormous expectations, but also disappointment, conflict, and contempt. Like a child who shows her unpleasant, undisciplined side to her mother to test the limits of her love, a woman who is extremely close to her friend will risk being totally herself when with her; this means she will show her weaknesses and irritating qualities as well as her strengths and likable traits. The friend is expected to accept both the negative and the positive side of the individual, just as the mother was expected to accept her daughter's less-than-perfect behavior.

Since women's wants and needs never correspond exactly, some conflict in a long-term, close friendship is inevitable. As relationships between mothers and daughters are often filled with ambivalent feelings, so, too, are women's friendships. A tolerance of such ambiguity, an ability to accept the mixed emotions of loving some aspect of a friend's nature and disliking other facets of her character, is necessary for intimate friendship to endure.

Besides tolerating ambiguity, long-term, intimate friends must also be able to understand that reciprocity is not always immediate. In any friendship, but particularly in intimate friendships, when there is much to gain as well as much to lose, a feeling of balance, or equity, must be in effect for it to survive. For example, when Anne babysits for her friend Gwen, drives her to the garage when her car breaks down, and a week later invites her to dinner, she expects something in return for her efforts—not exactly the same services or favors she provided, but something equivalent. Perhaps Gwen can feed Anne's cat when she goes on vacation, bring Anne home-made soup when she is sick, or take her to lunch for her birthday. In casual relationships, such reciprocity is expected within a short time, or the party who does all the giving will feel used; however, research by E. Hatfield and J. Traupmann suggests that the desire for repayment of favors soon after they are given diminishes as a relationship grows stronger.[1]

Equity in a friendship pertains to the emotional sphere, too. Steve Duck, in his book, *Friends, for Life,* states that "researchers have found that people will be happy with their relationships when they feel that their rewards are equitable with their efforts. If they put up with a lot in a relationship (e.g., if they have a friend who has very severe changes in mood, a quick temper and is often irritable) then the amount of love, help and advice or entertainment that they receive from the partner will also have to be a lot."[2]

Generally, women are more attentive to their friendships than men; as lifelong caretakers they are keenly responsive to subtle changes in a friend's personality. Because their friendships are often so intimate and so important to them, women analyze them and try to repair and renew relationships more often than men. But women also tend to blame themselves rather than external circumstances, if a friendship deteriorates or fails.

With the new wave of feminism, the power and promise of women's friendships is only starting to be recognized. If we are to examine women's friendships, we must understand how closely related are the positive and negative sides of intimacy. We must acknowledge that women's friendships, just like other highly charged emotional relationships, have a dark side.

FRIENDSHIP TROUBLES

Jealousy

If there is a negative trait most frequently attributed to women, it probably is that "green-eyed monster": jealousy. When women are raised to be supportive, and when they know it is crucial for them to stick together because of their inferior status in our society, why are they prone to be divided by jealousy? Or is it a myth that women are more jealous of each other than men are?

If women are more jealous than men, it may be because they rightfully feel more deprived than men. As numerous sociologists of both sexes have pointed out, women are as capable of showing scorn for each other as any oppressed people—blacks, Jews, or Hispanics, to name a few. To a woman living on the periphery of male society and longing to be accepted by the dominant group, the safest recipients of rage are others of her sex. This sometimes occurs to the woman who breaks sex-role barriers and climbs to a high-level professional position; instead of being warmly received, she is ostracized and penalized. It is one of the ironies of our times that women of accomplishment, pioneers who need supportive friendship, experience a good deal of rejection from other women. A thirty-seven-year-old attorney's experience:

It is difficult for me to find friends who delight in my success instead of resenting it. More than once I have found myself the unexpected target of another woman's wrath concerning my achievements. One woman went so far as to claim that I had no right taking a man's job! I really don't know how to react when this occurs. It is not that I brag about my work or draw attention to my accomplishments; I don't. As a matter of fact, for a while I fell into a pattern of placating other women by deprecating myself. That was stupid and I no longer do it. Now I seek only women who are my professional equals as friends. I see this as unfortunate and a form of elitism, but there is just too much resentment the other way.

Women constantly assess how they are faring, socially and professionally, by their friends' progress. If one friend leaps ahead while another gets stuck in the status quo, the less fortunate friend may feel threatened and jealous. The more deprived and hopeless she feels about improving her lot, the more likely that she will feel jealous.

Pangs of jealousy may be particularly strong in an unattached woman when her friend meets a man. If we look at the dynamics in terms of the mother-daughter relationship, it is easy to understand why a friend's lover can be so threatening; he will bring back feelings of jealousy concerning the original family threesome of mother, father, and daughter. Just as the daughter felt abandoned when her mother received her father's attention, so, too, she feels left out of the love triangle when her friend becomes seriously involved with a man.

In addition, a woman who has found a man, according to the values of our society, is validated; her relationship with him is viewed by society as primary—more important than relationships she may have with women. Thus, even though her friend may reassure the left-out woman that she still cares for her as much as ever, she is bound to feel particularly lonely, discarded, and jealous.

Dependency

Dependency is not necessarily destructive; we are all dependent on others for the exchange of goods and services as well as for companionship and emotional gratification. Men generally gain all the nurturing they require from women, but, as we have noted previously, women must often turn to other women for their nurturance. It is only when women find their dependency need insatiable, when they can't get enough emotional support from others no matter how much they receive, that they need be concerned about their dependency.

If a woman did not receive the nurturing and direction she needed in childhood to develop an independent identity separate from her mother she may, in later life, unconsciously strive to fuse with others. She will not respect the boundaries of privacy that most individuals construct; she may not understand the need to be alone, because she is not comfortable in her own company. Emotionally healthy individuals, unlike the overdependent person, enjoy their friends for a time but also look forward to solitude and other activities; otherwise the relationship becomes wearing. Indeed, there is evidence that the most integrated personalities need and actively seek solitude in order to contemplate and discover their authentic feelings and beliefs.

Women tend to have a wider "range of caring" than men. Men often shrug off a friend's affairs, a neighbor's financial problems, or a cousin's marital split. Women, in contrast, take these problems to heart and are drained by them; they turn to a friend to recharge themselves. When a woman cannot get the emotional nurturance she needs from friends, she may sometimes deny the need, but it surfaces in less direct ways. The woman may feel that there is something lacking in her life, but she won't be able to pinpoint what it is; she may become depressed or self-destructive, depending on alcohol or drugs to fill the void.

When the overdependent woman seeks friends, she often looks for a woman whom she considers "strong," believing that she will gain the emotional ability she needs to stand on her own—but she will be sorely disillusioned. Emotional strength comes from within the individual; it is not absorbed from others.

For example, Sue, a twenty-eight-year-old secretary and struggling part-time artist, created distance between herself and her friend, Violet, a thirty-five-year-old owner of a retail clothing business, by attempting to become too close; her incessant clinging became suffocating. The two women met at a university seminar on twentieth-century art, and because of their mutual interest in abstract expressionism, they struck up a conversation that led them to have coffee together after class. Violet thought Sue was a funny, self-effacing, sensitive woman, and Sue admired Violet for her intelligence and independence. After several pleasant lunches, Violet, who needed a sales manager in her store, asked Sue if she would like the job. Sue accepted immediately. Violet was very pleased with Sue's dedication to her job. The women increasingly confided in each other, and Sue, a single woman, told Violet, who was divorced, about her many failures at love. It seemed that Sue's men friends often complained that she was "too clinging" or "expected too much too soon."

When Sue first started to confide in Violet, Violet was pleased that her friend trusted her and heeded her counsel. Sue, in some ways, reminded Violet of her thirteen-year-old daughter, who, unfortunately, was at the stage of adolescence when she never willingly followed her mother's advice. Yet after several months Violet's pleasure wore off; Sue's need for attention and direction was becoming consuming. When Violet began to give her friend polite excuses for not having lunch or dinner with her, Sue felt hurt and said so. She played on Violet's guilt, saying, "I need a friend so badly, and lately, you're not there when I most need you."

Within a year, Sue and Violet's friendship disintegrated to

the point where they barely talked to each other. Sue felt "rejected," and Violet felt "tired and put-upon." Sue left for another sales job in an art supplies store, never quite forgiving her friend for her "neglect."

Sue had been searching for a mother, not a friend. The oldest and only girl in a family of three children, Sue was raised by a mother who "doted on the boys" and expected Sue to help take care of her younger brothers. Sue lacked the nurturance she needed in childhood and sought to find it in Violet. Sue eventually gained a greater sense of self through psychotherapy and a supportive network of friends she met at a women's group.

In some instances, particularly in a crisis, dependency may be only temporary and not based on earlier deprivation. For example, when Bernadette, age thirty, broke up with her live-in lover, she felt so painfully lonely that she could not bear to be alone at times; she would then call her friend Joanne at odd times, day or night. Joanne unfailingly provided solace and understanding, even though at times she resented the intrusion on her family life.

After about three months of almost daily calls, Bernadette's need for assistance subsided. She was getting over her grief and was circulating socially again. When she hadn't heard from Joanne for a couple of weeks, she decided to call, not to ask for solace this time but simply to chat. Bernadette was shocked when the normally mild-mannered Joanne attacked her angrily. "Don't you know when enough is enough? You're always on my back. You're always wanting me to rescue you. Don't you realize that I have a life of my own?"

After listening to a torrential outpouring of anger, Bernadette meekly apologized and suggested that her friend might have told her sooner if she felt put upon by her calls.

Joanne then admitted that she had difficulty being assertive, especially with friends. She realized later that she had allowed Joanne to become dependent on her by not letting her know her own needs. By asserting her need for privacy, a woman can often avoid the destructive effects of overdependency in a friendship.

And a woman who temporarily needs a large amount of emotional tending because of some traumatic event she has suffered would do well to seek solace from a large network of friends rather than just one. It is a mistake to believe that only one particular person can help or understand you.

Whether it is done out of guilt or genuine concern, a woman who encourages dependence is doing her friend an injustice. Catering to excessive dependency will do nothing to bolster a friend's self-confidence; she may, in fact, regress to a state in which she feels helpless without you. A woman who wishes to take care of her friends may have her own dependency problems; she may need others to depend on her to feel important or needed. For her own emotional growth as well as her friends', it is best for her to let go and allow others to handle their own lives.

Approval Seeking

From earliest childhood, girls are taught to define themselves in terms of others. They are told by society that to be truly feminine they must be nurturing, appealing, and pleasing to others. It is not surprising, then, that some women equate their self-worth with how much they are able to satisfy those who are important in their lives. An overdependent woman believes that approval from those she depends on will assure her of her very survival. Because an overdependent woman has lacked the nurturance she needed earlier in her life, she is not likely to risk losing her current source of emotional sustenance by asserting her own needs. It's too risky.

In this way, a woman becomes prisoner to the needs of her family and friends, yet she is doing no one—not them, not herself—any favor by being obsequious. By not allowing her true needs or feelings to surface even if they cause displeasure in others, she is denying herself, and those with whom she comes in contact, any genuine friendship.

For example, Genevieve, a thirty-six-year-old homemaker and mother of two, complained to her physician of chronic depression, although she was physically well and by all outward standards was a fortunate woman. She considered her marriage "happy," and she claimed to love her family dearly. It was not until a neighbor gently suggested to Genevieve that she "never seemed to disagree with anyone" that she started to understand that her self-imposed sentence of having to be agreeable at all times might be contributing to her depression. Genevieve would never acknowledge outright that her constant amiability was counterfeit; that would be too threatening. After all, how could she tell her husband, for instance, that she found having sex every other night before going to sleep routine and boring? It would probably lead to a fight, and she could not tolerate the gulf it would cause between them. At the worst, he would abandon her, and Genevieve felt she could never get along on her own.

With her women friends, Genevieve also pretended to go along with their ideas. She would offer her own opinion only if she was certain her friends would agree with her. Genevieve had never formed any deep or lasting friendships; it seemed her friends sensed a hollowness and a lack of spontaneity that drove them away. It was not until she entered psychotherapy that she learned to understand that she was a worthwhile person in her own right, that she could disagree with others if she wanted to and that disagreement didn't necessarily lead to abandonment. With supportive therapy, she was eventually able to dare to be herself, and she found that her honesty and integrity brought her a flood of friends. With open discussion of her sexual differences with her husband, Genevieve's marriage improved also, and her depression lifted.

Dominance-Submissiveness

When one woman in a friendship continually feels the need to prove herself better than the other—either smarter, happier, richer, more beautiful, more powerful, or more popular—the relationship is destructive. If a friendship can't be enjoyed on its own terms as a mutual and relatively equitable give-and-take relationship, it is headed for failure. If a friendship includes a user and giver, a master and a slave, an advice giver and an advice seeker, a critic and a "mistake maker," then there is no equity in the relationship, and unless an attempt is made to improve it, antagonism and hostility are bound to result.

Nadine, a homemaker with three young children, explained how her friendship with Blanche started with a certain ambivalence on her part. Later, she found her defensive reaction to Blanche's critical nature and her uneasiness with Blanche's competitiveness well founded. In Nadine's words:

When I met Blanche at a PTA meeting, we discovered we lived around the block from each other. We soon started a casual friendship; we'd have coffee together occasionally, and talk about our kids, who were the same ages, four and nine, about community events, and sometimes about other people we knew. I guess it was the way Blanche had to build herself up by putting others down that bothered me. She spoke viciously about some women whom I didn't know well but who I thought didn't deserve such harsh criticism. If Blanche judged them so sharply, I wondered if she talked that way about me. But she bent over backward for me at first, and when I became pregnant again, she gave me a lovely baby shower.

Soon after I gave birth, Blanche told me she was going back to work. Both her daughters would be in school full-time, and she was anxious to resume her career as a real estate agent. She asked me, then, if I could babysit for her. She said she would pay me, but she couldn't afford very much. As a favor to her, I took her up on her offer.

After about two months, it was obvious that my children and Blanche's just weren't getting along. On top of that, I felt drained. I worked my schedule around her kids, and believe me, I was getting paid so little for the work I put into taking care of those children, it was laughable. I was doing Blanche a favor, but she acted as if she were doing me a favor, since, she said, she was sure I could use the money. I let the insult pass, but one day, when Blanche's nine-year-old daughter told my children, "My mom said you're not as rich as us because you don't really own your house—you rent it," I had had it. I quit, and Blanche was furious. She had the nerve to say I was ungrateful.

I realize now Blanche was very competitive with other women; she always wanted to be on top, and she always wanted more: more power, more status, more money. She wanted to make me into her submissive servant while she strutted around in her business suits and high heels and acted as though I was lucky to know her.

I'm more cautious about whom I make friends with now. I look for women who are happy with themselves, women who I feel can give me some wisdom. I don't want to get into the rut of keeping up with my friends materially. I don't think that's what friendship is about. And I certainly don't need friends like Blanche.

Women like Blanche, who need to feel superior even at the expense of causing hurt, have never developed trust and confidence in themselves. They cannot accept themselves as they are—in some respects probably superior to their friends, and in other ways inferior. They missed the support and praise they needed as they were growing up to feel worthy of love despite their failures and imperfections. Before she can accept others as they are without being judgmental, Blanche will have to feel better about herself. Nadine refrained from objecting to Blanche's underhandedness until she could no longer tolerate it. But if Nadine had felt any part of the friendship was worth saving, she might have stood up for her principles at the beginning of their relationship. Without directly attacking Blanche, she could have explained how odious she considered gossip; she could have mentioned she was not particularly interested in babysitting. Through her polite protests, Nadine might have given Blanche some insight into her grasping behavior, and perhaps she might have gained respect from Blanche.

The advice giver or critic who feels she is always right and who will become downright hostile in proving her superiority is a suspect friend. For instance, Kelly, a thirty-four-year-old magazine photographer, viewed her three-year-long friendship with her coworker Gloria as destructive in retrospect:

Gloria and I seemed to have a lot in common, and our relationship started out in a promising way. We traded ideas about photography a lot, and we went out together—to discos mostly, where we could meet men. But when Gloria met somebody whom she eventually married, our relationship changed. We still got together because her husband worked on Saturdays, and she liked my company. But I know she felt superior to me after she was married. When I sometimes spoke of my loneliness, she would say, "Well, I'm glad I'm married." And when I talked about my dates, she'd tell me what to do about the men in my life—who was worth pursuing, and who was "no good" in her opinion. I wouldn't have minded her advice, but I resented the way she gave it—as though she knew what was best for me, as if someone gave her the power to run my life. When I didn't do what she told me, she'd badger me about it.

After a while, she started to become sarcastic at my expense. She said she was just being funny, and she didn't understand why I was so sensitive that I couldn't take a joke now and then, but it didn't feel that way to me. I remember one day at work, the women in the office were having a little going-away party for me because I was taking a vacation in France. Well, we all had a good time, but just as I was leaving, Gloria said loudly so everyone could hear: "This is Kelly's last hope. If she can't find a man in France, she won't be able to find one anywhere." I was so embarrassed I could have fallen through the floor. Even though Gloria had let out a little giggle after her remark, no one else thought it was funny. It really wasn't funny at all. I left without saying anything, and I cried in the taxi going home. Afterward I just let our friendship cool; I didn't respond to her invitations to spend Saturdays with her anymore, and soon she stopped asking me.

Women who are covertly aggressive are angry at their target of attack or at some unresolved difficulty in their lives. Kelly later discovered through the office grapevine that Gloria's marriage was quickly disintegrating; the anger she felt toward her husband was probably being vented on her close friend Kelly, a safer target. For women, direct aggressiveness is traditionally taboo, and so Gloria vented her rage in disguised form: in "jokes" and sarcasm directed at Kelly. Kelly recalled: "Gloria was always angry underneath, but she never said so directly. She had a great anger toward men, but she would only let women know about it. Actually, I feel sorry for her now."

In dealing with a highly critical or covertly hostile friend, it is best to bring her anger to the surface, and with it the unresolved difficulty in the relationship or in her life. The next time a friend offers you negative criticism or offhanded sarcasm, ask her pointblank: "Is something bothering you? I hear a bit of hostility in your voice." Your covertly hostile friend will either confirm it, which will allow you to discuss constructively why she feels the way she does, or deny it, but with some discomfort or embarrassment, which may cause her to alter her behavior next time.

Sexual Betrayal

Sisterhood may be powerful, but is it marred by competition for men and an ancient tradition of betrayal? American society has certainly encouraged women to compete for men; a husband is still coveted by some women as proof of their desirability, their very identity. Particularly for older women, the odds against finding an eligible man are so frightening that "stealing" a man from a friend may be an act of desperation for some women, yet it is never admitted as such; instead, chemistry is blamed— a sexual excitement that cannot be ignored. Yet, in the recesses of her mind, the woman who chooses her friend's man for an affair may be unconsciously harboring hostile thoughts toward her friend, or she may be choosing a man who is "taken" because she is ambivalent about a long-term love commitment.

Competitiveness among women is never supposed to be out in the open; outwardly, women are expected to be compliant, agreeable, and trustworthy, particularly in sexual matters, so that when a betrayal is discovered, it is unexpected and has a shocking effect. Often women's betrayals receive considerable attention, while men's philandering is considered commonplace.

The double standard is so strong and so pervasive in our society that when a woman and a man are caught in a betrayal, the woman is often blamed for her "promiscuity." And the woman who is caught rarely blames the man for his part in the affair; she is more likely to blame his wife or other lover. After all, she asks, if her friend had "taken care of" her man, could he have been so easily seduced?

Shirley Eskapa, in *Woman versus Woman*, contends that the "other woman" is often the cause of marital breakup, which is not necessarily the result of a failing marriage.[3] While this is arguable, the main issue is that it is just as much a male prerogative to say "no" to an affair as it is the other woman's choice. Sexual betrayal in a friendship cannot realistically be justified, but to blame it solely on a woman, either the betrayer or the betrayed, is sexist.

Nevertheless, a husband may be forgiven for his "straying," but a woman who betrays another woman by having a sexual relationship with her man destroys the friendship. Lisa, an accountant in her mid-thirties, offered her testimony:

When I turned thirty, my life took a sharp turn. Not only was I shaken by leaving my twenties behind, moving into being a "grownup," but the man I loved, my husband, was involved with another woman. My friend Marion, a bit younger but worldly, listened patiently as I poured my heart out. She was there when I needed her; at two in the morning or mid-afternoon, she listened and gave me advice. I told her of my suspicions and his denial. She encouraged me to believe him and trust him. "That's the only way the relationship can progress," she advised. Despite my efforts to look the other way, I was besieged with distress. I felt as if my life were falling apart—I would think about losing my husband, moving, and starting from scratch and panic would set in. Knowing that Marion was there enabled me to survive. It was not easy allowing myself to rely so heavily on her; I am very protective of my vulnerability. Nevertheless, I leaned on Marion, and she came through; she was like a rock in my life, very supportive. We ate together and talked well into the night on several occasions when my husband was "out of town." We really drew very close. Just as I had calmed down and started to believe my husband, he confessed. I was right all along. He packed his things that night and left.

After I was divorced, I found that Marion was once his lover. *Betrayed* isn't a strong enough word for how I felt. *Knifed in the back* is more like it. When I confronted Marion, she was open about it. She had not been his lover all along, she said, but she had been lured into a brief affair by his charm, just prior to becoming my confidant. That was six years ago. Marion is married now—no, not to my ex-husband—and I am still single. Owing to our different life-styles and to my dormant hurt and anger, I no longer see Marion, but occasionally I think of her. I don't blame her for my marital split, but I still feel betrayed. Along with these feelings—and this may sound crazy since Marion took advantage of my trust—is the recognition that she actually did help me; I think her original motives for comforting me were basically sincere, based on our friendship. I don't think Marion planned to hurt me, but it happened. Nevertheless, for some time, I found myself guarded with people, looking for a friend who came with a guarantee of trust. I realize there is no such thing, but Marion was a real setback; I was emotionally naked with her, and the hurt touched my core. These days, I'm "brave" again, more relaxed with other women, but I don't know if I'm quite the same. I've lost my innocence; I'm more skeptical.

Symbiotic Friendships

When a friendship is based on gratification of neurotic needs rather than genuine interest in the other person's welfare, it is destructive. When a woman does not feel complete within herself, when she needs a friend to feel whole, she is seeking the impossible from friendship. A woman must feel worthwhile on her own, or she will find it difficult to establish a worthwhile friendship.

Sometimes we search for qualities in our friends that we lack ourselves; we've all heard the cliché "Opposites attract." This is often true not only in love relationships but in friendships, too. A friendship between women with complementary personalities (when, for example, one is outgoing, the other introverted) can be constructive and healthy, as long as neither woman feels inferior or incomplete because she lacks her friend's qualities.

When one woman needs another to bolster her self-esteem on a continual basis, she is merely using her friend for her own ends. For example, Paula, who is shy and short on confidence, was immediately attracted to Joan, a striking woman who always had a smart answer and a take-charge attitude. They met at a party at the public library and within weeks were talking to each other almost daily. Joan liked being with Paula because she derived a feeling of instant superiority when she compared her-self to her reticent, indecisive friend. Paula, on the other hand, liked being in the company of someone whom she regarded as a winner.

The friendship was doomed to failure. Paula and Joan were in fact using each other; neither had real respect for the other. But neither of them recognized these facts; they were clouded by surface gratification.

It was a friendship based on false premises: Joan wasn't such a winner, or she wouldn't have needed to feed her ego on Pau-la's inadequacy, and Paula was not entirely a loser. The rela-tionship perpetuated Joan's false sense of superiority and al-lowed Paula to continue to let another woman take charge of her life. Neither woman was coming to terms with her personality deficit. When a friendship stunts growth and perpetuates needi-ness, it is destructive.

On the other hand, when a woman's life appears dull com-pared to that of her friend, who is barraged with invitations to exciting social events, the woman who is bored may live vicar-iously, for a time, through her friend. This is not necessarily destructive if it is only temporary. If a woman can learn to im-itate the behavior in her friend that allows her to be so popular, she is growing and coping constructively with her boredom. In the meantime, her contact with her friend makes her life less monotonous.

The key to determining whether a friendship between seem-ing opposites is destructive or healthy is respect—respect for oneself and for the friend. If a plain-looking woman admires the beauty of her friend and actually feels enhanced being with her, there is no destructive element in the relationship, so long as the two women truly appreciate each other as whole human beings. But if they think of themselves as one-dimensional, as "Beauty and the Beast," their relationship will not be based on respect, and their own integrity will be compromised. Each woman must choose a friend because of a genuine and deep interest in the other person, not out of a neurotic need to bolster her self-esteem.

Unrealistic Expectations

Sometimes friendship is burdened by hidden expectations. In these instances, one friend may expect the other to transform her into more than she is. While mutual growth is frequently a benefit of friendship, paradoxically, it is hardly ever beneficial when it is demanded. When we insist, even in undertones, that another person must take charge of our lives, fix our faults, banish our limitations, or solve our problems, the relationship usually takes a downhill course. In a symbiotic relationship, one woman wants another to fill in a gap in her personality, but sometimes the idea of being completed by another is taken one step further, and a woman expects to be transformed by her friendship. For instance, Edith's experiences:

> When Arlene and I initially met, we were immediately attracted to each other. We both had experienced unhappy marriages that ended in divorce, and we seemed to fill a gap of loneliness in each other's life. We saw each other very frequently, socialized a great deal, and became very tight friends in a short time. This was particularly suitable to me at the time. I always considered myself an outsider; I felt awkward with people in general, and I was especially uncomfortable being a lone figure in a singles scene, so Arlene was my passport. I see in retrospect that she was as insecure as I am, but she handled her insecurities by becoming socially gregarious. She surrounded herself with a large network of friends and acquaintances, mostly the latter. Arlene felt most comfortable in a crowd. Initially, Arlene viewed me as a person at peace with herself—a woman who could stand alone, a good listener, and someone she could rely on who was stable. As for me, I felt she was the

answer to my prayers. My anxieties about the singles scene were quieted by her. She did most of the leading and talking when we socialized; she generally cleared a path I wouldn't dare enter alone.

So here we were in a friendship that seemed destined to rival Butch Cassidy and the Sundance Kid. But it turned into a disaster. Because we both lacked important qualities in our own personalities, we each mistook the other's weakness for strength. We each had entered the friendship with a hidden agenda. Arlene interpreted my shyness and withdrawal as being a sign of self-sufficiency; she thought I was a "Rock of Gibraltar" type. And my needs resulted in seeing her as everything I wasn't—social, at ease with people, secure. In fact, she was insecure; she simply expressed it differently. Needless to say, within a few months the relationship began to unravel. My uneasiness around people disappointed her, and once the novelty wore off, Arlene's inability to be away from others drove me to distraction. She wasn't able to alter my personality one bit, and I could no longer accept her the way she was—and she certainly wasn't going to change.

I guess when I look back at it now, I expected some miracle—that Arlene would inspire me to be more sociable, more at ease with people. It didn't work. Instead, I withdrew further and became increasingly critical of Arlene's need for constant companionship. Arlene reacted defensively to my withdrawal, her insecurity escalated, and characteristically, she redoubled her social efforts, which only served to anger me more. We both felt trapped in an escalating cycle. After a while, we were in a relationship where resentfulness, despair, and bitterness had replaced the original ecstasy. There was no real communication, and whatever feeling we once had for each other soured. We parted enemies.

Potentially as destructive as Edith and Arlene's relationship is that of the self-appointed improver and her friend—the woman to be transformed. Anyone who sets out to improve a friend, whether she wants to be subjected to an improvement campaign or not, is seeking not a friend but someone whom she can manipulate. Similar to the advice giver, the improver has difficulty separating her own needs from those of others. Often she lacks self-esteem and needs someone else to make over, so that she will not have to consider her own inadequacies.

For example, Jenny, a thirty-eight-year-old speech therapist, befriended Deborah, a music teacher, because they had similar interests but also because Jenny subconsciously knew that Deborah would be a malleable subject; she had some obvious faults, and she was shy and unassertive. The two women enjoyed many lunches together and a few evenings out to movies and concerts; they truly enjoyed each other's company. But within a couple of months, Jenny offered Deborah free speech lessons because, she asserted, Deborah had a thick New York accent. Deborah accepted, but half-heartedly; she really didn't think she had to change her way of talking after thirty-five years. She felt her voice was distinctive; she didn't have to sound like a radio announcer.

Jenny, who believed she was being generous, also offered to "help" Deborah quit smoking and lose weight. She refused to allow her friend to smoke in her presence, and when they went to a restaurant together, Jenny reminded Deborah about calories—even though Jenny, who never had a weight problem, ordered whatever she wished. Jenny was surprised when, instead of being grateful for her attentions, Deborah one day blew up at her, shouting, "I'll eat whatever I want, smoke whenever I feel like it, and talk any damn way I please from now on—whether you like it or not." The rebellion was the beginning of the end of the friendship.

True friends accept each other the way they are. Women who are friends must accept each other's idiosyncrasies and limitations if they are to enjoy each other's strengths. No one can force another person to change. Nagging a friend or pushing her to change what you consider a "bad habit" usually does not lead to change—it leads to anger and the possible termination of the friendship.

On the other hand, it is equally unrealistic to expect a friend to stay the same forever. Relationships evolve; they are not static, and friends who cannot adapt to changes in another's life are not likely to keep a friend for long. Envy and fear of abandonment are the feelings behind not wanting a friend to move ahead. It is sometimes difficult for a woman who has been supportive of a friend in a crisis to show the same support when she is striving for success. Particularly if the friend does not feel fulfilled herself, the other woman's success may be a threat. According to Luise Eichenbaum and Susie Orbach in *What Do Women Want: Exploding the Myth of Dependency,* our sexist society encourages women to fear growth and change in each other: "As long as women do not feel good in themselves, whole within themselves, and substantive, and as long as they are encouraged to look to other people (especially men) to derive their place in the world, then women will feel frightened of other women's successes. They will feel less by comparison, they will feel abandoned and left behind, they will feel what is missing in their own lives." [4]

WARNING SIGNALS: POTENTIALLY TOXIC FRIENDSHIPS

While no close friendship is conflict-free and no friend is perfect, some feelings and behavior patterns are particularly indicative of possible trouble ahead. Feeling drained, frustrated, and depleted by a friendship, not once in a while but usually, is a sure sign something is amiss. Frequently, this is a consequence of being in a relationship with someone who is overly demanding or in chronic distress. Her suffering is becoming contagious;

you are probably too involved as a helper and are suffering along with her. If these feelings persist despite efforts to balance the giving and receiving in the relationship, it is time to ask the question "What price friendship?"

An abrupt change in your friend's personality or actions may mean difficulties are brewing. If your friend suddenly turns cold or miserly toward you, you would certainly be concerned, but if she is suddenly overly affectionate or much more generous than usual, consider her motives. Is her expression one of strained congeniality because she is really angry with you but afraid to acknowledge it? Is she suddenly all-giving because she feels guilty about a betrayal, or because she feels rejected by you and wishes to gain your approval? It would be cynical to question every generous or affectionate gesture a friend makes, but if positive actions become exaggerated over a period of time or if all the giving is one-sided, you are bound to feel uncomfortable; at that point a discussion with your friend to consider her true intentions may be in order. If your friend is angry with you or has a problem that she is not ready to discuss, badgering her to confide in you will only be destructive; let your friend know that you care about her, and simply be available when she is ready to talk.

While a certain amount of misunderstanding and retreat is unavoidable in any relationship, attempts at promoting guilt and anxiety in a friend through withdrawal, manipulation, and veiled, indirect statements are destructive. Take, for example, a seemingly innocent observation: "Phyllis told me you called her when you came in from California." Rather than stating directly, "I am hurt that you didn't call me when you came home" and discussing the issue, the intent here is to promote guilt and thereby motivate the friend to greater responsiveness. The result is much more likely to be resentment.

Self-destructive actions or addictions like alcoholism are also potentially deleterious to friendships. Don't feel personally rejected if your troubled friend does not respond to your support or overtures to help. No one can change someone else if she does not want to be changed; each person in a friendship is responsible for her own actions.

While different personalities sometimes complement each other in a friendship, great differences in morals or values will probably lead to conflict. If a friend asks you to act in a way that you feel is morally wrong or demeaning, don't; a relationship based on one individual's compromising her integrity is bound to be destructive. There will be loss of respect for herself and for her friend.

A woman who can't tolerate being alone will probably surface as an overdependent friend. Yet a woman who is difficult to get close to may also lack an independent self; she may have an identity so weak that she is wary of getting too close to anyone emotionally for fear of losing herself.

A betrayal of trust, such as breaking a confidence, may be a sign that your friend is angry with you or jealous of you. Or perhaps she had other motives for initially pursuing the friendship. Beware of the friend who attaches herself to you when you're successful and loses interest when your fortunes turn. The status-climbing friend is more interested in your power, position, or wealth than she is in you personally. Any true friendship is based on the enjoyment of a relationship for what it is, not for what it can accomplish. If you mistake a status seeker for a friend, you're bound to be hurt. As increasing numbers of women enter the career world, they will have to be attuned to so-called friends at work who try to gain a business advantage while pretending to desire friendship.

The best friendships were described by a woman in her late thirties who had been hurt many times by destructive friendships but who had also managed to find several enduring, loving friends. She said: "The best friends accept each other, in good times and in bad, through success and failure. And they are happy with themselves, blemishes and all. But some women, because they are unhappy with themselves, can suck you dry emotionally, like vampires. I believe I can spot those now, and I stay far away from them. Certainly, if a friendship drains me more than it replenishes me, it is destructive, and I'll end it. If I lose respect for a friend—if she has used me or betrayed me—I'll end the friendship.''

Often an investment in time is needed to determine the course of a friendship. But many women trust their first instincts to steer them away from potentially destructive alliances. Women trust their unconscious; they believe ''instant liking'' or ''chemistry'' is an indication that a relationship would work out well. Explained a forty-two-year-old housewife: ''Some women I know I should like because we have similar interests, but I just don't feel one way or the other about them. But there are others I like instantly. I guess I believe in good vibrations.''

And a twenty-seven-year-old department store buyer suggested: ''Maybe it's woman's intuition, but I can sense right away whether a friendship will go well or not. I'm right 99 percent of the time.''

Trusting their first instincts is the way most women enter friendships; after all, there is no test to guarantee compatibility. Most, in fact, are correct in determining, right from the start, how well they will get along with an acquaintance. But as acquaintances transform themselves into friends, and as friendships progress through various stages, it is beneficial to heed potential danger signals. If you feel exploited in any way or uncertain about your friend's integrity or intentions, then begin an honest dialogue with her. Only by thoroughly understanding your friend's needs and your own can you successfully resolve difficulties or destructive elements in your friendship.

CHAPTER

10

HOW TO TEND,
MEND, AND END
FRIENDSHIPS

There's a lot of talk and an abundance of printed words about the need to ''work at'' marriage, but when has anyone suggested that women similarly need to work at their friendships? There is a feeling that somehow friendships flourish like weeds, without care or effort. But friendships erode when no one is tending them on a day-to-day basis; then the psychological termites creep in.

Our research has shown that friendships follow a definite course, that they pass through stages of increasing intimacy, but that each new level is reached only when both women in the friendship exhibit the necessary desire, social skills, and interaction to enable their bond to deepen. If, for instance, a woman does not know how to offer and accept confidences at appropriate times in a relationship, it is doubtful that she will have close friends. If she does not know how to listen effectively, how to show affection or displeasure openly, or how to reciprocate in dispensing favors, invitations, or empathy, she is likely to have difficulty in forming enduring friendships.

An important social skill required to forge fulfilling friendships is the ability to keep friends despite inevitable conflicts. It is a mistake to believe that an intimate friendship will run smoothly. Indeed, in contrast to more casual, shallow relations, long-term, rewarding friendships have their difficult periods; what makes them endure is not an absence of conflict but the skill of each friend in handling anger and resolving conflicts constructively.

Unfortunately, no one can guarantee that a friendship will last forever; as a result of changing needs, even the most intense, long-term relationships sometimes fade away. When a friendship offers you little emotional return or enjoyment, or when it begins to be based on guilt and obligation rather than genuine concern and a desire to please each other, it is time to reevaluate it. When a friendship drags on even though it is no longer meeting your needs, it depletes energy that could be spent in more productive relationships. It's hard to say goodbye to anyone with whom you have shared enjoyment and confidences and pain, but it's sometimes the most constructive way to get on with your life.

TENDING FRIENDSHIPS: SOCIAL SKILLS, COMMITMENT, AND CARING REQUIRED

Forming a strong and healthy friendship takes effort. Being a friend means you assume some responsibilities; friendship requires that you make some concessions and some sacrifices. Close friends care enough about each other to attempt to fulfill each other's needs, as long as each friend's expectations are realistic. Friends understand that they cannot be totally responsible for each other, but they can be supportive and helpful.

In order to gain increasing intimacy with a friend, certain skills and attitudes are necessary. Here we will explore the modes of interaction that facilitate friendship.

Listening

Joanna, a forty-four-year-old accountant, explained that she measured the worth of a friendship by the ability of her friend to listen without interrupting, contradicting, or offering advice. She explained: "Sometimes friends aren't all-giving, they aren't very amenable at all because of difficulties in their own lives. Sometimes, when one of my close friends is depressed, I'll listen to her talk obsessively about her problems every day for weeks, and believe me, it's not easy to stick with her, because sometimes I strongly disagree with the things she says and does, but I care for her deeply, and she would do the same for me. When we listen to each other without offering advice unless it's asked for, we confirm to each other that we're understood. We accept each other through listening, we make things clearer, we get rid of troubling feelings, and it feels very, very good."

The ability to listen in an empathic, nonjudgmental way is one of the most important friendship skills. Listening does not include offering your opinion or trying to fix a problem. Friends don't have to make life right; they just have to listen, understand, and be there for each other. When a friend starts telling you her problems, she often simply wants a sympathetic ear. She wants validation and support, someone to confirm that she is indeed capable of handling her own difficulties.

Some women find it extraordinarily difficult to listen without doing anything more to help a friend. Women, after all, are raised to be responsible for others: Traditionally, women are supposed to be helpful; they are supposed to do "good deeds." But attempting to solve a friend's problem for her may undermine the friend's confidence in her own ability, a tactic she is likely to resent.

Sometimes a woman who needs someone to listen to her just to share her burdens asks, instead, for an opinion or advice. She may be confused about what she wants or embarrassed about asking for "nothing but sympathy." But that may be all she really wants—a little sympathy and a lot of reassurance.

Listening empathically means not making assumptions about your friend's motives or feelings but trying to understand her point of view. Sometimes repeating her thoughts in your own words helps you to understand her better and further clarifies for your friend the ideas she expressed. This may be the start of a solution to a problem.

Priscilla, a thirty-eight-year-old librarian, recalled an argument she recently had with her close friend Dorothy. One Monday evening when Priscilla was feeling restless and bored, she called Dorothy to "chat." Priscilla asked Dorothy how her weekend was, and her friend, a sculptor, said she had gone to a gallery opening, and to a restaurant for dinner afterward with her husband and friends on Saturday night. Priscilla responded, "Oh, I wish I could have gone with you. You must have had so much fun. I just sat home this weekend, but you always seem to have such exciting things to do."

Dorothy became infuriated, saying, "I don't like your assumption that I'm having a great time all the time, Priscilla. In fact, my weekend was kind of dull."

Priscilla, taken aback, said she was sorry.

"I don't think you're sorry," Dorothy shot back, angrier than before. "You don't know the things that bother me. No matter what I say, you have this image of my life as glamorous."

"You take everything so literally, Dorothy. I'm just enthusiastic, that's all," Priscilla said, feeling rebuffed.

"No, it's more than that. You don't really *know* me, even though we've been friends for—how long is it—three years? You seem to have your own very private ideas of who I am," Dorothy countered.

The argument was smoothed over but not really settled. It was not until Priscilla realized, after considerable self-examination, that she had a preconceived idea about what her friend's life was like and that she often disregarded Dorothy's silence or dismissed her gentle protests against Priscilla's assumptions of her grandiose life-style as modesty. Because of her need for an idealized image of her friend, Priscilla failed to objectively listen or to understand her friend's hints that life, from her viewpoint, was not paradise. If Priscilla had been more objective and less eager to gloss over her friend's moods with her forced optimism, Dorothy would have felt understood and validated. On the other hand, Dorothy, if she were a more empathic listener, as concerned about her friend's feelings as her own, might have understood how Priscilla's enthusiasm masked her true feelings of loneliness and jealousy. Then open discussion of these feelings might have eased the difficulties between the two friends.

Besides stereotyping a speaker, as Priscilla did, another roadblock to listening effectively is contradicting a friend's expression of feelings. For example, when Julie confides in her friend Eve, saying, "I feel so angry at my daughter right now that I wish she'd never been born," and Eve responds, "Oh, no, you couldn't feel that angry. You're exaggerating," she is negating Julie's feelings and implying that they are wrong.

But, of course, feelings are not right or wrong, and denying them often causes them to become stronger. Angry feelings such as Julie's can best be dispelled when they are accepted rather than contradicted by a friend. It often takes great self-control to listen without contradicting, interrupting, or stereotyping. But, with practice, it can be done, and those who are effective listeners are usually considered treasured friends.

Open Expression of Feelings

Expressing true feelings, even positive ones, is risky. After all, if a woman tells a friend, "I think you're wonderful" or "I love you," and her bosom buddy does not reciprocate with a similar show of affection, the communication can be embarrassing, and hurtful. Moreover, our society inhibits superlative expressions of emotion between women, just as it does between men. Saying "I love you" to a friend of the same sex may be viewed as a message with homosexual undertones. Yet, whether we demonstrate them through words or through gestures, showing our deepest feelings to a friend is an important step in establishing intimacy.

Jennifer, a thirty-eight-year-old secretary, expressed sentiments about openness that were echoed by several other women: "I have a great need to keep the atmosphere clear with my female friends. We are seldom content to lay a problem aside or to gloss over difficulties in our lives or between ourselves. My experience has been mostly positive; I have not been hurt by my honesty. Quite to the contrary, being expressive about loneliness, anxiety, or my joys has made it easier for friends to relate to me.''

Expressing negative emotions is particularly troublesome for women, since they have been traditionally conditioned to be acquiescent and appeasing. The growing girl often feels that if she is not always kind and warm, she is somehow a failure or unfeminine. In fact, women learn to call their own anger bitchiness. Conflict is bound to occur with this anger constraint because anger is an inevitable factor in any close relationship, and suppressing rather than discussing it usually results in a distancing tension and strain between friends.

Since women have been socialized to keep the peace, conflict between two women can be threatening. Any significant disagreement can be experienced by one or both friends as a break with the feminine code. Occasionally, petty arguing about which is the better diaper service or who sells the finer cuts of meats are outlets for anger about more significant issues that neither friend dares to express more directly. That is, arguing about traditionally feminine issues is more acceptable than confronting more consequential areas of conflict, which may be too threatening for some women, particularly those who cling to their traditional upbringing.

Anger turned inward not only interferes with intimacy but can also lead to self-blame and depression. Simply put, anger that is not dealt with effectively promotes isolation. Women who allow each other to express anger and frustration as well as joy and exuberance, however, are likely to form a close attachment.

A woman's upbringing will determine to a great extent how she will handle her anger, but she can reeducate herself later in life to deal with it more constructively. The way we handle anger is not innate; it is a skill that is learned. Consider the commentary of two friends who share a six-year friendship on the atmosphere in their childhood homes and its impact on their relationship. Marsha stated:

> We fought often in my household; you could hear us four blocks away. I remember many of the fights between my parents or between me and my sister being followed by making up. We said things to each other in anger that we apologized for. Apologies came easily in my family. Also, when my parents were mad at me as a child, I was told, "Being angry doesn't mean we don't love you." When they were mad at each other I was reminded of the same thing: "We may disagree about some things and feel very angry but that doesn't mean we hate each other." They taught me that a person may not like something about you but still like you. This is a lesson that's made a critical difference in my friendships. Anger, speaking my mind, for instance, isn't as traumatic to me as it is to many women. I know, on an emotional level, that I don't have to be pleasing all the time; I can risk a friend's disapproval. Being wrong or possibly incurring a friend's wrath doesn't frighten me. I've seen wrath; it's not so terrible. This allows me the freedom to get past conflict and to pursue closeness.

Rita commented:

> I know Marsha's family. I like them and I agree with her view of their impact on her. I think she was very fortunate to grow up in a household where people don't believe in facades. Her parents don't censor themselves and display only their best side; they're *real*. My family, on the other hand, was petty, bickering, and indirectly hostile to each other. The demonstration of emotion was taboo. I picked up a lot of bad habits. First of all, in contrast to Marsha, my tendency is to withdraw

when something bothers me. I would stew about it rather than confront her. When I did say something, it was aimed at provoking guilt in her. I tried to get to her through emotional blackmail. It's only been in the last year or so of our friendship that I have learned, mostly through Marsha's example, to speak up and say what I want and what's bothering me. No camouflaging. No beating about the bush.

There are constructive ways of expressing negative feelings that Rita discovered from her friend. Communicating feelings and needs effectively is a skill that improves with practice. It you have difficulty making close friends, it might be helpful for you to reevaluate the way you communicate with them. Consider these rules for effective communication:

1. *It is important to take clear responsibility for your feelings, for this is the only way to enter into personal dialogue.* The essential step in personalizing conversations is to begin statements with a form of the pronoun *I (me, my, mine)*. *I* statements are expressions of responsibility: ''I am angry'' is a personal statement saying something about your feelings; ''You make me mad'' is an accusatory statement, shifting responsibility to another person. It is more likely that the *I* statement will be positively received; *you* statements, accusations, and critical comments about the person to whom you are speaking are generally met with defensiveness.

2. *When something is wanted, whether it is change, clarification, reassurance, companionship, or support, it is important that a request be made that is direct and to the point.* Often women expect their friends to intuit their feelings and wants; this can lead to misunderstanding and disappointment. Rather than expecting ''mind reading'' from each other, friends need to push past the fear of rejection and the image of appearing ''needy'' to ask for what they want.

3. *Style of delivery is at least as important and probably even more influential than content.* When words convey one

message but tone or gestures another, communication becomes muddled. For example, if a woman asks her friend how she feels about their relationship and her friend replies, "You are very important to me" as she looks at the floor and leans away, her response does not have the strength of impact it would if she maintained good eye contact and moved forward.

4. *When behavior is described ("I would like you to spend more time with me") rather than labeled ("You are just plain selfish") the outcome is likely to be more positive.* Not only does descriptive language provide a means for communicating more effectively, it also establishes a vehicle for expanding one's own awareness. In this regard, an important element of descriptive language is the expression of one's inner experience. Often, this will convert a confusing or harsh statement into one that is more understandable and acceptable. "I hate you" becomes "My heart is pounding as I say this, but when you make demand after demand of me I feel myself tightening up and resenting you."

Self-disclosure

Revealing ourselves—our failings as well as our successes, our quirks and our interests, our likes and dislikes, our less than endearing qualities as well as our strong, likable ones—is essential for drawing closer to a friend. Unless a friend knows your true self, she will not know how to respond to you appropriately and meaningfully.

A woman who censors much of what she tells her friend is not being emotionally fair to her friendships. To understand why she is not revealing more of her true self to her friend, she will have to consider her feeling about herself and her friend. Does she believe her true self is not likable? Does she expect harsh judgment? Does she fear that her friend will take advantage of her self-disclosures? Does she fear that her self-disclosure will make her friend feel embarrassed or uncomfortable? Relationships in which self-disclosure is minimized are lacking in trust. If trust is not increased, it is unrealistic to expect greater intimacy.

An important skill involved in self-disclosure is timing. If a woman's pace is not right she is likely to alienate her friend rather than draw her closer. If she makes her friend feel uncomfortable by disclosing intimate facts about her life too soon, her friend may feel she is indiscriminate rather than friendly; but if she withholds too much about herself for too long, her friend may sense that she is too difficult to get close to or surmise that she does not wish the friendship to grow.

Researchers E. E. Jones and E. M. Gordon report in the *Journal of Personality and Social Psychology* that if someone reveals positive information about herself early in a relationship she tends to be disliked, but if she discloses negative information about herself and takes the responsibility for it, she is most often liked.[1] This research suggests that the fears many women have concerning rejection, if they reveal their weaknesses and "bad" points, are unfounded; in fact, the opposite is true. Friends are often warmly accepted if they are vulnerable enough to own up to their faults, but they are shunned if they try to make a favorable impression, especially in the beginning of a relationship, by bragging about their good fortune and positive qualities. Showing your good qualities through your actions and attitudes is much more impressive than self-congratulation.

Time and Caring

The ability to structure time so that we can enjoy friends, unhampered by the stresses of everyday living and work obligations, is a necessity in maintaining close friendships. If true intimacy is to be achieved, relaxed, unfettered time together is important; if small segments of time or preoccupied moments are the only periods one can spare for a friend, the relationship is bound to falter. Spending time with another involves commitment and caring. "Let's go to lunch sometime" is vague and lacks commitment, but if you find time to make specific dates with friends they will understand that you care about them.

Research suggests that the more we like a person, the more varied the number of activities we do with her in more varied settings. Women who have only recently met may not know enough about each other's interests to suggest meeting in specialized settings. At first, socializing is often done at home or at a restaurant. Later, the friends may go to sporting events, plays, movies, discos, PTA meetings, or career-oriented seminars; whatever interests they hold in common they will often enjoy pursuing together.

Friends enjoy spending structured time together; they like a companion to share activities with. But to foster intimacy, unstructured time is also important; when there is no other activity on which to focus, friends can give their full attention to each other. They can talk, uninterrupted. They can, in a relaxed way, discover themselves and each other.

Ruth, a fifty-eight-year-old registered nurse, who has several lifelong close female friends, gave her prescription for tending friendships:

> Probably because I have no family (both my parents died when I was a teenager, and I was only a child) I've always cherished my friends and have worked hard at being a friend, with the philosophy that a good, warm friendship, like a good, warm fire, needs continual stoking. I think that the secret ingredient of tending friendships is listening and really hearing what each other says, being truly concerned, nonjudgmental, available. It doesn't necessarily have to do with the quantity of time spent together (as in parenting) but more with the quality of time. Thus, my friends and I often meet sans husbands and families for heart-to-heart talks. It means bringing a pot of chicken soup to a friend who's in bed with the flu, checking up on someone's eighty-five-year-old mother when a friend is away on a business trip, remembering birthdays and special events (including their kids' big occasions). Yes, it's time-consuming—but what joyous time!

Moving Closer

Suppose you know the ABCs of friendship tending. You're a good listener and an honest communicator, you risk revealing your foibles and you're willing to spend uninterrupted time with friends, but you're still not as close as you would like to be with your female friend. Perhaps you are expecting too much from the friendship too soon. Perhaps your friend is not ready to reciprocate for reasons of her own that have nothing to do with you. Perhaps the friendship does not yet have a solid foundation on which to build the relationship. To increase intimacy and derive the maximum emotional benefits from your friendships, consider these suggestions for moving closer:

1. *Relating closely is bound to be unsettling at times.* Rather than automatically regarding periods of emotional distress as a signal to back away from a friendship, reconsider: Are you being too protective of your vulnerability? It is important to recognize that intimacy always involves some risk; consequently, it is unrealistic to expect an absence of conflict, ambivalence, and emotional turmoil.

2. *Discard any preconceived timetable for developing a close relationship with another woman.* Friendships require time to blossom. The surest guarantee that a relationship will collapse is to impose in advance a prescribed period of time for it to flourish.

3. *Just as rushing a friendship is often self-defeating, it is foolish to persistently pursue a friendship with a woman who isn't interested in you.* Friendship involves a complete interplay of values and interests as well as a nonanalyzable bond between people—a "chemistry"—many women simply do not match and never will. Aside from incompatibility, some women either have other demands on their time and literally don't have time for you, or they are defensive, overly shy, and generally unavailable. It is wise to accept such women as the strangers they wish to be so that you have the time and energy to invest in friendships with women who want you as a friend.

4. *Trust is one of the necessary ingredients for true intimacy.* The exchange of trust encourages friends to be generous, consoling, and comforting. Trust is developed as two women practice honesty in communication; it requires a mutually shared risk. For example, if a woman can admit her envy of her friend's success instead of attacking her for being overzealous in her career, support and understanding are possible. Tolerance and generosity of spirit become easier when an individual openly acknowledges her fallibility. Similarly, if a woman is courageous and honest enough to admit her mistakes and finds forgiveness in her friend, it then becomes easier for her to be tolerant of her friend's foibles.

CONFLICT AND ALIENATION: MENDING THE COLD WARS OF FRIENDS

"Why would I have a fight with a girlfriend?" Sheila, a forty-year-old teacher asked rhetorically. "I have fights with my husband, my kids, and my parents, but I can't think of anything my female friends and I would disagree about. We have much more to agree about. Even if a friend wants to argue with me—I can think of one who picks arguments—I don't allow it."

Denise, a twenty-eight-year-old secretary, remarked: "If a friend and I disagree, I'll usually drop the issue. Or we'll skirt around the topic, or joke about it. Mostly, I accept differences in my friends. I believe you can be friends with someone even though you disagree with them about some things."

Like Sheila and Denise, many women have difficulty facing disagreements with friends. Women are taught to "get along," to "be sweet"; they're not socialized to constructively deal with differences, competition, or conflict. Hence, many of them tend to withdraw from a conflict even before they attempt resolving the difficulty. Denise's acceptance of differences is healthy, but if she withdraws from a touchy issue even before it is discussed, the way Sheila handles conflicts with her friends, she is not giving herself or her friend a fair chance at resolving it.

While starting an argument over every minor difference would certainly be considered picky at best and hostile at worst, friends must speak up if they are hurt by each other or if a small grievance continually annoys them. For example, if Leah's friend Margie is a smoker and Leah gets nauseated from cigarette smoke, explaining this to Margie is the best course of action. Chances are Margie will volunteer not to smoke in a closed room with Leah, if she truly values her friendship. At least, the issue can be discussed, and perhaps some compromise will be reached.

Jean, a thirty-two-year-old dental assistant, discovered that when she aired her grievances rather than kept silent, her friendships more often remained on firm ground. She explained: "If I'm annoyed about something a friend does, I'll tell her about it right away. I've learned from experience that if I don't, I inwardly steam about it, and I start to show my displeasure in different ways. In the past, sometimes I just let the friendship end, rather than confront the issue at hand. Now I realize I lost a lot of friends unnecessarily. Even though there's risk involved, I speak up now if something a friend does really bothers me."

According to a study by Keith E. Davis and Michael J. Todd reported in *Psychology Today,* spouses and lovers are more often ambivalent about their relationship and more often in conflict than friends.[2] Perhaps friends are more inhibited about saying what is on their mind, or perhaps they have less to argue about than lovers. Several women we interviewed said they didn't expect to have arguments with their female friends because they selected them carefully on the basis of their similarities; they expected support from women with whom they had so much in common. For these women, an argument with a friend was extremely upsetting because it was so unexpected. However, it is unrealistic to expect to be in complete agreement with anyone in a long-term close relationship.

In any intimate relationship, the potential for conflict exists at all times. Indeed, conflict is inevitably introduced into a friendship and will test the extent of involvement in the relationship. Frequently, the manner in which conflict or crisis is handled influences feelings of loyalty in the friendship. A woman may be in distress and ask her friend's aid, even though the friend is drowning in work responsibilities. The issue of contention is most often based directly on the value of the friendship; the friend is asked to choose between the friendship and her own priorities. Those who "pass the test" become closer friends, while those who do not may be unofficially demoted from friends to acquaintances.

Quarrels often erupt when least expected, and if they are not dealt with directly or if an agreement can't be reached, friends drift apart. Sometimes, there is no outright disagreement or quarrel, but a friend slowly withdraws from your life. She is busy whenever you call, she forgets appointments with you, or she decides she has "other priorities" when you suggest activities together. To avoid losing a friend because of unspoken or unresolved conflicts, it is best to take preventive measures. There are signposts that indicate a friendship is in danger.

1. *The feeling by one friend that she is giving much more than the other, that the rewards of the friendship are not worth the cost.* In these circumstances, one woman may feel unable to meet the needs of the other, or a friend may feel unappreciated. In either case, there are usually feelings of loneliness and isolation as well as resentment, all of which warrant discussion.

2. *Arguments that are frequent and unproductive.* This pattern involves an escalating series of nasty verbal exchanges— accusations, insults, frequent criticism, recriminations, and the like. Also included in this pattern is the inability to move from inflexible, conflicting positions. Friends caught in this difficulty behave as though they have a vested interest in rejecting each other's point of view; each refuses to acknowledge there could be merit to any perspective but her own.

3. *Frequent excuses to avoid each other's company.* If one

or both friends find they rarely have time to spend together, it is obvious that their relationship has become a low priority.

4. *A lack of enjoyment in a friend's company.* A friendship is in trouble when you feel better without your friend than with her. If you would rather be alone or with somebody else, not sometimes but usually, chances are the friendship is over except for the formality.

5. *Overdependence on the part of one or both friends.* This can be expressed by jealousy, not feeling confident or worthwhile without a friend's companionship, resentment of a friend's independent interests, and being overly sensitive to a friend's criticism.

RECONNECTING:
GAINING NEW PERSPECTIVE

If any of friendship's danger signals are present, and one wishes to stop further erosion of the friendship, how does she reconnect? It's best to examine one's own input into the silent (or not so silent) conflict. Did the friends really "just drift apart" or did one neglect the other?

Some women find it less threatening to write a letter to an estranged friend in an attempt to reconstruct the friendship; there is less risk involved and more time to choose words carefully. When you don't have to confront your friend directly and there is no fear of immediate judgment or interruption, feelings flow more easily and sentiments can be expressed more exactly. Becky, a twenty-four-old social worker, shared her experience of reconnecting with a friend:

> When my friend, Jan, hadn't called or written to me for six months, I got angry. I had written her a few letters after she first moved to Florida, about a year ago. She answered one, and then sent a post card, and that was it. We were best friends in college, and when she moved,

she promised to keep in touch. I really didn't want to lose her. I had thought of calling her, but I felt uncomfortable saying what I had to say on the telephone. Instead, I wrote her a long letter telling her how much I missed her and how hurt I was that we had lost touch. I reminded her of some of the good times we had together. It worked; she answered my letter by inviting me down to Florida for a couple of weeks vacation with her.

When a reconnection is made, it isn't wise to immediately bring up old conflicts. Friends might try to renew the friendship from a fresh perspective, perhaps by discussing "the good old times" together. They might give themselves time to rebuild trust by allowing each other the distance to discover if time has changed the relationship or each other before old issues of contention are brought up.

Reconnecting with a friend does not mean reliving all your past hurts. If past disagreements have not been resolved and the friendship is worth saving, the past should be left alone.

ENDING FRIENDSHIPS:
WHAT WENT WRONG?

When lovers part or spouses divorce, there is usually a clear understanding of what went wrong in the relationship. The end of a love affair brings with it much anguish; there is a clear, definitive parting, often preceded by a confrontation. Friends, on the other hand, often cannot pinpoint how their relationship failed, and frequently, even though they know they no longer share the same closeness, women don't know if a friendship has ended or not. There's a sense of unfinished business in some friendships that drift along without direction or definition when the caring has gone out of them; there's a vague sense of something missing, a loss that can't be mourned, or forgotten, until there is some finality in the relationship.

Since there are no formal or clear-cut ways to part as friends, each individual must decide for herself when and how to end a friendship. But regardless of how it is made final, ending a friendship is associated with painful feelings: hurt, anger, bewilderment, guilt, remorse are all common reactions. In this respect, the parting of intimate friends is similar to a divorce.

While women often anticipate that their relationships with lovers will be stormy and transient, they expect their female friendships to endure. "Lovers come and go, but I can always count on my women friends," a thirty-five-year-old divorced secretary commented. And a forty-five-year-old homemaker, when asked if she had ever ended a friendship, replied, "No, I never consciously ended a friendship. Friends are supposed to be for keeps."

According to popular myth, a good friend is supposed to be forever; but in real life, friendships fade, or end abruptly, probably as often as they are formed. According to a survey of 40,000 women and men reported in *Psychology Today,* the most important psychological reasons for friends' parting were feeling betrayed and discovering they held widely divergent views on issues important to them.[3]

There are a myriad of other reasons for ending friendships. When a friendship starts, it is forged out of mutual need. When it ends, the needs of one woman or the other, or the needs of both, are no longer being met in the relationship; or sometimes the friends' needs have changed.

Fulfilling a friend's needs has to be a reciprocal process if a friendship is to endure. When one friend readily meets the needs of the other but there is no reciprocation, it may be nearly impossible to continue the friendship; the sense of injustice will be too strong.

Career changes and geographical moves also can change the delicate balance of needs in a friendship. Whether a friendship will weather such changes depends, to a large extent, on the emotional foundation on which it is based. For instance, while some deep friendships can endure even though the friends move thousands of miles apart geographically, others that are emotionally shallow dissolve if a friend moves to the next town. The extent of commitment to the relationship, as well as the need for regular contact are a few of the other variables that determine what will happen to a friendship when distance separates friends.

While many friendships survive geographical barriers, moving up the career ladder usually means dropping some friends along the way. An abrupt change in status is often a factor in failing friendships. It is difficult, for example, for a company's vice president, whose colleagues lunch either in the executive dining room or at certain expensive restaurants, to order deli sandwiches along with her old friends in the secretarial pool.

But friendship failure is also linked to a woman's perception of her past. Often a woman who has worked her way to the top dislikes being reminded of the low-status, low-paying job she once had. Or she'd like to forget the humilities she suffered; perhaps she had to deal with discrimination or sexual harassment, or perhaps she had to toil endlessly over boring or trivial work, even though she knew she was capable of making executive decisions. Whether they intend to remind her of "the old days" or not, friends-from-way-back-when bring back memories that are simply too painful and too humiliating. The friends, along with the memories, are consequently left behind.

We often hear the expression "They've grown apart" applied to spouses who have marital difficulties, but the same can be said for women in a failing friendship. When friends can no longer fulfill each other's needs or validate each other's identity, no matter how much they once loved each other, the friendship loses its reason for being. When friends sense an inevitable end to their relationship is approaching, it is best to let go gracefully—a particularly difficult task for women.

Saying Goodbye: Why It Is So Difficult for Women Friends

When a woman outgrows a friend, she finds herself in an awkward situation. It is arrogant and hurtful to say to a friend, "I've moved beyond you" or "You are no longer necessary to my life." Women feel indebted to their friends the way a daughter feels toward her mother. Her mother, like her intimate friend, is a significant influence in her life; a woman derives her identity from her caregiver. When women leave behind a close friend of their own sex, they often feel as if they are leaving behind a part of themselves.

If a woman has been cast aside by her friend, the hurt and guilt can be equally intense. Like a child who wonders what she did wrong when her mother is angry with her or inattentive to her, a friend may vaguely feel guilty, as well as confused about what went wrong in the relationship. And the hurt goes deep, particularly if the friendship was a long-term, intimate one.

Adrienne, a thirty-five-year-old journalist who had been an adopted child, disclosed the critical link between female friendship and her mother. She had searched for her birth mother for years, but when she finally was able to locate her (her mother was a successful actress), she was rejected. Adrienne persisted with phone calls and letters, but soon, instead of curt notes from her mother asking to be left alone, she received no response at all. This rejection from her mother left Adrienne particularly sensitive to female friends who slighted her or became distant. She confided: "I've come to realize I can't take my mother's rejection personally. She has her own problems, I suppose, and they have nothing to do with me. But there's something I still don't know how to do—let go.

"No one likes to be rejected," she continued, "but the worst hurt in the world is being rejected by your own mother. Because of my past experience, I believe I appreciate my friends more than most women, but when I have a falling out with a female friend, it hurts more, too. In fact, I really never say goodbye to a friendship without harboring some hope that maybe some day it will be renewed."

If a woman missed feeling loved and nurtured by her mother, she may seek to fulfill these emotional needs through her female friends; indeed, these needs become so important to her that it is difficult for her to let go of a friendship, even when it is showing signs of failure. Women who are not as emotionally needy may find ending friendships not quite as traumatic. Predictably, it is easiest to end a new friendship, in which less of a woman's self is invested than in more intimate, long-term friendships. Indeed, some friendships are ended in embryo. Wendy, age forty-four, shared this experience:

> I guess there are people who make good acquaintances and bad friends. Susan is like that; an engaging, gregarious, very bright woman, she has a large social network. Susan is forever organizing something, dreaming up elaborate plans and projects involving other people. On several occasions I have approached Susan and she has enthusiastically agreed to get together for a night out. My intent was to get to know her better, to develop a friendship. The problem was that Susan invariably canceled our meeting for another appointment, forgot about our meeting or, as sometimes happened, she showed up hours late apologizing profusely: "Oh, I'm terribly sorry, something came up."
>
> At first, I thought maybe it was me, but after listening to several other acquaintances we have in common voice similar complaints, I became curious. "Susan, what's with you?" I asked one day. "Why do you overcommit yourself like that?" After a brief conversation, the answer was clear: Susan is one of those people who think you have to be all things to all people in order to be liked. As a result, she doesn't seem to realize that she is nothing special to anyone. She is a social chameleon. Because she is so clever and charming, she thinks any understanding friend will forgive her. I'm sorry, but she's in no danger of being my friend. I've stopped pursuing her; she is relegated to the category of social acquaintance.

In addition to personality factors, "breaking up" is affected by the nature of the friendship; a relationship only moderate in involvement may waste away and die quietly. Close, emotionally entangled friendships, if they end, die hard. Some women experience the loss dramatically. They cannot sleep, or they sleep fitfully; they cannot eat, or they eat constantly. Many become plagued by gastrointestinal or other psychosomatic disorders, or their work suffers, household chores pile up, and the children are ignored—all indications that depression has set in. In the past, such dramatic reactions to loss were associated with romantic relationships. Our research suggests, however, that emotion runs at least as high between intimate female friends.

Unfinished Business
versus
Final Resolution

Since women have been raised to be kind and agreeable, their friendships often end without any final quarrel or confrontation. Letting a friendship wither is less frightening than confrontation, but if a silent denouement is not mutual, walking away from a friendship without formally ending it can result in awkward situations. If one woman fails to sense the relationship is over and she persists in calling to make dates as usual, the other woman is faced with endless excuses for being unable to get to their Friday night tennis game.

Yet the other often-used alternative, the angry farewell, tends to leave a bitter emotional aftertaste. A final explosion is often provoked when friends let their petty annoyances and angry grievances pile up; the final argument is only the climax of an erosion process that has been occurring over a period of time.

There is no easy way to end a friendship, the women we interviewed agreed, but if they had to choose a way to part, most women said they would prefer an honest discussion of their differences. Then, if the differences couldn't be resolved, they at least knew they had made an effort at reconciliation, and their friendship had a final resolution.

"If I don't know why a friendship ended," said a forty-two-year-old homemaker, "I have a sense of unfinished business hanging over me. I feel confused. I wonder endlessly why it happened. I think that perhaps I did something wrong. Sometimes I attempt to have a talk with a friend who is acting distant. I ask outright, 'What's wrong? I don't see you anymore.' Unfortunately, when this happens, I often get vague answers."

Women often avoid revealing their feelings to a friend from whom they've grown apart, since they are often ambivalent about the relationship. Memories of the rewarding parts of the friendship are intertwined with the minor annoyances or changes in attitude that have brought about its erosion. It is difficult for many women to be assertive about what is bothering them with strangers or acquaintances, but it is even more frightening and guilt-producing to tell someone you once loved and admired, and whom you still find agreeable in many respects, that she is no longer needed. There are few, if any, tactful ways of conveying these mixed feelings.

These are Sandy's sentiments as she struggles to cut the last ties to a friend she has moved beyond:

> Every year around the holidays, I get a card and a letter from my friend, Sara. I greet her life update with mixed feelings. We were friendly about a dozen years ago as undergraduates; we lived in the same dormitory. In those days we did some drinking together, talked of our futures, and worked the same part-time job. Sara is now divorced; she holds a job as a teaching assistant, her life is in kind of a shambles. I think she had some kind of a breakdown a few years back, following her divorce. In contrast, I hold a very responsible position, I have a husband, two children, and all the trappings of success—a large house, expensive cars, and the like. I feel awkward relating to Sara; I struggle with a simple reply to her once-a-year letter. We seem to be worlds apart and each year, as she documents her problems, I find

myself feeling guilty. How can I respond to her hard-luck story with "I am better than ever"?

I suppose a once-a-year awkwardness can be managed, but this year Sara mentioned that she is coming into town and would relish getting together; maybe, she hinted, she could even stay with us for a few days. I remember reading this and thinking, "Oh, no, how do I get out of this?" Thank goodness for small things—at least she wrote, giving me time to react. If she had called I would probably have had an instant case of stammer. As it is, Sara wrote again, about a month later, while I was still working on a tactful excuse; she sent her regrets for she was not able to make it due to some problems at her new job. So I've been given a reprieve for another year. But the whole thing brought up a real problem for me: I have a hell of a time breaking clean. In a situation like this, I'm a sitting duck. I feel as if I have no control—I'm at the mercy of my 'friend.'

Sandy felt as if she were at her friend's mercy, but she was really at the mercy of her own ambivalence. She had shared an important part of her life with Sara; they had been close once, and telling Sara directly that they had grown apart would mean that Sandy had lost a part of herself, a connection to her past. Sandy allowed the shell of a once full friendship to exist because she believed she did not want to hurt Sara. This is probably true, but she also did not want to hurt herself.

At other times, when friends part, there is no ambivalence; at least one friend, or sometimes both, are glad to be rid of a relationship which is beginning to bring more grief than fulfillment. For instance, Kay, a thirty-six-year-old dietitian, said she was "relieved" to move to a different state to get away from her former friend, Sally. Kay explained:

I met Sally when our children were both going to the same play group about ten years ago. It was a very intense time for both of us; we both had similar stresses, and we "took" to each other right away. We would have very long and candid conversations. We even confided in each other about our marital problems. But there were things about Sally that got on my nerves, and the longer I knew her the worse her annoying habits got. For instance, she'd ask me occasionally if she could drop her kids off for a few minutes, and then she wouldn't come back for hours, or she'd ask me to drive to wherever we happened to be going together, because she was tired or because she couldn't trust her car. She never offered to reciprocate.

When my husband changed jobs and we moved out of state, I never made an attempt to keep in touch with Sally. Her annoying habits had gotten so bad that they completely canceled whatever good points I had once seen in her. But when I think about it in retrospect, if I could have been more assertive, just for my own self-respect, I would have felt better. For all I knew, maybe Sally never understood how unfair it was for her to always ask for a free ride. I don't know.

There's one thing I learned from the relationship— it's to stand up for myself. Maybe if I had let Sally know what bothered me about her behavior sooner, she would have stopped taking advantage of me, and our friendship could have been saved. In any event, you have to respect yourself. And if you end a friendship, you have to do it in a way in which both friends can keep their respect for each other and for themselves. I didn't handle it right. If I saw Sally now, I'd be embarrassed.

An angry confrontation, like unexpressed pent-up anger, can lead to the end of a friendship. When raw feelings spill over and accusatory remarks are made without taking time for reflection, the pleasure and comfort of the friendship may be buried in hurt. Here the goodbyes are definite; there are no nagging thoughts concerning why the friendship ended. But occasionally there are "what ifs" and regrets. At other times, only relief and a need to forget the past prevails. Consider forty-five-year-old Erica's experience:

> Joyce and I knew each other even before our children were born, some twenty years ago. We planned our pregnancies together, and later we shared a full-time job together before time sharing was even heard of. We had a long history, and we were very close.
>
> But when we went into the retail clothing business together three years ago, our relationship changed. We became business partners first, friends second. Joyce put up most of the money to get the business started, and she thought she could call all the shots. It turned out that our attitudes about money and business risks, our ideas about hiring and marketing, and our work habits were totally different. The two years that we worked together we were in constant battles—it was hell. When the business failed and we parted, going our separate ways, many people we knew thought it was sad the relationship had ended. But the friendship didn't really end at that point. Three years ago, it had shifted from a friendship to a business relationship. It was so emotive, so awful, that I have no ambivalence about it. I'm glad it ended.

Erica's once intimate friendship with Joyce was soured by the new demands placed on it. Both women went through many unpleasant experiences together. Seeing each other reminded them of their failures at business—a common dream that had been shattered. Further, their vehement arguments erased any empathy or any hope of reconciliation.

Still other friends who have shared primarily good times together, who are torn apart by a disagreement, may mourn the loss of friendship deeply. For instance, Peg, age fifty, feels morose when she remembers her friendship with Kate, which ended seven years ago. Peg confided:

> Kate had been a neighbor, a friend in my childhood. I was the delivery-room nurse when she had Dawn. We spent holidays together, en famille, before and after marriage. Dawn calls me Aunt Peg, and we truly were each other's surrogate families. Dawn took a job out of town and met and married someone who was not of the same religion. Kate and her husband refused to accept this and actually dissolved their relationship with their only child. I was the only one who, as family, went to her wedding—and we remain devoted to each other. I begged Kate to reconsider, to take the train down with me, but she refused. When I came back from the wedding, she called me, told me that she considered me disloyal to her and that our friendship was over. I tried to conciliate but she stood firm. She remains estranged from me as well as from her daughter and two grandchildren. Dawn and I have long talks about it, but any attempts by either of us to work things out with Kate are all failures. I've learned to live with it, but the hurt is still there.

Indeed, Peg's loss of her lifelong friend was as hurtful as Dawn's loss of her mother. The two women, daughter and friend, still cling to each other in hope and pain.

There is no pain-free way to end a friendship. But if friends are to survive each other's loss, they must abandon faded dreams, false hopes, and lingering bitterness. They must mourn and then move on. No friend comes with a lifelong guarantee; as women appreciate the dual nature of their friendships, the fragility as well as the richness and strength, they will more fully value their time together.

BIBLIOGRAPHY

Allport, Gordon W. *The Nature of Prejudice*. Reading, Mass.: Addison-Wesley Publishing, 1954.

Argyle, Michael and Furnham, Adrian. "Sources of Satisfaction and Conflict in Long-term Relationships." *Journal of Marriage and the Family* 45 (August 1983): 481 493.

Arlings, Greg. "The Elderly Widow and Her Family, Neighbors and Friends." *Journal of Marriage and the Family* 38 (November 1976): 757–768.

Bell, Robert R. *Worlds of Friendship*. Beverly Hills, Calif.: Sage Publications, 1981.

Bem, Sandra L. "The Measurement of Psychological Androgyny." *Journal of Clinical Psychology* 42 (1974):155–62.

Bernard, Jesse. *The Female World*. New York: The Free Press (Macmillan), 1981.

Block, Joel D. *To Marry Again*. New York: Grossett and Dunlap, 1979.

———. *Friendship: How to Give It, How to Get It*. New York: Macmillan, 1980.

Booth, Alan. "Sex and Social Participation." *American Sociological Review*, 37 (1972): 183–92.

Booth, Alan and Hess, Elaine. "Cross-Sex Friendship." *Journal of Marriage and the Family*, 36 (1974): 38–47.

Bouton, Katherine. "Women and Divorce." *New York*, (October 8, 1984): 34–41.

Bramson, Robert M. *Coping with Difficult People.* New York: Ballantine Books, 1981.

Brandt, Anthony. "Leaving People Behind." *Esquire,* (October 1983): 20–24.

Cantwell, Mary. "The American Woman: Interviews with Susan Brownmiller, Nora Ephron, and Erica Jong. *Mademoiselle* (June, 1976): 121–.127.

Caplan, Paula. *Between Women: Lowering the Barriers.* Toronto: Spectrum, 1981.

Champagne, Marion. *Facing Life Alone.* New York: Bobbs-Merrill, 1964.

Clawson, James G., and Kram, Kathy E. "Managing Cross-Gender Mentoring." *Business Horizons* (May–June 1984): 22–32.

Collins, Nancy W. *Professional Women and Their Mentors.* Englewood Cliffs, N.J.: Prentice-Hall, 1983.

Cunningham, Mary. *Power Play: What Really Happened at Bendix?* New York: Linden Press, 1984.

Davis, Keith E. "Near and Dear: Friendship and Love Compared." *Psychology Today* (February, 1985): 22–30.

Donelson, E. and Gullshorn, J. *Women: A Psychological Perspective.* New York: Wiley, 1977.

Douvan, Elizabeth and Adelson, Joseph. *The Adolescent Experience.* New York: Wiley, 1966.

Duck, Steve. *Friends, for Life.* New York: St. Martin's Press, 1983.

Duck, Steve, and Gilmore, Robin, eds. *Personal Relationships,* Vol. 2: *Developing Personal Relationships.* New York: Academic Press, 1981.

Eichenbaum, Luise, and Orbach, Susie. *What Do Women Want.* New York: Berkley Books, 1983.

Eskapa, Shirley. *Woman versus Woman.* New York: Franklin Watts, 1984.

Fischer, Claude, S. *To Dwell among Friends: Personal Networks in Town and City.* Illinois: University of Chicago Press, 1982.

———. "The Public and Private Worlds of City Life." *American Sociological Review* 46, no. 3 (June 1981): 306–316.

Franck, Karen A. "Friends and Strangers: The Social Experience of Living in Urban and Non-urban Settings." *The Journal of Social Issues* 36, no. 3 (Summer 1980): 55–71.

Frank, Francine and Frank, Ashen. *Language and the Sexes.* Albany, N.Y.: State University of New York Press, 1984.

Friday, Nancy. *My Mother/My Self.* New York: Dell, 1977.

Friedan, Betty. *The Feminine Mystique.* New York: W. W. Norton, 1963.

Fury, Kathleen. "Mentor Mania." *Savvy* (January, 1980): 42–47.

Gamer, E., Thomas, J. and Kendall, D. "Determinants of Friendship across the Life-span.'' In F. Rebelsky, ed., *Life the Continuing Process.* New York: Knopf, 1976.

Gibbs-Candy, Sandra, Levy, Sheldon and Troll, Lillian. ''A Developmental Exploration of Friendship Functions in Women.'' *Psychology of Women Quarterly*, 5, no. 3 (Spring 1981): 456–72.

Gilligan, Carol. *In a Different Voice.* Cambridge, Mass.: Harvard University Press, 1982.

Gladieux, Johanna Dobkin. ''Pregnancy—the Transition to Parenthood: Satisfaction with the Pregnancy Experience as a Function of Sex Role Conceptions, Marital Relationships and Social Network.'' In Warren B. Miller and Lucille F. Newman, eds., *The First Child and Family Formation.* Chapel Hill, N.C.: Carolina Population Center, 1978.

Harlow, Harry F. and Harlow, M. ''Learning to Love.'' *American Scientist* 54 no. 3 (1966): pp. 190–201.

Harragan, Betty Lehan. *Games Mother Never Taught You: Corporate Gamesmanship for Women.* New York: Warner Books, 1977.

Harris, Janet. *Thursday's Daughters.* New York: Harper and Row, 1977.

Hatfield, E. and Traupmann, J. ''Intimate Relationships: A Perspective from Equity Theory.'' In: *Personal Relationships, Vol. 1; Studying Personal Relationships*, ed. S. W. Duck and R. Gilmour. New York: Academic Press, 1981.

Hellman, Lillian. *The Children's Hour.* New York: Dramatists Play Service, 1953.

Hunt, Morton. *The Divorce Experience.* New York: McGraw-Hill, 1977.

———*Her Infinite Variety.* New York: Harper and Row, 1962.

Huston, T. L. ''A Perspective on Interpersonal Attraction.'' In: T. L. Huston, ed., *Foundations of Interpersonal Attraction.* New York: Academic Press, 1974.

Jacobson, Gerald. *Multiple Crises of Marital Separation and Divorce.* New York: Grune & Stratton, 1983.

Jones, E. E. and Gordon, E. M. ''Timing of Self Disclosure and its Effects on Personal Attraction.'' *Journal of Personality and Social Psychology*, 24 (1972): 358–65.

Koile, Earl. *Listening as a Way of Becoming.* Waco, Tex.: Regency Books, 1977.

Komarovsky, Mirra. *Blue Collar Marriage.* New York: Vintage Books, 1967.

Levinson, Daniel J. *The Seasons of a Man's Life.* New York: Alfred A. Knopf, 1978.

Levinson, Harry. *The Exceptional Executive.* Cambridge, Mass.: Harvard University Press, 1981.

Lowenthal, Marjorie Fiske and Haven, Clayton. ''Interaction and Adaptation:

Intimacy as a Crucial Variable." *American Sociological Review,* Vol. 33 (February 1968): 20–38.

Luce, Clare Boothe. *The Women,* In: *20 Best Plays of the Modern American Theatre.* John Gassner, ed. New York: Crown Publishers, 1939.

Maccob, E., and Jacklin, C. *The Psychology of Sex Differences.* Stanford, Calif.: Stanford University Press, 1974.

Marty, Martin E. *Friendship.* Niles, Ill.: Argus Communications, 1980.

Mead, Margaret. *Male and Female: A Study of Sexes in the Changing World.* New York: William Morrow, 1949.

———*Blackberry Winter.* New York: Pocket Books, 1975.

Milgram, Stanley. "The Small World Problem." *Psychology Today,* (May, 1967): 61–67.

Missirian, Agnes K. *The Corporate Connection.* Englewood Cliffs, N.J.: Prentice-Hall, 1982.

Montgomery, James E. "The Housing Patterns of Older Families." *The Family Coordinator* (January 1972): 41.

Napolitane, Catherine and Pellegrino, Victoria. *Living and Loving after Divorce.* New York: Rawson Associates, 1977.

O'Neill, Nena and O'Neill, George. *Open Marriage.* New York: M. Evans, 1972.

Parkes, Colin M. *Bereavement.* Harmondsworth, England: Penguin, 1975.

Parlee, Mary Brown. "The Friendship Bond." *Psychology Today* (October 1979): 43–54, 113.

Phillips-Jones, Linda. *Mentors and Protégés.* New York: Arbor House, 1982.

Roche, Gerard R. "Much Ado about Mentors." *Harvard Business Review* 57 (January–February 1979):14, 20–28.

Rogan, Helen. "Take My Mentor—Please." *Harper's* (October 1983): 6–8.

Rubin, Lillian B. *Intimate Strangers: Men and Women Together.* New York: Harper and Row, 1983.

Safilios-Rothschild, Constantina. *Love, Sex and Sex Roles.* Englewood Cliffs, N.J.: Prentice-Hall, 1977.

———. "Toward a Psychology of Relationships." *Psychology of Women Quarterly* 5, No. 3 (1981):337–85.

Scarf, Maggie. *Unfinished Business.* New York: Ballantine Books, 1980.

Schmidt, Peggy. "Big-City Loneliness," *Glamour,* (August, 1983): 91–92.

Seiden, Anne M. and Bart, Pauline B. "Women to Women: Is Sisterhood Powerful?" In: *Old Family/New Family.* N. Glazer-Malbin, ed., New York: D. Van Nostrand Co., 1975.

Sheehy, Gail. "The Mentor Connection: The Secret Link in the Successful Woman's Life." *New York* (April 5, 1976): 33–39.

Sherman, Mark A. and Haas, Adelaide. "Man to Man, Woman to Woman." *Psychology Today* (June 1984): 72–78.

Simon, Rita James, Crotts, Gail and Mahan, Linda. "An Empirical Note about Married Women and Their Friends." *Social Forces* 48 (June 1970):520–525.

Smith-Rosenberg, Carroll. "The Female World of Love and Ritual: Relations Between Women in Nineteenth Century America." In: *A Heritage of Her Own*. Nancy F. Cott and Elizabeth H. Pleck, eds. New York: Simon and Schuster, 1979.

Speizer, Jeanne J. "Role Models, Mentors and Sponsors: The Elusive Concepts." *Journal of Women in Culture and Society* 6, no. 4 (1981): 692–712.

Stamell, Marcia. "50 Ways to Leave Your Mentor." *Savvy* (September 1983): 20–22.

Steinem, Gloria. *Outrageous Acts and Everyday Rebellions*. New York: Holt, Rinehart and Winston, 1983.

Todd, Janet. *Women's Friendships in Literature*. New York: Columbia University Press, 1980.

Van Druten, John. *The Voice of the Turtle*. New York: Dramatists Play Service, 1943.

Weiss, Robert S. *Loneliness*. Cambridge, Mass.: MIT Press, 1973.

Welch, Mary Scott. *Networking: The Great New Way for Women to Get Ahead*. New York: Harcourt, Brace, Jovanovich, 1980.

Wheeler, Ladd, Reis, Harry and Nezlik, John. "Loneliness, Social Interaction and Sex Roles." *Journal of Personality and Social Psychology*, 45 (1983): 943–53.

Wickham, Glynal. *Early English Stages: 1300 to 1660*. London, England: Routledge and Kegan Paul Ltd., 1963.

Wolfe, Linda. "Friendship in the City." *New York* (July 1983): 20–27.

Wollstonecraft, Mary. *A Vindication of the Rights of Woman* (1792). Charles W. Hagelman, Jr., ed. New York: W. W. Norton & Co., 1967.

Woolf, Virginia. *A Room of One's Own*. New York: Harcourt, Brace and World, 1957.

Wright, Paul, H. "Men's Friendships, Women's Friendships and the Alleged Inferiority of the Latter." *Sex Roles, A Journal of Research* 8 no. 1 (1982): 1–20.

NOTES

CHAPTER 1

1. Joel D. Block, *Friendship*, 82–83.
2. Alan Booth, "Sex and Social Participation," *American Sociological Review*, 186–187.
3. Mirra Komarovsky, *Blue Collar Marriage*, 148.
4. Paul H. Wright. "Men's Friendships, Women's Friendships and the Alleged Inferiority of the Latter," *Sex Roles, a Journal of Research*, 19.
5. Johanna Dobkin Gladieux, "Pregnancy—the Transition to Parenthood: Satisfaction with the Pregnancy Experience as a Function of Sex Role Conceptions, Marital Relationships and Social Network," 292.
6. Jesse Bernard, *The Female World*, 292.
7. Glynne Wickham, *Early English Stages: 1300 to 1660*, 14.
8. Virginia Woolf, *A Room of One's Own*, 86–87.
9. Janet Todd, *Women's Friendship in Literature*, 58.
10. Ibid, 271.
11. Sally Ridgeway, Professor of Sociology, Adelphi University, Garden City, New York, personal communication, March 19, 1985.
12. John Van Druten, *The Voice of the Turtle*, 143.
13. Clare Boothe Luce, *The Women*, 452.
14. Ibid, 455, 457.
15. Francine Frank, and Frank Ashen, *Language and the Sexes*, 74.
16. Paula Caplan, *Between Women: Lowering the Barriers*, 18–19.

17. Carroll Smith-Rosenberg, "The Female World of Love and Ritual," 313–314.
18. Ibid, 314.
19. Ibid, 314.
20. Ibid, 315.
21. Ibid, 319.
22. Ibid, 318.
23. Ibid, 320.
24. Gordon Allport, *The Nature of Prejudice,* 152.
25. Block, op. cit., 29–31.
26. Mary Wollstonecraft, *A Vindication of the Rights of Woman,* 91–92.
27. Ibid, 91–92.

CHAPTER 2

1. Michael Argyle and Adrian Furnham, "Sources of Satisfaction and Conflict in Long-term Relationships," *Journal of Marriage and the Family,* 490, 492.
2. Ladd Wheeler, Harry Reis and John Nezlik, "Loneliness, Social Interaction and Sex Roles," *Journal of Personality and Social Psychology,* 951.
3. Robert R. Bell, *Worlds of Friendship,* 60.
4. Block, *Friendship,* 14.
5. Sandra Gibbs-Candy, Sheldon Levy and Lillian Troll, "A Developmental Explanation of Friendship Functions in Women." *Psychology of Women Quarterly,* 466–469.
6. Harry F. Harlow and M. Harlow, "Learning to Love," *American Scientist,* 198–201.
7. Elizabeth Duvan and Joseph Adelson, *The Adolescent Experience,* 188.
8. Block, op. cit., 6.
9. Marjorie Fiske Lowenthal and Clayton Haven, "Interaction and Adaptation: Intimacy as a Crucial Variable," *American Sociological Review,* 30.
10. Greg Arlings, "The Elderly Widow and Her Family, Neighbors and Friends," *Journal of Marriage and the Family,* 761–762.
11. James E. Montgomery, "The Housing Patterns of Older Families," *The Family Coordinator* 42.

CHAPTER 3

1. Stanley Milgram, "The Small World Problem." *Psychology Today,* 63.

CHAPTER 4

1. Claude S. Fischer, *To Dwell among Friends: Personal Networks in Town and City,* 56–57.
2. Peggy Schmidt, "Big-City Loneliness," *Glamour,* 92.
3. Karen Franck, "Friends and Strangers: The Social Experience of Living in Urban and Non-urban Settings," *The Journal of Social Issues,* 56–57.
4. Betty Lehan Harrigan, *Games Mother Never Taught You: Corporate Gamesmanship for Women,* 38–65, 67, 79–83.
5. Linda Wolfe, "Friendship in the City," *New York* 23. Also, Janet Lee Barkas, "Friendship Patterns among Young Single Women," Dissertation Abstracts International (1983).
6. Mary Scott Welch, *Networking: The Great New Way for Women to Get Ahead.* 32.

CHAPTER 5

1. Block, *Friendship,* 105.
2. Margaret Mead, *Male and Female, A Study of Sexes in the Changing World,* 53–54.
3. Sandra Bem, "The Measurement of Psychological Androgyny," *Journal of Consulting and Clinical Psychology,* 160–161.
4. Mark A. Sherman and Adelaide Haas, "Man to Man, Woman to Woman," *Psychology Today,* 72.
5. Constantina Safilios-Rothschild, *Love, Sex and Sex Roles,* 94.
6. Carol Gilligan, *In a Different Voice,* 8–9.
7. See "A Woman's Work is Never Done," *The New York Times* (March 6, 1983), 29.
8. Caplan, *Between Women,* 134.
9. Bell, *Worlds of Friendship* 107.
10. Lesta M. Tucker and Robert C. Tucker, "Lovers and Other Friends," *Essence* (October, 1980), 118.

CHAPTER 6

1. Lillian B. Rubin, *Intimate Strangers: Men and Women Together,* 122–125.
2. Block, *Friendship,* 131.
3. Rita James Simon, Gail Crotts and Linda Mahan, "An Empirical Note about Married Women and Their Friends," *Social Forces,* 522–523.

CHAPTER 7

1. Gerald Jacobson, *Multiple Crises of Marital Separation and Divorce,* 230.
2. Shirley Eskapa, *Woman Versus Woman,* 159.
3. Katherine Bouton, "Women and Divorce," *New York* 37.
4. Colin M. Parkes, *Bereavement,* 105.
5. Catherine Napolitane and Victoria Pellegrino, *Living and Loving after Divorce,* 278.
6. Robert S. Weiss, *Loneliness,* 215.
7. Joel D. Block, *To Marry Again,* 6.

CHAPTER 8

1. Gail Sheehy, "The Mentor Connection," *New York* 34.
2. Linda Phillips-Jones, *Mentors and Protégés,* 162–163.
3. Nancy W. Collins, *Professional Women and Their Mentors,* 119.
4. Gerald R. Roche, "Much Ado About Mentors," *Harvard Business Review,* 20.
5. Agnes K. Missirian, *The Corporate Connection,* 77.
6. Daniel J. Levinson, *The Seasons of a Man's Life,* 100.
7. Ibid., 97.
8. Mary Cantwell, "The American Woman: Interviews with Susan Brownmiller, Nora Ephron, and Erica Jong, *Mademoiselle,* 123–124.
9. Harry Levinson, *The Exceptional Executive,* 162–163.
10. Sheehy, op. cit., 34.
11. Ibid., 34.
12. Margaret Mead, *Blackberry Winter,* 122.
13. Collins, op. cit., 158.
14. Ibid, 73.
15. James G. Clawson and Kathy E. Kram, "Managing Cross-gender Mentoring," *Business Horizons,* 22–32.
16. Ibid., 27.
17. Kathleen Fury, "Mentor Mania," 45.
18. Sheehy, op. cit., 35.
19. Marcia Stamell, "50 Ways to Leave Your Mentor," *Savvy,* 20, 22.

CHAPTER 9

1. Cited in Steve W. Duck and Robin Gilmore, eds., *Personal Relationships 2: Developing Personal Relationships,* 32.

2. Steve Duck, *Friends, for Life,* 109.
3. Eskapa, *Woman Versus Woman,* 17–18.
4. Luise Eichenbaum and Susie Orbach, *What Do Women Want?: Exploding the Myth of Dependency,* 169.

CHAPTER 10

1. E. E. Jones and E. M. Gordon, "Timing of Self-disclosure and Its Effects on Personal Attraction," *Journal of Personality and Social Psychology,* 361–362.
2. Keith E. Davis, "Near and Dear: Friendship and Love Compared," *Psychology Today,* 27.
3. Mary Brown Parlee, "The Friendship Bond," *Psychology Today,* 50.

INDEX